Challenger

SECOND EDITION

7

ADULT READING SERIES

Corea Murphy

New Readers Press

Acknowledgments:

"The Good Lord Will Provide" by Lawrence Treat and Charles M. Plotz. Adapted with permission of Scott Meredith Literary Agency, New York, NY.

"Mr. Manning's Money Tree" copyright © 1958 by Robert Arthur. Adapted by permission of the estate of Robert Arthur.

Quotations for "Money" page 40, are from various Penny Press puzzle magazines and are used by kind permission of the publisher.

"The Choice" copyright © 1926, copyright renewed 1954 by Dorothy Parker, from *The Portable Dorothy Parker* by Dorothy Parker, edited by Marion Meade. Used by permission of Viking Penguin, a division of Penguin Group (USA) Inc.

"All the Years of Her Life" copyright © 1934 by Morley Callaghan; renewed 1962 by Morley Callaghan. Adapted and used by permission of the estate of Morley Callaghan.

"Prelude" by Albert Halper. Copyright © 1938 by Harper's Magazine. All rights reserved. Adapted and reprinted from the August 1938 issue by special permission.

"March, 1938" copyright © 1938 by The New York Times Company. Reprinted by permission.

"The Test" by Angelica Gibbs reprinted by permission; © 1940, 1968 The New Yorker Magazine, Inc.

Adaptation of "Charles" from *The Lottery* by Shirley Jackson. Copyright © 1948, 1949 by Shirley Jackson. Copyright renewed 1976, 1977 by Laurence Hyman, Barry Hyman, Mrs. Sarah Webster, and Mrs. Joanne Schnurer. Reprinted by permission of Farrar, Straus & Giroux, Inc.

"On Golden Pond" reprinted by permission of Dodd, Mead & Company, Inc. from *On Golden Pond* by Ernest Thompson. Copyright © 1979 by Ernest Thompson.

"The Execution" adapted from *Dostoyevsky: A Human Portrait* by Robert Payne. Copyright © 1958, 1961 by Sheila Lalwani Payne. New York: Alfred A. Knopf, 1961. pp. 86-93.

Ernest Hemingway, "A Day's Wait" from *Winner Take Nothing.* Copyright 1933 Charles Scribner's Sons; copyright renewed © 1961 Mary Hemingway. Reprinted with the permission of Scribner, a division of Simon & Schuster.

"The $24 Swindle" by Nathaniel Benchley adapted by permission of Marjorie Benchley. "The $24 Swindle" first appeared in *American Heritage,* December 1959.

Excerpt from "Moriturus." Copyright © 1928, 1955 by Edna St. Vincent Millay and Norma Millay Ellis. Reprinted by permission of Elizabeth Barnett, Literacy Executor, The Millay Society.

"To Have or To Be" approximately 1500 words passim (abridged and adapted) from *To Have or To Be?* by Erich Fromm. Volume Fifty in the World Perspective Series planned and edited by Ruth Nanda Anshen. Copyright © 1976 by Erich Fromm. Reprinted by permission of Liepman Agency.

"The Woman Who Willed a Miracle" adapted from Arthur Heinemann's screenplay, *The Woman Who Willed a Miracle.* Reprinted with permission of the dick clark company, inc.

Images courtesy of:
p. 8: DoD photo by Petty Officer 1st Class Aaron Glover, U.S. Navy; p. 12, p. 14, p. 35, toothpaste: p. 44, p. 47, p. 62, p. 64, p. 70, p. 72, p. 86, p. 108 , p. 128, p. 135, p. 146, p. 170, p. 176 p. 178, p. 188, p.199: © 2008 Jupiterimages Corporation; p. 22, cosmetics: p. 44, p. 55, p. 87, p. 110, p. 158, p. 208: istockphoto.com; p. 53, p. 60, p. 93, p. 94, p. 95, p. 98, p. 117, p. 138: Public Domain (Wikimedia Commons)

Challenger 7, 2nd Edition
ISBN 978-1-56420-574-2

Developmental Editor: Terrie Lipke
Contributing Writer: S. Dean Wooton
Creative Director: Andrea Woodbury
Production Specialist: Maryellen Casey
Art and Design Supervisor: James P. Wallace
Cover Design: Carolyn Wallace

Table of Contents

UNIT 1
Love and Money

Most of us have heard the saying, "The love of money is the root of all evil." Is there any truth in this saying? In this first unit, we shall see how the desire for money affects the lives of three different groups of characters.

In the story for Lesson 1, "Storm at Sea," a young man is faced with a difficult decision. He needs money to help someone he cares about, but just how far is he willing to go to get it?

"The Good Lord Will Provide," the reading for Lesson 2, is a series of letters written between a husband and wife. Like many couples, they have problems with money, and their letters describe their efforts to get ahead of the bills.

"Mr. Manning's Money Tree" is the story for both Lesson 3 and Lesson 4. Henry Manning, the main character in this story, experiences many changes as he begins to think about what is really important in his life.

All the lessons in Book 7 begin with a word chart in which rules you have studied for sounding out words in previous *Challenger* books are reviewed. By completing the definitions that follow each word chart, you will learn words that appear in future stories and word exercises in Book 7.

Review of Long and Short Vowels

ā	ē	ī	ō	ū
sane	eke	awhile	tote	Judy
quake	gene	rival	rove	tulip
labor	senior	riot	romance	rumor
maze	regain	lilac	motive	puny
bass	impede	finance	oval	unity

ă	ĕ	ĭ	ŏ	ŭ
sap	ebb	imp	tot	muss
fashion	yen	kindle	romp	juggle
pasture	zest	quiver	comic	unjust
pastor	temple	wicked	olive	hub
bass	pedal	equip	option	humdrum

1 Definitions. Match the words listed below with the correct definitions.

ebb	humdrum	kindle	opt	tot
eke	imp	maze	puny	tote
hub	impede	olive	rove	yen

_____ **1.** a center of activity or interest; the center part of a wheel or fan

_____ **2.** to make a choice

_____ **3.** a confusing network of walled pathways; any situation in which it is easy to get lost

_____ **4.** a longing for something; also, the basic unit of money in Japan

_____ **5.** a small, bitter fruit with a hard stone that grows on a Mediterranean evergreen tree

_____ **6.** a small child

_____ **7.** a troublesome or extremely playful child

_____ **8.** boring; dull; uninteresting

_____ **9.** to block the way

_____ **10.** to build or fuel (a fire); to ignite

_____ **11.** to fall back; a period of fading away

_____ **12.** to haul or lug

_____ **13.** to make a living, for example, with great effort or strain

_____ **14.** to roam or wander about

_____ **15.** weak; low in strength, size, or importance

Words for Study

gradually	continuous	mulling	desperation	downplayed
crescent	bursar	options	collapsed	solemnly
horizon	ruthless	Shanghai	transported	casually

Storm at Sea

by S. Dean Wooton

The lights of New York City rose slowly, dimly, out of the ocean, gradually brightening into a crescent that filled the horizon. Kyle stood watching, breathing in the rich salt air, listening to the waves breaking on the ship's hull and the gulls screaming. After nine months of almost continuous sea duty, he was ready for time on shore and to face whatever awaited him.

Salama, the assistant bursar, walked up and leaned against the railing next to Kyle. He held out a thick brown envelope to Kyle. "You should take this," he said and placed his hand on Kyle's. "You need it. You're not going to be able to help your sister without it."

"I don't need that," Kyle replied. "I'll figure it out somehow."

"How you gonna do that?" Salama said. "I know you; you don't have two nickels to rub together, and you're not smart enough to get a big job on Wall Street. So you'll try to get money on the street, and you don't know a thing about the street, how to survive there."

"I grew up on the street," Kyle cut him off.

"Not the street where you can get money," Salama insisted fiercely. "You'll try to sell drugs or stick up a liquor store or something, and you'll be over your head the moment you get involved. You'll at least get thrown in jail and might get killed, and you know it. This," he said indicating the envelope in his hand, "this won't cost you your life."

"It'll cost you," Kyle said, and he pulled his hand away. "It'll cost you more than you're willing to admit . . . and it might cost me as well."

"Only if I get caught," Salama said, "and I won't because I know what I'm doing, and they'll never figure it out. And it won't cost you anything, because no matter what happens, no one will ever trace it to you."

"You don't know that, Salama," Kyle replied. "You think you can get away with it and no one will find out, but you can't be sure. These are intelligent people who operate this business—they wouldn't have stayed in operation this long if they weren't. And they're tough and ruthless as well—as tough as anyone I'll run into on the street."

"The difference is, I know what I'm doing," Salama said coldly. "I say I'll be all right, and you can believe that."

Kyle remained silent, staring moodily down into the sea, his face creased with anxiety and uncertainty. Salama looked at him a moment. "Think about it, my friend," he said. "If you decide, it's here for you."

Kyle had been mulling over his options for a month now, ever since he got the call from Maggie, his little sister, when he was in Shanghai. She was the only one in the family he heard from anymore. Mom, Dad . . . a long time ago they'd cut him off, or maybe he had cut them off. He just didn't care much about them. They'd never done much for him, and when he became eighteen, he ran off to sea. But Maggie, she was special. He'd always felt that about her, and they'd stayed in contact. She was ten years younger than him and had all the family's brains and all of its sweetness too, as far as he could see.

Three years ago, while he was at sea, there'd been a car accident. Mom hadn't made it, and Dad ended up in a wheelchair, pent up with anger and depression. Kyle hadn't made it home, and he couldn't imagine how difficult it had been for Maggie dealing with all that. "Poor Maggie," Kyle thought, "like usual, she had to carry it all on her own shoulders."

But now, Maggie needed help herself. Kyle couldn't get the conversation out of his head when he'd first heard about it—the strain and desperation in her voice.

"I don't know what to do," Maggie had cried into the phone. "The doctor said I'd probably be okay, but I'm scared, Kyle. I'm really scared. And Dad . . . what'll I do? He doesn't know anything."

Kyle knew it was even worse than she led him to believe. She tried to be strong and to protect him from what happened at home. Little by little, port by port, as the ship worked its way home, Kyle gathered more information from Maggie. She had collapsed one day while she was on her way to class at the university. Strangers called 911, and she was transported to the hospital where a battery of tests gave grim news. There could be no surgery the doctors said, but it wasn't hopeless, they insisted. The doctors said there were things they could do, but she'd probably need long-term care. Maggie downplayed it, but Kyle knew this was the time for him to get home.

As the ship came into port and approached the dock, Kyle stood looking to see if anyone would meet him. Then he spotted Maggie, looking small and frail in a long gray coat. She stood alone there on the dingy dock, her eyes searching the *Longdale Vincent* for her long-absent brother's face.

"That Maggie?" Salama said, reappearing as the ship docked.

"Yea," Kyle said. "That's Maggie." He looked over at Salama. "I can't let her down," Kyle said solemnly.

"I know," Salama said. "Take it. You've got to help her. I can see that, and I can't let you let her down. You know what you have to do." He pushed the envelope into Kyle's hand, and turned and walked away. Kyle looked after him and called, "So what are you gonna do?"

Salama waved casually over his shoulder and walked on.

2 Understanding the Story. Put the letter of the correct answer on the line.

1. Why has Kyle returned to New York? _____.
    a. to take care of his sister
    b. to spend time with his father
    c. to get away from Salama
    d. to escape the crime bosses operating the ship

2. Which of the following is *not* a reason that Salama offers Kyle the envelope? _____
    a. He knows Kyle needs money.
    b. He's certain that Kyle will pay him back.
    c. Kyle is his friend and he wants to help him.
    d. He thinks Kyle will get killed if he tries to get money on his own.

3. Why doesn't Kyle want to take the envelope Salama offers him? _____
    a. He doesn't trust Salama.
    b. He doesn't need it.
    c. He doesn't know what it is.
    d. He thinks Salama will get in trouble.

4. Why did Maggie call Kyle when he was in Shanghai? _____.
    a. to tell him about their mother's death
    b. to warn him about Salama
    c. to tell him about her illness
    d. to ask him for money

5. The most likely reason that Kyle left home and went to sea was because _____.
    a. he wanted to become a ship's captain
    b. he couldn't get along with his parents
    c. he wanted to make money
    d. he had gotten in trouble and needed to get away

6. Kyle probably needs money in order to _____.
    a. pay off his gambling debts
    b. pay off the owners of the ship so he can leave
    c. pay for Maggie's medical care
    d. pay for Maggie's schooling

7. Which of the following does not describe Kyle's reaction to Salama's offer? _____.
    a. gratitude
    b. uncertainty
    c. concern
    d. disappointment

3 What Do You Think? Answer the following questions in good sentence form.

1. What do you think Salama is trying to give Kyle? Where do you think he got it?

_____

_____

_____

2. What are the possible consequences of Kyle's decision to accept the envelope on himself, on Maggie, and on Salama?

_____

_____

_____

_____

4 Which Word Does Not Fit? Choose the word that does not fit with the other words in each row, and write it on the line.

1.	bass	guitar	banjo	piano	violin	_____
2.	drift	roam	romp	rove	wander	_____
3.	amusing	creative	humorous	laughable	funny	_____
4.	bar	block	dam	foam	impede	_____
5.	daisy	fern	lilac	rose	tulip	_____
6.	coil	curl	twine	twist	crawl	_____
7.	humdrum	occurrence	ordinary	normal	routine	_____
8.	cruel	fierce	heartless	vicious	thoughtless	_____
9.	flutter	murmur	quiver	shiver	shudder	_____
10.	gradually	step by step	little by little	suddenly	slowly	_____

5 More about New York Harbor. Use the words listed below to complete these sentences about
New York Harbor.

busiest	common	manufactured	serves
cargo	handle	passenger	ships
commercial	human	recreational	swimmers

New York Harbor covers about 650 square miles and is one of the world's _____

ports. More than 5,000 _____ and _____ ships stop off in the port

each year. Altogether, the port _____ about 35 percent of the United States. Almost

$100 billion in consumer goods, food, _____ goods, and oil are shipped through the

port each year. To _____ all this traffic, the port hires about 230,000 workers in the

New York City area.

Besides all the _____, or business, traffic, the harbor is also a popular

_____ site. People play along the shores in kayaks, jet skis, and other small boats.

_____ even take to the water close to land. Farther out, squads of sailboats use

the harbor.

Although _____ are constantly moving into and out of the port, the harbor is

home to hundreds of animal species. These include many kinds of fish, birds, and mammals. Although the

_____ activity makes the harbor a busy place, these animals find refuge in marshes and

swamp forests that are surprisingly _____ along the shores.

Review of Consonant Blends: Part 1

bl	cl	fl	gl	pl	spl
blazer	clan	flank	glacier	plaza	splat
bladder	clarinet	flavor	glamour	plasma	splay
blemish	clergy	flimsy	glamorous	plaid	splice
blizzard	cleanliness	flog	glee	plaster	splendor
blockade	clique	florist	glide	plod	split-level
blunt	nucleus	flutter	glimpse	plush	
blunder	nuclear	inflict	Gloria	Plymouth	

1 Definitions. Match the words listed below with the correct definitions.

blazer	blunder	clergy	flog	glee	plasma	Plymouth
blemish	blunt	clique	glacier	nucleus	plaster	

_____ 1. a core; a thing or part forming the center around which other things or parts are gathered

_____ 2. a slowly moving mass of ice and snow

_____ 3. a single-breasted sports jacket in a solid, often bright color or with stripes

_____ 4. a small circle of people who tend to be snobbish and exclude others from their company

_____ 5. a stupid and serious mistake; a clumsy, foolish act or remark

_____ 6. town in southeastern Massachusetts where the Pilgrims from the *Mayflower* landed in 1620

_____ 7. any mark that damages the appearance, such as a stain, spot, or scar

_____ 8. having a thick, dull edge or end; not sharp or pointed

_____ 9. lively joy; merriment

_____ 10. men or women who have been given the office of some religious service, such as pastors

_____ 11. the fluid part of blood which is used for transfusions

_____ 12. a soft mixture of lime, sand, and water that hardens as it dries

_____ 13. to beat harshly with a whip or a rod

Words for Study

penitentiary	mortgage	R.F.D.	Ernie	allowance
parole	generous	awhile	bushel	acquire
plumb	sheriff	liable	deputies	rheumatism

The Good Lord Will Provide
by Lawrence Treat and Charles M. Plotz

STATE PENITENTIARY

April 3

Dear Judy,

It's been a whole year now a whole long year without you. But I been a real good prisoner staying out of trouble like a cat stays away from water. They all say I'll get my parole next April, plenty of time to put in a crop. So hang on, you and Uncle Ike. The only thing bothering me is I ain't heard from you in so long. Why? What's happening?

Judy, it's not like I done anything wrong. All I did was drive that car. I didn't know they had guns and itchy fingers. I didn't even know them good. They was just a couple of city fellas hanging around a bar. I musta told them I could just about drive a car up the side of a wall and down the other side and if they wanted to see how good I was, why come on out and look. Which they did.

Maybe I was a little stupid but when they allowed they'd pay me right then and there to take them to the bank next day and then on out to the back hills—well all I did was ask how much. And when they told me I plumb near keeled over. Because it was almost as much as we needed for that mortgage payment. I figured money was money and if they was taking a lot of it out of the bank, why wouldn't they be generous? What I didn't know was they didn't have no account there.

So I reckon I was real stupid. But stupid or not I sure was lucky because if I'd stayed with that pair much longer I'da got killed too. But they paid me to get them out of town and up into the hills and after I done that I took off and come straight back to you.

When Ike heard the news on the radio he knowed right off it was me at the wheel of the car. Nobody else could have outdrove and outsmarted the cops and I bet I could have got clear off to Mexico or maybe China if I'da wanted to. And if the planes hadn't spotted me like they did that pair. But I done what I was paid for, and if they took fifty thousand like the papers said or a million I wouldn't know. I was waiting out in the car and all the money I ever seen was what I give you. And like I said, I got it the day before and it wasn't stolen from the bank. Not that bank anyhow.

The sheriff kept asking me where the stolen money

was. After all the two bank robbers was dead with no trace of the money and all the sheriff had was me. Just a poor dumb farmer with a knack for handling a car.

But I don't want to worry you with all this. I'm real lonesome for you like I said. So when are you coming up here to visit me? And how are you and how's Ike and the farm?

Your loving husband
Walt

R.F.D. 2, Hadley

April 10

Dear Walt,

I got your letter and the reason I ain't come to see you is that I just don't have the money for the trip. Besides I got to do all the chores now. Uncle Ike's down with the rhumatiz again. And when Ike's feeling puny he wants me around all the time and all he does is complain and tell me everybody's out to take the skin off me. He even tried to chase George off the place when George come around in his new car to ask me out for a ride. And I sure needed to get away from the farm for awhile.

George was real nice to me too. I told him right out that we was liable to lose the farm unless we got that mortgage installment paid and how could I pay it until I got a crop in? And I said that what with George getting promoted to be vice president of the bank he could maybe do something. He said he'd see what he could manage and that was about as far as we got. Anyway, it was nice getting away from Ike for awhile, specially when George took me to dinner at that new place in town.

Walt, I wish you was a banker too.

Your loving wife
Judy

April 15

Dear Judy,

I know it's hard on you with Ike to take care of it's even worse. But the good Lord will provide, Judy, and I know what I'm saying.

About George and the bank holding off—you want to get it writ down. So next time you see him you want to ask him about Ruthie Watkins which I found out about from a guy up here named Ernie. Ernie, his business is selling letters. And like he says, if I got a cow or a bushel of wheat I can sell them, can't I? So why can't he sell letters?

Ernie and me get along fine because the both of us we're innocent men and we shouldn't ought to be here. But as long as we are we talk about things and Ernie happened to mention some letters he got hold of which George writ to this Ruthie Watkins. So maybe you better mention them to George next time you see him.

Your loving husband
Walt

R.F.D. 2, Hadley

April 22

Dear Walt,

George took me out to dinner again. And like you told me to I just happened to mention Ruthie Watkins and then I said about the mortgage and how it ought to be writ down. And the very next day I got a letter from the bank promising to hold off until autumn but I don't know what good it's going to do. Because Ike got a hold of that white mule stuff and got the idea he ought to go riding in the tractor. You ought to see what's left of that tractor. So how do I make that mortgage payment in the fall with no crop coming in?

I'm tired, Walt. I'm plumb tired. You said the good Lord will provide—but how? How?

Your loving wife
Judy

STATE PENITENTIARY

April 28

Dear Judy,

You got to be patient like I said and if you're real patient the Lord *will* provide. Because He come to me in a dream and He said that there was something buried in the south field that would take care of us. So you tell Ike to get over that rhumatiz of his. Tell him I got only a year to go and then I'm going to dig up that something in the south field and after that everything's going to be all right.

Your loving husband
Walt

R.F.D. 2, Hadley

May 4

Dear Walt,

I don't know just how to tell you this but I guess I'll just set it down the way it happened.

You know how Ike hates the law ever since they come around and took you away. So when the sheriff and six deputies showed up the day before yesterday Ike tried to chase them away. He yelled at them and called them all kinds of names and they finally grabbed him and tied him up, so he never did see what they done.

Walt, they went down to that south field and the six of them spent the whole day digging and then they come back the next day and kept on until they dug up just about every inch of that field. And I never did see any six men look so tired and they sure was mad. I asked them lots of questions and one of them—I think he come all the way down from the prison—he allowed as how all your mail gets read. Walter, what did he say that for?

Your loving wife
Judy

STATE PENITENTIARY

May 7

Dear Judy,

Now plant.

Your loving husband
Walt

2 Understanding the Story. Write the answers to these questions in good sentence form.

1. In his first letter, Walt claims he is "just a poor dumb farmer." What stupid thing did he do?

   _____

   _____

2. He also claims he didn't do anything wrong. What reasons does he give to support this claim?

   _____

   _____

3. Ernie, his fellow inmate, also claims to be innocent. Why is Ernie in jail?

   _____

   _____

4. Judy has two problems with the farm.

   a. One is getting the bank to wait for the mortgage payment until the crop is in. Describe how Ernie helps Walt and Judy with this problem.

   _____

   _____

   _____

   b. The second is getting the field ready for planting after Ike ruins the tractor. Describe how Walt solves this problem.

   _____

   _____

   _____

   _____

3 What Do You Think?

1. Is Walt the stupid farmer he claims to be? Give reasons to support your answer.

_____

_____

_____

2. Why is the story called "The Good Lord Will Provide"?

_____

_____

_____

4 Look It Up. Use a dictionary or the Internet to help you answer the first two questions in this exercise.

1. Judy writes to Walt that she is "plumb tired." What does the word _plumb_ mean as Judy uses it in her letter?

_____

2. What does _plumb_ mean in the following sentence?

When Justin _plumbed_ the depths of his mind, he finally thought of a way to solve his problem.

_____

3. A _plumb line_ is used around the home to make sure that things are vertically straight on a wall. For example, if you were hanging wallpaper, you could use a plumb line to be sure the wallpaper was vertically straight before you pasted it. Give another example of sometime you might use a plumb line in your home.

_____

_____

5 Standard English. Walt and Judy use certain words and expressions in their letters that people sometimes use when talking with family and friends. But people generally do not use them when they are in a situation in which they want to make a good impression. In more formal situations, people use what is called *standard English*. They do this so they will sound like they are skillful in using language and so they will be easily understood by everyone. Study the examples of standard English below, and then underline the correct word in the sentences that follow.

1. *Dumb* **and** *Stupid*

   Dumb means not having the power of speech, as in "deaf and dumb." *Stupid* means silly, foolish, or showing a lack of intelligence.

   a. Does Walt seem like a poor (dumb, stupid) farmer to you?

   b. Not realizing that the servant was (dumb, stupid), Lord Mansfield fired him for refusing to respond to his question.

   c. Do you think Ernie was (dumb, stupid) to try to sell the letters?

   d. The possibility of losing his farm struck Walt (dumb, stupid) for a while; then he developed a plan.

   e. Do you consider these rules about standard English (dumb, stupid)?

2. *Learn* **and** *Teach*

   Learn means to gain knowledge or skill or to acquire a behavior. *Teach* means to provide instruction.

   a. Many people believe that a penitentiary is strictly interested in punishing prisoners rather than (learning, teaching) them anything useful.

   b. Do you believe there is any truth in the old saying, "You can't (learn, teach) an old dog new tricks"?

   c. When Andrew asked his aunt why she was taking college courses at her age, she replied, "The older I get, the more I realize I still have a lot to (learn, teach)."

   d. The instructor tried to (learn, teach) his students how to spell better.

   e. While in prison, Walt didn't (learn, teach) a new trade.

3. *Set* **and** *Sit*

   Set means to put something in a certain place. *Sit* means to be seated.

   a. The thing Judy disliked most about getting dinner was having to (set, sit) the table.

   b. Uncle Ike's rheumatism was so painful that he couldn't do much but (set, sit) around all day.

   c. Judy was so exhausted from all her responsibilities on the farm that she wanted an opportunity just to (set, sit) and relax.

   d. When Uncle Ike returned from the store, he (set, sit) the groceries on the kitchen counter.

   e. Whenever Hiram lost his temper, he always recalled his grandmother's advice: "Never let the sun (set, sit) on an angry heart."

6 Common Expressions. Walt's expression "staying out of trouble like a cat stays away from water" is just one example of the many phrases and words in our everyday speech in which animals are mentioned in order to stress a point. Use the animals listed below to complete the following sentences correctly.

bug	butterflies	chicken	fleabag	goose	horse	pig's	skunk
bull	chicken	doghouse	goat	hog	horse	rat	tigers

1. Even though horror films gave Fred _____ bumps, he agreed to see *The Ghostly Haunting* because he didn't want his friends to think he was a _____.

2. Mr. Adams had always wanted to spend his two-week vacation in a big city, but when his wife pointed out to him that, on their tight budget, they'd have to stay in a _____, he hotly replied, "In a _____ eye!" And that was the end of that idea.

3. Mrs. Carver was such a clothes _____ that she decided to go whole _____ and spend her entire paycheck at Luella's High Fashion Dress Shop.

4. "This isn't an allowance! This is _____ feed!" cried Sonny as he stormed out of the house muttering, "Grown-ups always try to _____ us poor kids out of our money!"

5. Upon hearing that a new mob was trying to take over his operations on the South Side, Duke said with annoyance, "Those guys don't _____ me. They're nothing but a bunch of paper _____."

6. Watching her husband come home from work exhausted and upset for the fourth night in a row, Susan again considered trying to convince him to quit this _____ race and move to the country; but she kept quiet, realizing that she would only be beating a dead _____.

7. Whenever her daughter-in-law asked her to babysit, Louise would get a bad case of _____ in her stomach because her grandson was like a _____ in a china shop, and she knew by the end of the evening her lovely living room would be in shambles.

8. The foreman's nagging had really gotten Jesse's _____, so he decided to go out with his friends after work, even though he knew he'd be in the _____ when he got home.

Review of Consonant Blends: Part 2

br	**cr**	**dr**	**fr**	**gr**	**pr**
bravery	crayon	drab	frizzy	grid	prude
brief	cradle	dragon	frosty	griddle	prolong
brilliant	credit	drama	fray	gruff	profound
brilliance	credentials	dramatic	fragrance	gracious	privilege
brute	crock	dribble	fragrant	granola	precious
brutal	crocodile	drowsy	frustrate	gravity	predicament
umbrella	crumble	drudgery	frustration	agreeable	approve

1 Definitions. Match the words listed below with the correct definitions.

brilliant	crocodile	drowsy	fragrant	griddle	predicament	prude
credentials	drama	drudgery	granola	gruff	privilege	

_____ **1.** a letter or certificate that guarantees someone's position, authority, or right to be trusted

_____ **2.** a flat pan or other flat metal surface used for cooking

_____ **3.** a large reptile with thick skin and long jaws

_____ **4.** a person, especially a woman, who is overly concerned with being proper

_____ **5.** a play

_____ **6.** a special advantage granted to an individual or a class

_____ **7.** a troublesome situation

_____ **8.** boring or unpleasant work

_____ **9.** sleepy

_____ **10.** full of light; shining; splendid; excellent

_____ **11.** having a pleasant odor; sweet-smelling

_____ **12.** a snack mix usually made of oats, raisins, nuts, and other natural ingredients

_____ **13.** rough or harsh in manner or speech

Words for Study

cashier	subdivision	erect	suburb
briefcase	inwardly	unknowingly	patrols
thermos	burlap	mustache	disguised
intention	compost	mechanic	humorist

Mr. Manning's Money Tree: Part I
by Robert Arthur

At exactly noon Henry Manning, a sandy-haired, pleasant young man, closed the grilled window of his cashier's cage in the First National Bank. He picked up his briefcase and hat, let himself out of the cage, and strolled toward the front door of the bank. The briefcase held a thermos bottle and two sandwiches. Everyone knew that on nice days Henry, the promising young assistant cashier, took his lunch to eat in the park.

As Henry went out the door, two men in gray suits at the rear of the bank exchanged nods, and one started after him. Henry spotted him almost at once, and his heart began to beat faster. If they had a detective following him, it meant they were almost ready to arrest him. It also meant that he had no chance to hide the ten thousand dollars which at the moment was safely tucked away inside his innocent-looking thermos bottle.

Since Monday he had known they were on his trail. By now they must be just about certain that it was Henry Manning who had taken twenty thousand from the accounts during the past year. It was amazing, he thought, how a normally honest man could get the stock market fever and plunge in deeper and deeper, hoping at first for the lucky strike that would make him independent, then for the clever guess which would enable him to make up for his losses, then—

Well, the twenty thousand was gone, and he couldn't pay it back. So Henry, hardened by now to taking money that wasn't his, had taken ten thousand more. But with a detective who might arrest him at any moment at his heels, where on earth could he hide it?

As he reached the park, a Lakeside bus was just closing its doors. With a sudden inspiration Henry leaped on as the door slid hissingly shut. Through the window he saw the detective pound up to the bus stop and look helplessly after him. Henry smiled to himself. That was one problem solved.

But the biggest problem still lay ahead. He had no intention of trying to run for it. He'd take his punishment. Who wanted to spend the rest of his life a hunted man? But he did want to be able to count on the money in his briefcase to help him make a new start. How, then, could he possibly hide it where it would stay safe until he had served his sentence and was a free man again?

"Melwood Estates," the driver called presently. "End of the line."

Henry got out. They had stopped at one of the new subdivisions springing up all around the city. A hundred houses, all alike, were ranged up and down the slopes of newly planted lawn. He walked away briskly, as though he lived in one of the houses. But inwardly he felt a deep despair. It was all so naked and empty out here. Where could a man hide anything? Why couldn't he have had one more day? By now the alarm was out for him, but with one more day he could have—

As if stunned, Henry stopped in his tracks. He had reached a corner. Fifty feet away stood a pleasant little Cape Cod house surrounded by naked lawn. Almost beside Henry there was a deep hole in the lawn, and just beyond the hole a handsome spruce, roots wrapped in burlap, waited to be planted.

No one was in sight. Henry took off his hat, mopped his brow, and as if by accident let his hat drop into the hole. When he bent to get it, he slipped the thermos out of his briefcase and swiftly hid it beneath the loose soil and compost in the bottom of the hole.

It was all done in twenty seconds. Henry was standing erect, admiring the tree, when a cheerful, heavyset man with black hair came down the walk carrying a pail of water.

"Just admiring your tree," Henry said, his manner neighborly. "Beautiful spruce."

"Should be," the other chuckled. "They charged me a lot for it because I wanted a big one." He put down the bucket, and Henry stepped forward.

"Let me give you a hand," he said.

Henry stayed until the tree was planted and the soil packed down around it. A pretty young woman with light brown hair came to the door of the little house and watched them. A young couple, not doing too well yet—Henry saw the inexpensive car in the driveway. Mentally he wished them well. As he strolled away, to return to the bank and be arrested, he felt a certain fondness for these strangers who unknowingly had helped him solve his problem.

It was three-and-a-half years before Henry saw the tree again. By then he was heavier, looked older, had a mustache, and had a trade. In the prison garage he had become an expert mechanic.

The tree had changed too. It had grown into a handsome young spruce. And the house had grown also, Henry noted as he strolled by. A two-car garage had been added. The same old car stood in one half of it, but even as he watched, a much more expensive car drove in and the heavyset man Henry remembered got out, looking quite well-to-do. His wife came out to greet him, her brown hair blowing silkily about her ears, a healthy baby in her arms.

Good, Henry thought. They had done well. They'd be able to afford a new tree when he dug this one up and—suddenly confused, he stopped short. It had never occurred to him what a big job it would be to dig up a well-grown young tree. This was a busy suburb now, with regular police patrols, with people coming and going all the time—he could never do it, even at night, without being caught.

Henry gulped and resumed his walking. It looked as if he had outsmarted himself. He'd hidden the money so safely that now even he couldn't get at it.

Finally, he formed a plan. He'd have to get the tree legally. That meant he'd have to buy the house. Of course, he couldn't buy the house now. He had no money, and there was no sign the owner wanted to sell. But he could wait. For ten thousand dollars he could be patient. They were doing well, their family was growing. Sooner or later, they would want a bigger house. By then he'd have some money.

Having made his plans, Henry wasted no time. He dyed his hair and, feeling well disguised, got a job at a nearby garage, the one where Jerome Smith, the man who owned Henry's money tree, was a regular customer.

Continued in the next lesson . . .

2 Understanding the Story. Put the letter of the correct answer on the line.

1. At the beginning of the story, Henry's fellow employees think _____.
   a. he will probably have a successful career in banking
   b. he will never rise any higher than assistant cashier
   c. his eating in the park proves he is unfriendly
   d. his gambling on the stock market will lead to his ruin

2. Upon spotting the detectives, Henry _____.
   a. thinks they are after someone else
   b. wishes he had not stolen the money
   c. is shocked that they suspect him of any crime
   d. knows they have all the evidence they need to make an arrest

3. When he sees Melwood Estates, Henry is filled with despair because _____.
   a. he experiences a keen regret for the wrongs he has done
   b. he has always wanted to live in a place like this
   c. subdivisions have always depressed him
   d. the subdivision offers no hiding place

4. Henry has no intention of spending the rest of his life running from the law because _____.

   a. he doesn't think prison life will be that bad
   c. he doesn't want to live as a hunted man
   b. he feels he must pay for his crime
   d. he is fearful he might be killed

5. Henry suspects that the couple living in the Cape Cod house is struggling to make ends meet after he notices their _____.

   a. automobile
   c. naked lawn
   b. clothing
   d. spruce tree

6. The owner of the Cape Cod house seems _____.

   a. frantic
   c. distrustful
   b. friendly
   d. glum

7. Upon seeing Jerome Smith's neighborhood the second time, which sight distresses him? _____

   a. the child in Mrs. Smith's arms
   c. the police patrol
   b. the expensive car in the driveway
   d. the spruce tree

8. In what way does Henry's prison experience help him as he forms his future plans? _____

   a. He has a new trade.
   c. He now knows how to disguise himself.
   b. He is able to enjoy the Smiths' success.
   d. His moral values have changed completely.

3 What Do You Think? Robert Arthur writes, "So Henry, hardened by now to taking money that wasn't his, had taken ten thousand more." Do you think that committing one crime usually leads to committing more crimes? Be sure to include reasons to support your answer.

_____

_____

_____

_____

_____

_____

4 Synonyms. A *synonym* is a word that has almost the same meaning as another word. Match each word listed below with its synonym.

acquire	effortless	inflict	recently
attraction	flimsy	mess	reflection
comical	generous	possibly	unity

_____ **1.** amusing   _____ **7.** oneness

_____ **2.** charm   _____ **8.** perhaps

_____ **3.** impose   _____ **9.** easy

_____ **4.** muss   _____ **10.** thought

_____ **5.** newly   _____ **11.** unselfish

_____ **6.** obtain   _____ **12.** weak

5 Standard English. Study each rule below, and then underline the correct word in the sentences that follow it.

1. *Can* and *May*

   Can indicates the knowledge or ability to do something. *May* is used when permission is sought to do something, most often in the form of a question.

   a. "If I (can, may) be so bold," began Andy's advisor cautiously, "I would suggest that unless you take your homework assignments more seriously, you should forget all about getting a college degree."

   b. Because Karen (can, may) speak five languages, she was chosen to go to Europe.

   c. As the instructor was passing out the tests, one of the seniors asked sweetly, "(Can, May) we abbreviate our answers, or do we have to write them out?"

   d. "You (can, may) go to the movies if you (can, may) finish mowing the lawn before five o'clock," Dennis said to his son.

2. *In* and *Into*

In is used to indicate that something is already at a place. *Into* is used to indicate that someone or something is moving from the outside to the inside of a place.

a. "I was (in, into) the cellar selecting the wine for dinner, so you certainly can't suspect me of the murder!" the maid replied scornfully to the detective's first question.

b. "It figures," Sally sighed, when the telephone started ringing just as she was about to step (in, into) the bathtub.

c. As he sifted the flour and salt (in, into) the mixing bowl, Bart wondered if he shouldn't have simply followed his sister's suggestion and picked up a birthday cake at Mama's Bakery.

d. Anthony was (in, into) his closet searching for his all-time favorite sneakers when his mother walked (in, into) his room.

3. *Borrow* and *Lend*

Borrow means that an individual is on the taking end of a transaction. *Lend* means that an individual is on the giving end of a transaction.

a. An American humorist wrote, "Let us all be happy and live within our means, even if we have to (borrow, lend) the money to do it."

b. "I am not in the habit of (borrowing, lending) my clothes," said Alexis to her friend, "but if you really have nothing to wear skiing, you may use my turtleneck if you promise to wash it."

c. "May I (borrow, lend) your newspaper for a few minutes to kill time?" Mary asked the stranger seated next to her on the bus. "I promise to return it."

d. Herb grew increasingly annoyed with his boss for (borrowing, lending) money from him just before payday and then giving the staff lectures about how (borrowing, lending) money to fellow workers creates nothing but ill feelings in the office.

4. *About* and *Around*

About should be used when size or number is indicated. Used correctly, *around* indicates direction in a circle around an object.

a. The most recent ice age ended (about, around) 10,000 to 15,000 years ago.

b. Dr. Adams spends most of his time studying the earth's orbit (about, around) the sun.

c. Most glaciers range in thickness from (about, around) 300 to 10,000 feet.

d. After Nancy had lost (about, around) twenty pounds, she was once again able to button her favorite skirt (about, around) her waist.

6 Can You Crack the Code? Each group of letters spells the name of a tree, but the names have been concealed by a code in which a new set of letters has been used in place of the normal letters. The code is the same for all the trees. When you have guessed the name of a tree, use those letters to help you figure out the names of the remaining trees. The brief descriptions of these trees may help you solve this puzzle. The first one has been done to get you started.

<u>S</u> <u>P</u> <u>R</u> <u>U</u> <u>C</u> <u>E</u>
V A H D Q R

J T G

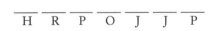
C T A Z R

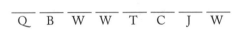
K B H Q F

O B Z Z J O

A B W R

Q B W W T C J W

H R P O J J P

Q F R V L W D L

X D P T V

1. An evergreen tree in the pine family, its wood is widely used for wood pulp by the paper industry. Sometimes the twigs from a young tree are used to make beer.

2. The male flowers of this tree, which lives from 200 to 400 years, produce pollen which is carried by the wind to female flowers. Once fertilized, a female flower will become an acorn.

3. Many people in the United States may not know that the leaf of this tree is the national emblem of Canada, but they do know that the delicious golden-brown syrup that comes from the sap of one type of this tree is used on pancakes and waffles.

4. One type of this tree has a bark that peels in layers. Some Indians used the bark to construct canoes.

5. One of the many trees of this type is native to China. It is described as "weeping" because of its graceful, drooping branches.

6. This tree, which ranks as the world's most important source of timber, bears both male and female cones. The female cones are much larger and have woody scales.

7. The dried bark from this tree is sold in sticks or ground up into a powder which many people enjoy mixing with sugar and sprinkling over buttered toast.

8. Growing along the West Coast of the United States, this is among the world's tallest trees. In a forest, these trees grow so close together that they shut out most of the sunlight.

9. Most of these trees in the U.S. have been killed by blight, but the wood is so lasting that even dead trees are harvested for lumber and pulpwood.

10. Also called the redbud tree, this tree is named after the man who, it is believed, hanged himself from one after betraying Jesus.

Review of Consonant Blends and Digraphs: Part 3

scr	shr	spr	str	tr	thr
scrawny	shrew	sprayer	straddle	tremendous	thrice
scrimp	shrewd	spree	stricken	trial	thrive
scrimmage	shrewdness	sprite	strife	triple	threesome
Scrooge	shrinkage	sprightly	strum	trombone	throng
subscribe	shroud	sprinkler	strudel	trustworthy	throaty
subscription	shrapnel	sprocket	strategize	tantrum	threshold
prescribe		spry	strychnine	pastry	

1 Definitions. Match the words listed below with the correct definitions.

scrawny	shrapnel	shrewd	sprite	strife	threshold
Scrooge	shrew	shroud	sprockets	strychnine	throng

_____   **1.** a cloth sometimes used to wrap a corpse for burying; something that covers or protects

_____   **2.** a great number of people gathered together; a crowd

_____   **3.** a highly poisonous, colorless substance used in small doses to increase the activity of the nervous system

_____   **4.** a mean, selfish person (from the character of this name in Charles Dickens' *A Christmas Carol*)

_____   **5.** teeth, as on the rim of a wheel, arranged to fit into the links of a chain

_____   **6.** a shell filled with an explosive charge and many small metal balls that explodes in the air over the target

_____   **7.** a small mammal with a long, pointed nose and poor eyesight; this word also refers to a woman who scolds or nags frequently

_____   **8.** an elf or pixie; a small or mysterious supernatural being

_____   **9.** bitter struggle or conflict

_____   **10.** clever; tricky

_____   **11.** skinny; thin and bony; lean

_____   **12.** the entrance or beginning point of something

Words for Study

Constance	housekeeper	anxious	chum
Mozart	proposing	hurricane	humble
Nevada	stammered	topple	gratitude
divorce	frequently	glinted	involvement

Mr. Manning's Money Tree: Part II
by Robert Arthur

Henry did his best to become friendly with Jerome Smith, but Smith was gruff, as though his mind was on bigger things. His wife Constance, however, was charming. Henry was on duty when she brought her car in for gas and oil.

"You're new, aren't you?" she asked, her voice musical. Henry nodded.

"Just since last week, Mrs. Smith. Shall I check the radiator and battery?"

"Would you?" Constance Smith sat waiting patiently, the car radio playing.

"Mozart, isn't it?" Henry said.

"Why, yes. You know music?" Constance looked with interest at Henry.

"A bit," Henry said.

It was certainly part of his plan to become friendly with the Smiths so that when they were ready to sell he would be among the first to know. But it wasn't part of his plan to look forward to seeing Constance, to feel somehow gloomy when several days went by and she did not stop in the garage for some service on her car. Nevertheless, it happened. Instead of hoping the Smiths would soon decide to move, Henry began to wish they would stay.

By then Henry was manager of the repair department, and his friendship with Constance, though limited to brief chats while she waited for her car to be fixed or perhaps over a cup of coffee in her kitchen when he went to start the car on a cold morning, was a firm one, important to both of them. They talked about books and music and plays, and Henry knew that Constance enjoyed the talks as much as he did.

One morning Constance called the garage to ask Henry if he could stop in. Her voice sounded upset. She was pale as she led him into the living room.

"Something has happened, Henry," she said, trying to smile, "and I—well, I felt I had to talk about it to a friend."

"I'm glad you think of me as a friend."

"It's a little difficult to say it. You see—" her voice could barely be heard— "Jerry and I haven't been close for a long time. He's away so much and even when he's home . . . well, anyway, he's in Nevada now. He's starting some business out there. So . . . he suggests in a letter I got this morning that he might as well stay there and get a divorce."

"A divorce?" Henry stared at her in disbelief.

"I'm going to say yes, of course. Goodness, I certainly don't want a husband who doesn't want *me*." Her laugh was a little shaky, but it held back the tears.

Now Henry no longer confined himself to business visits, but dropped in at the little house whenever he could. He helped Constance find a job and got the mother of one of his mechanics to become a housekeeper for her son, Peter. He was so concerned with making sure that Constance and Peter were well looked after that it never occurred to him that he could get his money tree until the evening when, after taking Constance to a concert, he found himself proposing to her.

He was in the middle of telling her how much she meant to him when it suddenly struck him that if she married him, the tree was his. And he stopped, wondering in shame whether he really loved her or whether he just wanted to retrieve his hidden money. The possibility rattled him and he stammered, so that Constance laughed softly.

"Henry, are you trying to propose?"

"Yes, I am! I love you! I want you to be my wife, Constance, and Peter to be my son."

She was silent for a long moment, studying his face. "Yes, Henry," she said at last.

So Henry finally became the owner of the money tree. But to him this was unimportant. Now that he had a gracious and loving wife and a handsome son, what need did he have for stolen money?

Still the money proved useful a year later when the owner of the garage decided to retire. Henry didn't have the necessary cash to buy the business. But he knew where the cash was—in his front yard. So he recklessly signed notes. After all, if worse came to worst, he could always pay them off.

There were many nights when Henry strolled in the yard, figuring out how he could keep from digging up the spruce just yet. Somehow, he was unwilling to touch it and, in the end, he managed.

Meanwhile Jerome Smith's photograph appeared frequently in the newspapers. He had become part owner of a big new hotel and gambling casino in Las Vegas and married a stunning showgirl.

Henry and Constance couldn't have cared less. They had a daughter by now, Anne. The children grew from year to year.

Henry bought an auto dealership. Again, there were many anxious nights when he stood beside the tree, thinking this might be the last time he could smell its fragrance. But each time he pulled through somehow.

From then on business boomed. Henry saved for what he knew he must do. At last the day came— just such a sunny day as that one long ago when as a young man he had come out of the bank with stolen money in his briefcase. His hair was graying now, and there were lines of years and living in his face as he entered the bank once more, carrying a briefcase under his arm—the same briefcase.

When he came out, the briefcase was empty. He had returned thirty thousand dollars with interest to date. He went home at peace with the world.

That night he stood beneath his money tree and counted his blessings. The money he had hidden beneath the roots of the tree had done its work. He reached out to stroke the needles of the beautiful spruce.

"You've done a good job, old boy," he said. "You've guarded my stolen fortune even against me. I'll never touch you. You can stand forever."

But one day the following autumn an Atlantic hurricane swung in suddenly from the coast and struck the city. Henry was with Constance in the living room, listening to radio reports of the storm. From the yard there came a creaking and groaning.

Henry reached the window just in time to see his proud spruce topple over, leaving a gaping hole.

He felt as if a friend had died. Then he realized he would have to find the long-hidden thermos before anyone else came upon it. Up at dawn the next morning, he scrambled into the hole left by the roots of the spruce.

The rising sun glinted on something bright. He reached in gingerly. It was the silvered core of the thermos—the outer steel covering had rusted away long ago. He eased open the cork with his knife and shook the bottle. Two scraps of paper fell out. Nothing else. Just two scraps of paper. He picked them up.

One was an old newspaper clipping. With a shock he saw it was a picture of himself and the story of his arrest. The other was simply a bit of paper on which was written in Jerome Smith's jagged writing. *I guessed. Thanks, chum.*

A little dazed, Henry went into the house and sat down at the kitchen table. All these years, the money he had counted on hadn't been there! Slowly the shock passed, and it was followed by a feeling of deep and humble gratitude. Life was a curiously complex business. The money he had stolen and buried, but never used, had won him a family, success, contentment. For Jerome Smith it had led to ownership of a big hotel and casino and involvement in the national gambling rackets with illegal interests.

Henry shook his head and picked up the piece of paper on which Smith had written *Thanks, chum.* Beneath it Henry wrote neatly, *You're welcome.* Then he sealed it in an envelope and addressed it. From what he had been reading in the papers lately, he judged that if he simply sent it in care of the Federal Penitentiary at Atlanta, Georgia, it would get to him all right.

2 Understanding the Story.

1. Number these events in the order in which they occur in "Mr. Manning's Money Tree." The first one is done to get you started.

_____ Constance accepts Henry's marriage proposal.

_____ Henry helps Constance find a job.

_____ Henry becomes the manager of the repair department.

_____ Henry buys an auto dealership.

_____ Henry returns the money to the bank with interest.

_____ Henry finds an old newspaper clipping in his thermos.

_____ Henry writes a letter to Jerome Smith.

___1___ Jerome Smith leaves a note for Henry.

_____ Jerome Smith leaves his wife.

_____ Melwood Estates is struck by a hurricane.

2. In what sense is Henry Manning still a gambler in the second part of "Mr. Manning's Money Tree"?

_____

_____

_____

3. How does Henry's gambling in the second part of the story differ from his gambling in Part I?

_____

_____

_____

_____

4. Cite two examples that show that Henry's attitude regarding the stolen money has changed.

a. _____

_____

b. _____

_____

3 What Do You Think? According to an old saying, "The love of money is the root of all evil." Does Robert Arthur seem to agree with this saying? Be sure to include details from the story to support your answer.

_____

_____

_____

_____

_____

_____

_____

4 Words That End in -al. Use the words listed below to complete the following sentences.

| approval | brutal | intentional | personal | refusal |
| behavioral | disposal | mechanical | proposal | regional |

1. After a _____ four-hour workout at the gym, the heavyweight prizefighter relaxed by soaking in a hot tub and listening to classical tapes.

2. "I don't care whether your being late was _____ or accidental," Peggy shouted at her boyfriend. "The point is I don't like being kept waiting."

3. The safe _____ of nuclear waste is a problem that demands our immediate attention.

4. The cashier's _____ to admit he had given the customer incorrect change led to a highly emotional scene which almost resulted in a fist fight.

5. The teachers' _____ to increase the number of field trips was vetoed by the board of education.

6. Prudes are so judgmental that it seems as if even the saints in heaven couldn't win their _____.

7. Thomas so enjoyed having a computer at work that he bought one for his _____ use at home.

8. Times were so hard that every farmer in the area attended the monthly _____ meeting to discuss the agricultural problems confronting them.

9. Watching Mr. Jones try to repair his Volkswagen was a comical experience because he had no _____ ability whatsoever.

10. When Mr. Reed finished telling the third-grade teacher about his son's actions at home, she replied calmly, "I think if we work together, we can help him overcome his _____ problems."

5 Antonyms. An *antonym* is a word whose meaning is opposite to the meaning of another word. Match each word listed below with its antonym.

approve	detect	flustered	gradually	impede	precious	shrinkage
creditor	ebb	glamorous	idleness	play up	rumor	unity

_____ **1.** assist

_____ **2.** composed

_____ **3.** debtor

_____ **4.** downplay

_____ **5.** dull

_____ **6.** expansion

_____ **7.** fact

_____ **8.** flow

_____ **9.** labor

_____ **10.** overlook

_____ **11.** scorn

_____ **12.** strife

_____ **13.** suddenly

_____ **14.** worthless

6 Look It Up. Use a dictionary, an encyclopedia, or the Internet to answer the following questions.

1. In order for a storm to be called a hurricane, its winds must be blowing at a certain speed. What is the minimum speed the winds can be blowing in order for a storm to be called a hurricane?

_____

_____

_____

_____

2. Hurricanes begin in the warm regions of which ocean?

_____

_____

3. What is a *hurricane lamp*?

_____

_____

1 Word Review. Use the words listed below to fill in the blanks.

burlap	Dickens	Mozart	rheumatism
casino	finance	parole	rumor
compost	gratitude	plaza	suburb
credit	mortgage	reptile	temple

_____ **1.** a building or place devoted to worship; any place or building serving as the center for a special activity or something especially valued

_____ **2.** a community on the outskirts of a city

_____ **3.** a composer of more than 600 classical works who began composing music at the age of five (1756–1791)

_____ **4.** a claim on property, given as security for a loan

_____ **5.** a mixture of decaying matter, such as leaves, used to fertilize the soil

_____ **6.** a public room or house for entertainment, especially gambling

_____ **7.** a public square in a town or city; a paved area for automobiles, such as the widened roadway forming the approach to a group of tollbooths on a highway

_____ **8.** a rough woven cloth made of fibers of jute, flax, or hemp, used to make bags

_____ **9.** a thankful awareness for a gift or favor

_____ **10.** any of several diseased conditions of the muscles, tendons, joints, bones, or nerves that causes discomfort and disability; rheumatoid arthritis

_____ **11.** any of a variety of cold-blooded animals, usually egg-laying, having a covering of scales or horny plates and breathing by means of lungs

_____ **12.** gossip; information usually spread by word of mouth that has not been proven true

_____ **13.** a popular English writer who showed sympathy for the poor and helpless and mocked the selfish, greedy, and cruel in his books (1812–1870)

_____ **14.** the release of a prisoner before his term has ended on condition of continued good behavior

_____ **15.** trust; praise; confidence in a buyer's ability to pay money owed at some future time

_____ **16.** the use or management of money and other assets

2 Synonyms and Antonyms. Choose a synonym to fill in the first blank in each sentence. Choose an antonym to fill in the second blank. Study the example before you begin.

Synonyms

anxious
brilliant
frequent
glee
humble
humdrum
nucleus
prolong
puny
rival
trustworthy
✓wicked

Antonyms

boastful
calm
despair
drab
edge
faithless
inspiring
partner
✓saintly
seldom
shorten
strong

1. Evil and __wicked__ are antonyms for __saintly__ .

2. Extend and _____ are antonyms for _____ .

3. Glowing and _____ are antonyms for

   _____ .

4. Hub and _____ are antonyms for _____ .

5. Unaffected and _____ are antonyms for

   _____ .

6. Loyal and _____ are antonyms for _____ .

7. Happiness and _____ are antonyms for

   _____ .

8. Often and _____ are antonyms for _____ .

9. Challenger and _____ are antonyms for

   _____ .

10. Boring and _____ are antonyms for _____ .

11. Weak and _____ are antonyms for _____ .

12. Worried and _____ are antonyms for

    _____ .

3 Word Families. Use the words in each set at the left to complete these sentences correctly.

finances
financial
financially

1. After Leslie phoned her father on the East Coast to tell him how proud she was that she had finally gotten the household _____ in order and her budget was _____ faultless, her husband presented her with the latest _____ problem—last month's telephone bill.

unity
disunity
unify

2. Alarmed by the growing _____ in the neighborhood, Ernie urged the parents to _____ their efforts to supervise their children's conduct so that _____ could be restored.

curious
curiously
curiosity

3. Even though the museum's ancient shrunken head was such a _____ that Kenneth stared at it for a long time, _____, he was not _____ enough to ask the curator about it.

fashion
fashionable
unfashionable

4. Because Mrs. Miller had been taught that it is not _____ to waste one's time criticizing other women's choices in _____, she kept to herself her opinions about how _____ the senator's wife had looked at the art museum that morning.

gracious
graciously
graciousness

5. In spite of Mrs. Rich's _____, Tony decided to refuse _____ her invitation to stay at her home because he was not used to such _____ living.

shrewd
shrewdly
shrewdness

6. In Aesop's fables, the fox is usually a _____ character who _____ convinces others to do exactly as he wants; but sometimes he is outsmarted by his own _____.

wicked
wickedly
wickedness

7. In *The Wizard of Oz*, the _____ Witch of the West _____ plots Dorothy's destruction, but her _____ results in her own destruction instead.

| agreeable agreeably disagreeable | **8.** The Johnsons found the crowded and noisy restaurant so _____ that they _____ decided to order a large pizza to go and eat at home where the atmosphere was more _____. |

| instant instantly instance | **9.** As the network newscaster began to report an _____ of public scandal in their suburb, Mr. Scott _____ rose to his feet and angrily turned off the set so his family could enjoy their _____ coffee in peace. |

| generous generously generosity | **10.** When Mrs. Clark offered all the loose change in her purse to the panhandler wandering around the busy intersection, he bowed graciously and said, "Your _____ donation restores my faith, and I know you will some day be _____ rewarded for your _____." |

4 Which Word Does Not Fit? Choose the word that does not fit with the other words in each row, and write it on the line.

1. float	glide	plod	sail	skim	_____
2. haul	grasp	lug	tote	pull	_____
3. despair	sorrow	grief	sadness	frustration	_____
4. elf	angel	gnome	pixie	sprite	_____
5. disagree	disjoin	divide	divorce	separate	_____
6. amazing	brisk	lively	spry	sprightly	_____
7. silly	glum	solemn	serious	grave	_____
8. Wyoming	Illinois	Nevada	Utah	Colorado	_____
9. delight	zest	passion	spree	enjoyment	_____
10. blizzard	tornado	cyclone	hurricane	earthquake	_____
11. strategy	design	option	plan	blueprint	_____
12. blunt	gruff	abrupt	short	outraged	_____

5 Money. Identify the underlined word that is misspelled in each of the following sayings, and write it correctly on the line.

_____ 1. Although a dollar bill is only six inchs long, it is used to measure many things.

_____ 2. Striving to live within a budget is almost as hopeless as attemting to find a word that rhymes with "orange."

_____ 3. If you can't pay your debts, at least you can be thankfull you are not one of your creditors.

_____ 4. The way food prices are soaring, being overweight may soon become a sucess symbol.

_____ 5. The buget is a method of being anxious about money before you spend it, instead of afterward.

_____ 6. Whatever assets we possess can often become of double value when we simply share them with a freind.

_____ 7. Everything seems to be under fedral control except the national debt and budget.

_____ 8. Washington, D.C., is the seat of the United States goverment, and the American taxpayer is the pants pocket.

_____ 9. A nickel goes much farther nowadays; it is neccessary to carry it around awhile before you can discover something it will purchase.

_____ 10. A financial fool who excitedly discovers he has money to burn will usualy meet his match.

_____ 11. The reason money is called legal tender is that if you dont have it, it's tough.

_____ 12. The real measure of an individual's welth is how much he would be worth if he lost all his fortune.

6 A Final Note on Love and Money. Read the poem, and then answer the questions that follow.

The Choice
by Dorothy Parker

He'd have given me rolling lands,
    Houses of marble, and billowing farms,
Pearls, to trickle between my hands,
    Smoldering rubies, to circle my arms.
You—you'd only a lilting song,
    Only a melody, happy and high,
You were sudden and swift and strong—
    Never a thought for another had I.

He'd have given me laces rare,
    Dresses that glimmered with frosty sheen,
Shining ribbons to wrap my hair,
    Horses to draw me, as fine as a queen.
You—you'd only to whistle low,
    Gayly I followed wherever you led,
I took you, and I let him go—
    Somebody ought to examine my head!

1. The speaker in this poem talks about a choice she was faced with. She had to choose between two men.

    a. The first four lines of each stanza describe what one man could offer her. What did he have to offer?

    _____

    _____

    b. The rest of each stanza describes what the second man had to offer. What did he have to offer?

    _____

    _____

2. Which man does she choose? _____

3. Why does she choose this man? _____

    _____

4. If she were offered the same choice again, does it seem as if she would make the same decision? Be sure to include reasons to support your answer.

    _____

    _____

    _____

5. If you had to choose between love and money, which would you choose? Be sure to include reasons to explain your answer.

    _____

    _____

    _____

    _____

UNIT 2
Struggle

It has been suggested by more than one writer that people's characters are formed by their struggles with forces outside themselves. Struggle is the theme of this group of short stories in which the characters find themselves in situations that seem to be too much for them to handle. What are their struggles and how do they cope with them?

In "All the Years of Her Life," the story for Lesson 5, three characters struggle to deal with their reactions to stealing.

"Prelude," the story for Lesson 6, is set in New York City just before the United States enters World War II. The family in this story struggles to cope with prejudice.

Prejudice is also the cause of tension in "The Test," the story for Lesson 7. In this story the author encourages us to ask: Is there more than one way to fail a test?

We often tend to think that struggles are something that teenagers and grown-ups have to face—something that children know nothing about. In "Charles," the story for Lesson 8, the author sees things differently, however, as she describes one child's response to being sent off to kindergarten.

Review of Digraphs: Part 4

sh	**ch**			**th**	
shanty	chute	charity	chord	filth	thy
shawl	machinist	Chile	chorus	filthy	thyself
shepherd	chandelier	chili	choir	panther	thine
shiftless	chauffeur	chickadee	chemistry	thermometer	thou
shun	chiffon	merchant	characteristic	thoroughfare	bothersome
anguish	Cheyenne	spinach	orchestra	theory	fatherly
accomplish	Charlotte	parched	orchid	ether	motherly

1 Definitions. Match the words listed below with the correct definitions.

chandelier	chemistry	merchant	shanty	shun
characteristic	Chile	orchid	shawl	theory
chauffeur	chute	parched	shiftless	thoroughfare

_____ 1. a piece of cloth worn by women as a covering for the head, neck, or shoulders

_____ 2. a feature, trait, or quality

_____ 3. a main road or public highway

_____ 4. a person employed to drive a private car

_____ 5. a person whose occupation is the wholesale buying and retail selling of goods for profit

_____ 6. a branched fixture usually hung from the ceiling that holds bulbs or candles

_____ 7. a plant found chiefly in hot climates and often having showy flowers

_____ 8. a republic of western South America

_____ 9. a shack; a roughly built or ramshackle cabin

_____ 10. an idea that explains the causes for something

_____ 11. an inclined passage or channel down which things may pass; a waterfall or rapid

_____ 12. lazy; showing a lack of energy or goals

_____ 13. the study of the structure, characteristics, and reactions of substances

_____ 14. thirsty or very dry

_____ 15. to avoid a person, group, or thing

All the Years of Her Life
by Morley Callaghan

They were closing the drugstore, and Alfred Higgins, who had just taken off his white jacket, was putting on his coat and getting ready to go home. The little gray-haired man, Sam Carr, who owned the drugstore, was bending down behind the cash register, and when Alfred Higgins passed him, he looked up and said softly, "Just a moment, Alfred."

The soft, confident, quiet way in which Sam Carr spoke made Alfred start to button his coat nervously. He felt sure his face was white. Sam Carr usually said, "Good night," without looking up. In the six months he had been working in the drugstore Alfred had never heard his employer speak softly like that. His heart began to beat so loud it was hard for him to get his breath. "What is it, Mr. Carr?" he asked.

"Maybe you'd be good enough to take a few things out of your pocket and leave them here before you go," Sam Carr said.

"What things? What are you talking about?"

"You've got a compact and a lipstick and at least two tubes of toothpaste in your pocket, Alfred."

"What do you mean? Do you think I'm crazy?" Alfred blustered. His face got red and he knew he looked fierce with indignation. But Sam Carr only nodded his head. Then Alfred grew very frightened and he didn't know what to say. Slowly he raised his hand and dipped it into his pocket. With his eyes never meeting Sam Carr's eyes, he took out a blue compact, two tubes of toothpaste, and a lipstick, and he laid them one by one on the counter.

"Petty thieving, eh, Alfred?" Sam Carr said. "And maybe you'd be good enough to tell me how long this has been going on."

"This is the first time I ever took anything."

"So now you think you'll tell me a lie, eh? What kind of a sap do I look like, huh? I tell you you've been doing this pretty steady," Sam Carr said.

Ever since Alfred had left school he had been getting into trouble wherever he worked. He lived at home with his mother and his father, who was a printer. His two older brothers were married and his sister had got married last year. It would have been all right for his parents now if Alfred had only been able to keep a job.

While Sam Carr smiled, Alfred began to feel that familiar terror growing in him that had been in him every time he had got into such trouble.

"I liked you," Sam Carr was saying. "I liked you and would have trusted you, and now look what I got to do." While Alfred watched with his alert, frightened blue eyes, Sam Carr drummed with fingers on the counter. "I don't like to call a cop in point blank," he was saying as he looked very worried. "You're a fool, and maybe I should call your father and tell him you're a fool. Maybe I should let them know I'm going to have you locked up."

"My father's not at home. He's a printer. He works nights," Alfred said.

"Who's at home?"

"My mother, I guess."

"Then we'll see what she says." Sam Carr went to the phone and dialed the number. Alfred was not so much ashamed, but there was that deep fright growing in him, and he blurted out rudely, "Just a minute. You don't need to tell her." He wanted to sound like a swaggering, big guy who could look after himself, yet the old, childish hope was in him, the longing that someone at home would come and help him.

"Yeah, that's right, he's in trouble," Mr. Carr was saying. "You'd better come down in a hurry." And when he was finished, Mr. Carr went over to the door and looked out at the street and said, "I'll keep my eye out for a cop."

Alfred knew how his mother would come rushing in. She would rush in with her eyes blazing, or maybe she would be crying, and she would push him away when he tried to talk to her, and make him feel her dreadful contempt. Yet he longed that she might come before Mr. Carr saw the cop on the beat passing the door.

While they waited—and it seemed a long time— they did not speak, and when at last they heard someone tapping on the closed door, Mr. Carr, turning the latch, said crisply, "Come in, Mrs. Higgins." He looked hard-faced and stern.

Mrs. Higgins must have been going to bed when he telephoned, for her hair was tucked in loosely under her hat, and her hand at her throat held her light coat tightly across her chest so her dress would not show. She came in, large and plump, with a little smile on her friendly face. Most of the store lights had been turned out and at first she did not see Alfred, who was standing in the shadow at the end of the counter. Yet as soon as she saw him she did not look as Alfred thought she would look.

She smiled, and her blue eyes never wavered. With a calmness and dignity that made them forget that her clothes seemed to have been thrown on her, she put out her hand to Mr. Carr and said politely, "I'm Mrs. Higgins, I'm Alfred's mother."

Mr. Carr was a bit embarrassed by her lack of terror and her simple manner, and he hardly knew what to say to her, so she asked, "Is Alfred in trouble?"

"He is. He's been taking things from the store. I caught him red-handed. Little things like compacts and toothpaste and lipsticks. Stuff he can sell easily," the owner said.

When Sam Carr had finished, she said, "Is it so, Alfred?"

"Yes."

"Why have you been doing it?"

"I been spending money, I guess."

"On what?"

"Going around with the guys, I guess," Alfred said.

Mrs. Higgins put out her hand and touched Sam Carr's arm with an understanding gentleness and said, "If you would only listen to me before doing anything." Her simple earnestness made her shy. Then she said with a kind of patient dignity, "What did you intend to do, Mr. Carr?"

"I was going to get a cop. That's what I ought to do."

"Yes, I suppose so. It's not for me to say, because he's my son. Yet I sometimes think a little good advice is the best thing for a boy when he's at a certain period in his life," she said.

Alfred couldn't understand his mother's quiet manner. If they had been at home and someone had suggested he was going to be arrested, he knew she would be in a rage and would cry out against him. Yet now she was standing there with that gentle pleading smile on her face, saying, "I wonder if you don't think it would be better just to let him come home with me. He looks a big fellow, doesn't he? It takes some of them a long time to get any sense," and they both stared at Alfred, who shifted away with a bit of light shining for a moment on his thin face and the tiny pimples over his cheekbone.

But even while he was turning away uneasily, Alfred was realizing that Mr. Carr had become aware that his mother was really a fine woman. He knew that Sam Carr was puzzled by his mother, as if he

had expected her to come in and plead with him tearfully, and instead he was being made to feel a bit ashamed by her vast understanding.

"Of course, I don't want to be harsh," Mr. Carr was saying. "I'll tell you what I'll do. I'll just fire him and let it go at that. How's that?" and he bowed low to Mrs. Higgins in deep respect.

There was such warmth and gratitude in the way she said, "I'll never forget your kindness," that Mr. Carr began to feel warm and friendly himself.

"Sorry we had to meet this way," he said. "But I'm glad I got in touch with you. Just wanted to do the right thing, that's all," he said.

"It's better to meet like this than never, isn't it?" she said. Suddenly they clasped hands as if they liked each other, as if they had known each other a long time. "Good night, sir," she said.

The mother and son walked along the street together, and the mother was taking a long, firm stride as she looked ahead with her stern face full of worry. Alfred was afraid to speak to her, so he only looked ahead too. He began to wonder what she was thinking of as she stared ahead so grimly. She seemed to have forgotten that he walked beside her.

Finally he said in his old blustering way, "Thank God it turned out like that. I certainly won't get in a jam like that again."

"Be quiet. Don't speak to me. You've disgraced me again and again," she said bitterly.

"That's the last time. That's all I'm saying."

"Have the decency to be quiet," she snapped. They kept on their way, looking straight ahead.

When they were at home and his mother took off her coat, Alfred saw that she was really only half-dressed, and she made him feel afraid again when she said, without even looking at him, "You're a bad lot. God forgive you. It's one thing after another and always has been. Why do you stand there stupidly? Go to bed, why don't you?"

When he was going, she said, "I'm going to make myself a cup of tea. Mind, now, not a word about tonight to your father."

While Alfred was undressing in his bedroom, he heard his mother moving around the kitchen. As he listened there was no shame in him, just wonder and a kind of respect of her strength and calmness. He could still see Sam Carr nodding his head encouragingly to her; he could hear her talking simply and earnestly. "She certainly was smooth," he thought. "Gee, I'd like to tell her she sounded swell."

He got up and went along to the kitchen, and when he was at the door he saw his mother pouring herself a cup of tea. He watched and didn't move.

Her face, as she sat there, was a frightened, broken face utterly unlike the face of the woman who had been so assured a little while ago in the drugstore. When she reached out and lifted the kettle to pour hot water in her cup, her hand trembled and the water splashed on the stove. Leaning back in the chair, she sighed and lifted the cup, swallowing the hot tea eagerly. Her hand holding the cup still trembled, and she looked very old.

It seemed to Alfred that this was the way it had been every time he had been in trouble before, that this trembling had really been in her as she hurried out half-dressed to the drugstore. He understood why she had sat alone in the kitchen the night his young sister had kept repeating stubbornly that she was getting married. Now he felt all that his mother had been thinking of as they walked along the street together a little while ago. He watched his mother, and he never spoke, but at that moment his youth seemed to be over. He knew all the years of her life by the way her hand trembled as she raised the cup to her lips. It seemed to him that this was the first time he had ever looked upon his mother.

2 Understanding the Story. The three characters in "All the Years of Her Life" experience many feelings and reactions as they deal with the fact that Alfred has been caught stealing. State a reason for each feeling or reaction listed below. Study the example before you begin.

Sam Carr

angry: <u>He has caught Alfred, whom he trusted, stealing from him.</u>

puzzled: _____

_____

softhearted: _____

_____

Alfred Higgins

blustering: _____

_____

frightened: _____

_____

astonished: _____

_____

Mrs. Higgins

polite: _____

_____

angry: _____

_____

trembling: _____

_____

3 What Do You Think? Answer the following questions in complete sentence form. Be sure to use examples to support your answers.

1. What do you think Morley Callaghan meant when he wrote, "It seemed to him that this was the first time he had ever looked upon his mother"?

   _____

   _____

   _____

   _____

2. In light of what happens in the story, do you think Alfred will change his behavior?

   _____

   _____

   _____

   _____

3. What feelings do you experience when you find yourself in a situation in which there is some kind of pressure?

   _____

   _____

   _____

   _____

   _____

4 Word Relationships. Complete each statement by writing out the best answer.

1. Shepherd is to flock as _____.
   - **a.** clotheshorse is to shopping
   - **b.** cowboy is to herd
   - **c.** inventor is to laboratory
   - **d.** merchant is to goods

2. Chile is to South America as _____.
   - **a.** China is to Europe
   - **b.** Egypt is to Africa
   - **c.** Iowa is to Midwest
   - **d.** Paris is to France

3. Theory is to idea as _____.
   - **a.** quiz is to assignment
   - **b.** organization is to details
   - **c.** flag is to emblem
   - **d.** strategy is to method

4. Container is to crock as _____.
   - **a.** fixture is to chandelier
   - **b.** fun is to drudgery
   - **c.** odor is to skunk
   - **d.** thermos is to coffee

5. Carol is to Christmas as _____.

    a. chord is to composer   **c.** hymn is to church

    b. conductor is to orchestra   **d.** melody is to choir

6. Cheyenne is to Wyoming as _____.

    a. Atlantic City is to New York   **c.** Cleveland is to Pennsylvania

    b. Baltimore is to New Jersey   **d.** Memphis is to Tennessee

7. Ruler is to inches as _____.

    a. cup is to pint   **c.** speedometer is to gasoline

    b. scale is to pressure   **d.** thermometer is to temperature

8. Yard is to measurement as _____.

    a. ether is to pill   **c.** sermon is to clergyman

    b. oval is to shape   **d.** snobbishness is to clique

9. Glee is to gloom as _____.

    a. approval is to assurance   **c.** silliness is to gravity

    b. generosity is to charity   **d.** strife is to disunity

10. Troublesome is to effortless as _____.

    a. bothersome is to convenient   **c.** wholesome is to healthy

    b. threesome is to trio   **d.** worrisome is to anxious

5 **Sounds for *ch*.** Classify each word listed below according to its sound for *ch*.

ache	chapel	Cherokee	choir	machinery	mustache
chalk	chef	Chicago	echo	mechanical	scorch
champagne	chemical	chief	lynch	Michigan	strychnine

china	**ch**andelier	**ch**aracter
1. _____	1. _____	1. _____
2. _____	2. _____	2. _____
3. _____	3. _____	3. _____
4. _____	4. _____	4. _____
5. _____	5. _____	5. _____
6. _____	6. _____	6. _____

6 Standard English. Study each rule below, and then underline the correct word in the sentences that follow it.

1. *All ready* and *Already*

All ready means just what the two words indicate—all prepared. *Already* means previously.

    a. Ralph was (all ready, already) for his first performance when he suddenly realized in horror that he had left his clarinet on the bus.

    b. Gloria's husband pleaded with her to work hard for a promotion, but she was (all ready, already) so frustrated that she decided to forget the whole idea.

    c. Justin's blunder had (all ready, already) cost the firm thousands of dollars, and he worked overtime for several weeks, hoping that it would not also cost him his livelihood.

    d. Charlotte was (all ready, already) to serve the chili when she realized that she had forgotten to buy any crackers to go with it.

2. *Beside* and *Besides*

Beside means at the side of. *Besides* means in addition.

    a. (Beside, Besides) being the best shooter on the basketball team, John was also a good sport.

    b. "How do you expect me to enjoy this juicy steak," roared Mr. Polk at the startled waiter, "when you place the bill right (beside, besides) my dinner plate!"

    c. (Beside, Besides) the mortgage and insurance payments, Wendy figured the bank loan would also have to cover the expense of her son's shoulder operation.

    d. Judy placed the vase containing the single fragrant rose her boyfriend had given her (beside, besides) his picture.

3. *Affect* and *Effect*

Affect most commonly means to influence. *Effect* usually means a result.

    a. Jerry hoped that the accident he had had two years ago would not (affect, effect) his chances of becoming Mr. Snow's chauffeur.

    b. Sir Isaac Newton's writings about the law of gravity had a great (affect, effect) on scientists both in his own time and in future generations.

    c. Defining work as honest toil rather than unjust drudgery can have a positive (affect, effect) on the way we view our jobs.

    d. The new tax laws did not (affect, effect) Steven's giving money to charities he considered worthwhile.

Review of Consonant Blends: Part 5

sl	sm	sn	sk	sch	sc	
slab	smartly	sniffle	skeleton	schedule	Scandinavia	scenic
slacken	smattering	snicker	skimpy	scholar	landscape	scissors
slender	smashup	snug	skirmish	scholarly	scurry	descend
slink	smug	snuggle	tusk	scholarship	scope	descent
sliver	smidgen	sneer	husk		microscope	descendant
slogan	smithereens	snoop	whiskers		telescope	

1 Definitions. Match the words listed below with the correct definitions.

> descend   microscope   scholarship   scurry   slacken   smithereens   telescope
> descendant   Scandinavia   scissors   skirmish   slogan   snicker

_____ **1.** a minor incident in a war

_____ **2.** a catch phrase used to advertise a product

_____ **3.** a gift of money or other aid given by a foundation, etc., to help a student continue his studies

_____ **4.** a person or animal descended from another

_____ **5.** a region in northern Europe which includes Norway, Sweden, Denmark, and sometimes Finland and Iceland

_____ **6.** a word used in informal speech to describe fragments or splintered pieces; bits

_____ **7.** an instrument that enlarges the images of objects too small to be seen by the naked eye

_____ **8.** an instrument used to observe distant objects

_____ **9.** to become less active or intense; to reduce the tension or relax

_____ **10.** to laugh in a sly and impolite way at someone

_____ **11.** an instrument used to cut

_____ **12.** to move from a higher to a lower place; to slope or incline downward

_____ **13.** to run hastily; to scamper

Words for Study

prelude	Silverstein	edition	Austria
Sylvia	respectable	hoodlums	dwindle
sergeant	communist	merely	prejudiced

Prelude

by Albert Halper

I was coming home from school, carrying my books by a strap, when I passed the poolroom and saw the big guys hanging around.

"Hey, Ike, how's your good-looking sister?" they called, but I didn't turn around. The guys are eighteen or nineteen and haven't ever had a job in their life. "What they need is work," my father is always saying when they bother him too much. "They're not bad; they get that way because there's nothing to do," and he tries to explain the meanness of their ways. But I can't see it like my father. I hate those fellas and I hope every one of them dies under a truck. Every time I come home from school past Lake Street they jab me, and every time my sister Sylvia comes along they say things. So when one of them calls, "Hey, Ike, how's your sister?" I don't answer. Besides, Ike isn't my name anyway. It's Harry.

I passed along the sidewalk, keeping close to the curb. Someone threw half an apple but it went over my head. When I went a little farther, someone threw a stone. It hit me in the back of the leg and stung me but it didn't hurt much. I kept a little toward the middle of the sidewalk because I saw a woman coming along the other way, and I knew they wouldn't throw.

I came up to the newsstand and put my school books inside. "Well, Pa," I said, "you can go to

Florida now." So my Pa went to "Florida," which was a chair near the radiator that Nick lets him use in his restaurant. He has to use Nick's place because our own flat is too far away, about a quarter-mile off.

The first ten minutes after coming home from school and taking care of the newsstand always excite me. I like everything about selling papers for my father. The fresh air gets me and I like to talk to customers and see the rush when people are let out from work. The only thing I don't like is those guys from the poolroom. But since my father went to the police station to complain, they don't come around so often. The desk sergeant there said, "Don't worry, Mr. Silverstein, we'll take care of it. You're a respectable citizen and taxpayer and you're entitled to protection." And the next day they sent over a patrolman who stood around almost two hours.

Well, all this happened three or four weeks ago and so far the gang has let us alone. They stopped pulling my sixteen-year-old sister by her sweater and when they pass the stand going home to supper all they give us is dirty looks. During the last three or four days, however, they passed by and kinda muttered, calling my father a communist banker and me and my sister Reds. My father says they really don't mean it; it's the hard times and bad feelings, and they got to put the blame on somebody, so they put the blame on us. It's certain speeches on the radio and the pieces in some of the papers, my father told us. "Something is happening to some of the people and we got to watch our step," he says.

I am standing there when my father comes out from Nick's looking like he liked the warm air in Nick's place. His cheeks look rosy, but they look that way from high blood pressure and not from good health. "Well, Colonel," he says smiling, "I am back on the job." My old man starts to stamp around in a little while and, though he says nothing, I know he's got pains in his legs again.

Then I see my sister coming from high school carrying her briefcase. She's a girl with a hot temper, and when she thinks she's right, you can't tell her a thing. When she comes by the pool hall, two guys come out and say something to her, but she just holds herself tight and goes right on past them both.

My old man went into Nick's once more for some "sunshine," and me and Sylvia got busy making sales to the men from the furniture factory which, lately, had been checking out early. Sylvia is a fast worker, faster than me, and we took care of the rush all right. Then we stood waiting for the next rush from the cocoa factory up the block to start.

Our old man returned from Nick's just as the *Times* truck, which was a little late, roared up and dropped the evening edition, which we were waiting for. Sylvia had to go home and make supper. "I'll be back in an hour," she told me. "Then Pa can go home and rest a bit and me and you can take care of the stand."

I said, "All right."

Then the guys from the poolroom began passing the stand on their way home to supper after a day of just killing time. One or two of them said something mean to us, but my old man and me didn't answer. "If you don't answer hoodlums," my father once told me, "sometimes they let you alone."

But then it started. In a flash I realized it was all planned out. My father looked kind of worried but stood quiet. There were about eight or nine of them, all big boys around eighteen or nineteen, and for the first time I got scared.

Finally one of them smiled and said, "Well, this physical fitness magazine you got here is mighty instructive, but don't you think we ought to have some of the exercises demonstrated?"

So another fella pointed to some of the pictures in the magazine and wanted me to squat on the sidewalk and do the first exercise. I wouldn't do it. My father put his hand on the fella's arm and said, "Please, please." But the guy pushed my father's hand away.

"We're interested in your son, not you. Go on, squat."

"I won't," I told him.

"Go on," he said. "Do the first exercise so that the boys can learn how to keep fit."

"I won't," I said.

"Go on," he said. "Do it. Do it if you know what's good for you."

Before I knew it, someone got behind me and tripped me so that I fell on one knee. Then another of them pushed me, trying to make me squat. I shoved someone, and then someone hit me. While they had me down on the sidewalk, Sylvia came running up the street. When she saw what was happening, she began kicking them and yelling and trying to make them let me up. But they didn't pay any attention to her, merely pushing her away.

"Please," my Pa kept saying. "Please let him up; he didn't hurt you. I don't want to have to call the police—"

Then Sylvia turned to the small crowd that had gathered and yelled, "Why don't you help us? What are you standing there for?" But none of them moved. Then Sylvia began to scream: "Listen, why don't you help us? Why don't you make them stop picking on us? We're human beings the same as you!"

But the people just stood there afraid to do a thing. Then while a few guys held me, about five others went for the stand, turning it over and mussing and stamping on all the newspapers they could find. Sylvia started to scratch them, so they hit her, then I broke away to help her, and then they started socking me too. My father tried to reach me, but three guys kept him away. Four guys got me down and started kicking me and all the time my father was begging them to let me up and Sylvia was screaming at the people to help. And while I was down, my face was squeezed against some papers on the sidewalk, telling about how people were fleeing Austria to escape Hitler's approaching army.

Then someone yelled, "The cops!" and they got off me right away. Nick had looked out the window and had called the station, and the guys let me up and beat it away fast.

But when the cops came, it was too late; the stand was a wreck. Newspapers and magazines were all over the sidewalk.

Then the cops came through the crowd and began asking questions right and left. In the end they wanted to take us to the station to enter a complaint, but Sylvia wouldn't go. She looked at the crowd watching and she said, "What's the use? All those people standing around and none of them would help!" They were standing all the way to the second post, and when the cops asked for witnesses none of them except one woman offered to give them names. Then Sylvia looked at Pa and me and saw our faces and turned to the crowd and began to scream: "In another few years, you wait! Some of you are working people and they'll be marching through the streets and going after you too! They pick on us Jews because we're weak and haven't got any country; but after they get us down, they'll go after you! And it'll be your fault; you're all cowards, you're afraid to fight back!"

"Listen," one of the cops told my sister, "are you coming to the station or not? We can't hang around here all evening."

Then Sylvia broke down. "Oh, leave us alone," she told them and began wailing her heart out. "What good would it do?"

The cops started telling people to break it up and move on. Nick came out and took my father by the arm into the lunchroom for a drink of hot tea. As the crowd began to dwindle, it started to snow. The woman who had offered to give the names and I were down on our hands and knees, trying to save some of the magazines. There was no use going after the newspapers, which were smeared up, torn, and dirty from the gang's feet. But I thought I could save a few, so I picked a couple of them up.

"Oh, leave them be," Sylvia wept. "Leave them be."

2 Understanding the Story. Put the letter of the best answer on the line.

1. Mr. Silverstein *says* that the basic cause of the tension between the gang and his family is that the gang members _____.
   a. are prejudiced against Jewish people   c. have not been raised properly
   b. are unemployed   d. suffer from poor educational opportunities

2. The *real* reason the poolroom gang doesn't like the Silversteins is because the Silversteins are _____.
   a. bankers   c. Jewish
   b. communists   d. prejudiced

3. The word that best describes Harry's attitude toward the gang is _____.
   a. amusement   c. hatred
   b. fear   d. indifference

4. As it is used in the story, *Florida* is a symbol of _____.
   a. escape   c. vacation
   b. retirement   d. warmth

5. Sylvia's resentment is directed mostly at _____.
   a. Adolf Hitler   c. the policemen
   b. the gathered crowd   d. the poolroom gang

6. The word that best describes the policemen's attitude toward Sylvia is _____.
   a. concern   c. duty
   b. contempt   d. indifference

7. Who demonstrates the least concern for the Silverstein family? _____
   a. Nick
   b. the policemen who arrive at the newsstand
   c. the woman who offers to give names
   d. the other people in the crowd who saw the incident

8. The word that best describes Sylvia's mood at the end of the story is _____.
   a. despair   c. scorn
   b. indifference   d. terror

9. A main theme presented in this story is that _____.
   a. people's fear of becoming involved is a major part of the problem of prejudice
   b. people who are unemployed are troublemakers
   c. prejudice is so widespread that nothing can really be done about it
   d. the American people generally agreed with Hitler's treatment of the Jews

10. This story takes place just before the United States entered _____.
    a. the Civil War   c. World War I
    b. the Spanish-American War   d. World War II

3 What Do You Think? Answer these questions in good sentence form. Be sure to include reasons to support your answers.

1. If you had been one of the crowd watching this situation, what do you think your response would have been?

   _____

   _____

   _____

   _____

2. *Prelude* means "an event or action that introduces and comes before a more important one." Using details from the story to support your answer, why do you think Halper has entitled his work "Prelude"?

   _____

   _____

   _____

   _____

3. How is the pressure which the Silverstein family experiences different from the pressure in the Higgins family in "All the Years of Her Life"?

   _____

   _____

   _____

   _____

4 Synonyms and Antonyms. If the pair of words is similar in meaning, write *synonyms* on the line. If the pair is opposite in meaning, write *antonyms*.

_____   **1.** accidental—intentional

_____   **2.** brute—sissy

_____   **3.** characteristic—trait

_____   **4.** descendant—offspring

_____   **5.** expansion—contraction

_____   **6.** filthy—spotless

_____   **7.** furious—outraged

_____   **8.** parched—thirsty

_____   **9.** scamper—scurry

_____   **10.** scenic—unsightly

_____   **11.** shiftless—hardworking

_____   **12.** smidgen—smattering

_____   **13.** smug—ashamed

_____   **14.** snicker—sneer

_____   **15.** snoop—pry

_____   **16.** utterly—totally

5 March 1938. In "Prelude" Halper mentioned that Germany invaded Austria. This happened in March of 1938. The items below are based on the March 1, 1938, edition of the *New York Times*. Although the facts, opinions, and ads might be different from what you would find in a current newspaper, the spelling should be the same. Identify the underlined word in each set that is spelled incorrectly, and write its correct spelling on the line.

_____   **1.** Raging winter weather returned to this city on a <u>fierce</u> gale that <u>caused</u> <u>widespread</u> damage yesterday as <u>furious</u> March weather came in like a lion a day ahead of <u>scedule</u>.

_____   **2.** All <u>German</u> officers ever in <u>service</u> before, during, or after the World War <u>learned</u> by a decree <u>issued</u> today that they might be drafted at any time. The decree is <u>planely</u> the result of the great need for officers to train the new troops.

_____   **3.** Back upon the Bench after a two weeks' <u>absence</u> the <u>Justices</u> of the Supreme Court were thought to have set a record for speed when today they handed down nineteen <u>formal</u> <u>decisions</u> in a little less <u>then</u> half an hour.

_____   4. Albert Warner, motion picture producer, reported to police today the theft of <u>jewlry</u> he valued at $90,000 from his winter home. <u>Detective</u> Chief Earl D. Carpenter said the <u>thief</u> gained <u>entrance</u> through a second-floor window by using an ice pick and walked past Mr. and Mrs. Warner's bed as they slept.

_____   5. <u>Transfer</u> of a part of an eye of a dead man in what was described by the attending <u>physician</u> as the first <u>operation</u> of its kind in the United States partly restored the <u>eyesight</u> of an 84-year-old <u>preist</u>.

_____   6. Big Charley Ruffing and Lefty Gomez signed Yankee <u>contracts</u> today. Manager McCarthy made no <u>referance</u> to terms in his <u>announcement</u>. It is <u>believed</u>, however, that each will receive about $18,500 for the season.

_____   7. Since the very <u>begining</u> Howard has worked hard to <u>tailor</u> clothes as fine as humanly <u>possible</u>. When you step out to buy your new clothes, <u>remember</u> that <u>style</u> is important. Suits, topcoats, and tuxedos—all $22.50 with ten weeks to pay.

_____   8. The <u>assistant</u> director of public <u>welfare</u> said that the <u>Republican</u> party had lost the <u>Negro</u> and labor vote because it failed to support legislation <u>helpfull</u> to the masses.

_____   9. Churches will hold special services <u>tomorrow</u> to <u>celebrate</u> Ash <u>Wendsday</u>, and there will be special services daily in many of the churches <u>throughout</u> the <u>forty</u> days of Lent.

_____   10. MILES AHEAD-This smart new chophouse. <u>Youll</u> agree when you dine at Longchamps Broilings Bar. <u>Select</u> your own steak, <u>hamburger</u>, chops, chicken, or lobster from the larder and watch it broil to your <u>exact</u> taste. A FLAVOR <u>SENSATION</u>! Oversize steak broiled to order—$1.75.

_____   11. To think is the crying need of our nation and in the opinion of us women it seems <u>increasingly</u> <u>evident</u> that all men have gone either haywire or numb in the <u>passed</u> few years. It is my firm <u>belief</u> that once enough women get really thinking, organized action will <u>surely</u> follow, and the results will make history.

_____   12. The following <u>telegram</u> was sent yesterday to General Pershing by a <u>comittee</u> representing twelve <u>veterans'</u> organizations: "We pray for your speedy <u>recovery</u>. To us you are the greatest American <u>commander</u>."

Question: How much do you think a copy of the daily edition of the *New York Times* cost in 1938? _____

6 Who Was General Pershing? Use an encyclopedia, a dictionary, or the Internet to help you answer the following questions.

1. What was General Pershing's full name? _____

2. What were the dates of his life? _____

3. In what wars did he fight? _____

4. During what years did World War I take place? _____

5. What was General Pershing's nickname? _____

sp	st	squ	sw
spatula	stable	squatter	swab
spectator	stampede	squiggle	swan
spectacles	stereo	squire	swap
spiritual	stocky	squadron	Swedish
wasp	sturdy	squabble	swine
wisp	quest		swoop

tw	dw	wh	ch
twelfth	dwarf	whew	chromium
tweak	dwell	whimper	chromosome
twerp	dwelling	whinny	Christine
twilight	Dwight	whisk	chronological
twiddle		whirlwind	
twinkle			

1 Definitions. Match the words listed below with the correct definitions.

chromium	quest	spectacles	squadron	swab	tweak
chronological	spatula	squabble	squatter	swine	whisk

_____ **1.** a group of aircraft or naval vessels

_____ **2.** a hard, grayish white element used in the production of stainless steel, etc.

_____ **3.** a petty argument; to engage in a minor quarrel

_____ **4.** a wad of absorbent cotton on the end of a stick used for cleansing or applying medicine

_____ **5.** a tool with a broad, flat blade used to mix, spread, or lift food

_____ **6.** eyeglasses

_____ **7.** arranged in order of time of occurrence

_____ **8.** pigs or hogs; a greedy or cruel person

_____ **9.** one who settles on land without legal claim

_____ **10.** the act of seeking something; a search

_____ **11.** to brush with a quick, light sweeping motion

_____ **12.** to pinch, pluck, or twist sharply; a sharp, twisting pinch

The Test

by Angelica Gibbs

On the afternoon Marian took her second driver's test, Mrs. Ericson went with her. "It's probably better to have someone a little older with you," Mrs. Ericson said as Marian slipped into the driver's seat beside her. "Perhaps the last time your Cousin Bill made you nervous, talking too much on the way."

"Yes, Ma'am," Marian said in her soft unaccented voice. "They probably do like it better if a white person shows up with you."

"Oh, I don't think it's *that*," Mrs. Ericson began, but quickly stopped after a glance at the girl's set profile. Marian drove the car slowly through the shady suburban streets. It was one of the first hot days in June, and when they reached the boulevard they found it crowded with cars headed for the beaches.

"Do you want. me to drive?" Mrs. Ericson asked. "I'll be glad to if you're feeling jumpy." Marian shook her head. Mrs. Ericson watched her dark, competent hands and wondered for the thousandth time how the house had ever managed to get along without her, or how she had lived through those earlier years when her household had been run by a series of untidy white girls who had considered housework beneath them and the care of children an added insult. "You drive beautifully, Marian," she said. "Now, don't think of the last time. Anybody would slide on a steep hill on a wet day like that."

"It takes four mistakes to flunk you," Marian said. "I don't remember doing all the things the inspector marked down on my blank."

"People say that they only want you to slip them a little something," Mrs. Ericson said doubtfully.

"No," Marian said. "That would only make it worse, Mrs. Ericson, I know."

The car turned right, at a traffic signal, into a side road and slid up to the curb at the rear of a short line of parked cars. The inspectors had not arrived yet.

"You have the papers?" Mrs. Ericson asked. Marian took them out of her bag: her learner's permit, the car registration, and her birth certificate. They settled down to the dreary business of waiting.

"It will be marvelous to have someone dependable to drive the children to school every day," Mrs. Ericson said.

Marian looked up from the list of driving requirements she had been studying. "It'll make things simpler at the house, won't it?" she said.

"Oh, Marian," Mrs. Ericson exclaimed, "if I could only pay you half of what you're worth!"

"Now, Mrs. Ericson," Marian said firmly. They looked at each other and smiled with affection.

Two cars with official insignia on their doors stopped across the street. The inspectors leaped out, very brisk and military in their neat uniforms. Marian's hands tightened on the wheel. "There's the one who flunked me last time," she whispered, pointing to a stocky, self-important man who had begun to shout directions at the driver at the head of the line. "Oh, Mrs. Ericson."

"Now, Marian," Mrs. Ericson said. They smiled at each other again, rather weakly.

The inspector who finally reached their car was not the stocky one but a friendly, middle-aged man who grinned broadly as he thumbed over their papers. Mrs. Ericson started to get out of the car. "Don't you want to come along?" the inspector asked. "Mandy and I don't mind company."

Mrs. Ericson was bewildered for a moment. "No," she said, and stepped to the curb. "I might make Marian self-conscious. She's a fine driver, Inspector."

"Sure thing," the inspector said, winking at Mrs. Ericson. He slid into the seat beside Marian. "Turn right at the corner, Mandy-Lou."

From the curb, Mrs. Ericson watched the car move smoothly up the street.

The inspector jotted notes in a small black book. "Age?" he inquired presently, as they drove along.

"Twenty-seven."

He looked at Marian out of the corner of his eye. "Old enough to have quite a flock of pickaninnies, eh?"

Marian did not answer.

"Left at this corner," the inspector said, "and park between that truck and the green car."

The two cars were very close together, but Marian squeezed in between them without too much difficulty. "Driven before, Mandy-Lou?" the inspector asked.

"Yes, sir. I had a license for three years in Pennsylvania."

"Why do you want to drive a car?"

"My employer needs me to take her children to and from school."

"Sure you don't really want to sneak out nights to meet some young blood?" the inspector asked. He laughed as Marian shook her head.

"Let's see you take a left at the corner and then turn around in the middle of the next block," the inspector said. He began to whistle "Swanee River." "Make you homesick?" he asked.

Marian put out her hand, swung around neatly in the street, and headed back in the direction from which they had come. "No," she said. "I was born in Scranton, Pennsylvania."

The inspector acted astonished. "You-all ain't Southern?" he said. "Well, dog my cats if I didn't think you-all came from down yondah."

"No, sir," Marian said.

"Turn onto Main Street and let's see how you-all does in heavier traffic."

They followed a line of cars along Main Street for several blocks until they came in sight of a concrete bridge which arched high over the railroad tracks.

"Read that sign at the end of the bridge," the inspector said.

"Proceed with caution. Dangerous in slippery weather," Marian said.

"You-all sho' can read fine," the inspector exclaimed. "Where d'you learn to do that, Mandy?"

"I got my college degree last year," Marian said. Her voice was not quite steady.

As the car crept up the slope of the bridge, the inspector burst out laughing. He laughed so hard he could scarcely give his next direction. "Stop here," he said wiping his eyes, "then start 'er up again. Mandy got her degree, did she? Dog my cats!"

Marian pulled up beside the curb. She put the car in neutral, pulled on the emergency, waited a moment, and then put the car into gear again. Her face was set. As she released the brake, her foot slipped off the clutch pedal and the engine stalled.

"Now, Mistress Mandy," the inspector said, "remember your degree."

"*Damn* you!" Marian cried. She started the car with a jerk.

The inspector lost his jolly attitude in an instant. "Return to the starting place, please," he said, and made four very black crosses at random in the squares on Marian's application blank.

Mrs. Ericson was waiting at the curb where they had left her. As Marian stopped the car, the inspector jumped out and brushed past her, his face purple. "What happened?" Mrs. Ericson asked, looking after him with alarm.

Marian stared down at the wheel and her lip trembled.

"Oh, Marian, *again*?" Mrs. Ericson said. Marian nodded. "In a sort of different way," she said, and slid over to the right-hand side of the car.

2 Understanding the Story. Answer the following questions in good sentence form.

1. At what point did you realize that the theme of this story deals with prejudice?

_____

_____

2. Why do you think Marian rejects Mrs. Ericson's suggestion that she bribe the inspector?

_____

_____

3. At what point in the story do you first realize that the inspector who rides with Marian is prejudiced?

_____

_____

4. Cite three ways in which the inspector goads Marian into losing her self-control.

    a. _____

    b. _____

    c. _____

5. At what point does Marian's self-control begin to crack?

_____

_____

6. Based on what happens in the story, do you think Marian had any chance of passing the driver's test? Be sure to use evidence from the story to support your answer.

_____

_____

_____

7. To what extent is Mrs. Ericson aware of what Marian is going through? Cite evidence from the story to support your answer.

_____

_____

_____

8. Could Mrs. Ericson have been of more assistance? If so, how? If not, why not?

_____

_____

9. The driver's test is not the only test that Marian fails. Describe at least one other test she fails.

_____

_____

_____

3 What Do You Think?

1. What advice would you give Marian regarding her next attempt to pass the driver's test?

_____

_____

_____

2. Do you think this story was written recently or a number of years ago? Be sure to support your answer with sound reasons.

_____

_____

_____

4 Word Review.
In the blanks at the right, write the word that is the best example of the first word or phrase in each line.

1. **fixture:**	landscape	chandelier	shroud	stereo	_____
2. **continent:**	Africa	Central America	Iceland	Scandinavia	_____
3. **dwelling:**	casino	subdivision	ramshackle	house	_____
4. **woodwind:**	bass	flute	trombone	trumpet	_____
5. **vine:**	beech	ivy	spruce	willow	_____
6. **country:**	Peru	Europe	Plymouth	Scranton	_____
7. **covering:**	core	stone	nucleus	husk	_____
8. **employee:**	creditor	debtor	machinist	squire	_____
9. **star:**	meteor	Milky Way	Pluto	sun	_____
10. **author:**	Dickens	Braille	Edison	Mozart	_____
11. **pastry:**	brownie	gingersnap	pizza	strudel	_____
12. **organ:**	spleen	vein	chromosome	skeleton	_____
13. **mammal:**	crocodile	robin	panther	wasp	_____
14. **fruit:**	eggplant	soybean	spinach	banana	_____
15. **blemish:**	cheek	eyebrow	pimple	face	_____

5 Chronological Order. If necessary, use an almanac or other reference book to help you put the following in chronological order.

James Garfield	Andrew Jackson	John F. Kennedy
Herbert Hoover	Thomas Jefferson	Abraham Lincoln

American Presidents

1. _____   4. _____

2. _____   5. _____

3. _____   6. _____

Columbus Day	Labor Day	Presidents' Day
Fourth of July	Memorial Day	Veterans Day

American Holidays

1. _____   4. _____

2. _____   5. _____

3. _____   6. _____

6 Standard English. Study the suggestions below for using standard English. Then correct the mistakes in the sentences at the end of the exercise by crossing out and/or adding words as necessary.

1. **Use *off*, not *off of*.**

   Right: John fell off the ladder.

   Wrong: John fell off of the ladder.

2. **Use *different from*, not *different than*.**

   Right: A movie director is different from a movie producer.

   Wrong: A movie director is different than a movie producer.

3. **Use *since* or *because* rather than *being that*.**

   Right: Since Helen was tired, she went to bed.

   Wrong: Being that Helen was tired, she went to bed.

4. **Use *this* or *that*.** *This here* and *that there* are not considered standard English.

   Right: Roger does not like to shop in that supermarket.

   Wrong: Roger does not like to shop in that there supermarket.

5. **Use *all right*.** *Alright* is not a word.

   Right: The change of plans was not all right with Adam.

   Wrong: The change of plans was not alright with Adam.

6. **Use *any* and *ever* with *scarcely* and *hardly*.** Do not use *no* or *never*.

   Scarcely and *hardly* are negative words even though they don't begin with *n*.

   Right: The Chapmans hardly ever went out for dinner.

   Wrong: The Chapmans hardly never went out for dinner.

1. Scarcely no Americans had heard of the Suwannee River until Stephen Foster made it famous in his song "Old Folks at Home" which he composed in the mid-1800s.

2. Stephen Foster spelled it *Swanee*, which is different than its correct spelling, *Suwannee*.

3. Stephen Foster was a Northerner and probably had hardly no knowledge of the Suwannee River.

4. The Suwannee River is important being that it helps to drain the Okefenokee Swamp, a vast swamp in southern Georgia.

5. This here word *Okefenokee* comes from an Indian word meaning "trembling earth," which refers to the quivering of the small bushes and weeds that float on water.

6. The Okefenokee was once a favorite hunting ground of local Indians who lived off of the animals that inhabited the swamp.

7. Today the swamp is a safe home for animals being that the United States government has set much of it aside as a wildlife preserve.

8. Those who want to conserve our natural resources do not believe it is alright to let people develop the Okefenokee.

Review of Vowel Combinations: Part 1

ai	au	ea	ea
aide	auburn	beacon	homestead
aimless	auditorium	cleaver	steadfast
maim	Australia	eavesdrop	treasury
campaign	precaution	queasy	treachery
maintain	sauna	New Zealand	treacherous
acquaint			

ee	oa	oe	oi
wee	moat	doe	oink
heed	bloat	foe	sirloin
peeve	petticoat	woe	loiter
feeble	goalie	hoe	poinsettia
beetle	coax	mistletoe	thyroid
referee	roach		

1 Definitions. Match the words listed below with the correct definitions.

auditorium	cleaver	heed	maim	peeve	thyroid	woe
bloat	foe	loiter	moat	queasy	treacherous	

_____ 1. a gland located in front and on either side of the windpipe

_____ 2. a heavy, ax-like knife or hatchet used by butchers

_____ 3. a building or large room designed for concerts or public meetings

_____ 4. a personal enemy; an enemy in war

_____ 5. a wide, deep ditch, usually filled with water, surrounding towns, fortresses, or castles in the Middle Ages as a protection against attack

_____ 6. an annoyance; to annoy or make resentful

_____ 7. deep sorrow; grief

_____ 8. not to be trusted; dangerous; disloyal

_____ 9. to cause to swell up or inflate, as with liquid or gas

_____ 10. to disfigure or disable; to deprive a person of the use of a limb

_____ 11. to loaf; to stand idly about; to linger aimlessly

_____ 12. to pay attention to; to listen and consider

_____ 13. uneasy; troubled; sickening

Charles

by Shirley Jackson

The day my son Laurie started kindergarten he renounced overalls with bibs and began wearing blue jeans with a belt. I watched him go off the first morning with the older girl next door, seeing clearly that an era of my life was ended. My sweet-voiced nursery-school tot was replaced by a long-trousered, swaggering character who forgot to stop at the corner and wave good-bye to me.

He came home the same way, the front door slamming open, his hat on the floor, and the voice suddenly become rough-sounding shouting, "Isn't anybody *here*?"

At lunch he spoke rudely to his father, spilled his baby sister's milk, and remarked that his teacher said we were not to take the name of the Lord in vain.

"How was school today?" I asked, striving to sound casual.

"All right," he said.

"Did you learn anything?" his father asked.

Laurie regarded his father coldly. "I didn't learn nothing," he said.

"Anything," I said.
"Didn't learn anything."

"The teacher spanked a boy, though," Laurie said. "For being fresh," he added with his mouth full.

"What did he do?" I asked. "Who was it?"

Laurie thought. "It was Charles," he said. "He was fresh. The teacher spanked him and made him stand in a corner. He was awfully fresh."

"What did he do?" I asked again, but Laurie slid off his chair, took a cookie, and left, while his father was still saying, "See here, young man."

The next day Laurie remarked at lunch, as soon as he sat down, "Well, Charles was bad again today."

He grinned broadly and said, "Today Charles hit the teacher."

"Good heavens," I said, mindful of the Lord's name. "I suppose he got spanked again?"

"He sure did," Laurie said. "Look up," he said to his father.

"What?" his father said, looking up.

"Look down," Laurie said. "Look at my thumb. Gee, you're dumb." He began to laugh insanely.

"Why did Charles hit the teacher?" I asked quickly.

"Because she tried to make him color with red crayons," Laurie said. "Charles wanted to color with green crayons so he hit the teacher and she spanked him and said nobody play with Charles but everybody did."

The third day—it was Wednesday of the first week—Charles bounced a seesaw on the head of a little girl and made her bleed, and the teacher made him stay inside all during recess. Thursday Charles had to stand in a corner during story time because he kept pounding his feet on the floor. Friday Charles was deprived of blackboard privileges because he threw chalk.

On Saturday I remarked to my husband, "Do you think kindergarten is too unsettling for Laurie? All this toughness and bad grammar, and this Charles boy sounds like such a bad influence."

"It'll be all right," my husband said. "Bound to be people like Charles in the world. Might as well meet them now as later."

On Monday Laurie came home late, full of news. "Charles," he shouted as he came up the hill. I was waiting anxiously on the front steps. "Charles," Laurie yelled all the way up the hill, "Charles was bad again."

"Come right in," I said as soon as he came close enough. "Lunch is waiting."

"You know what Charles did?" he demanded, following me through the door. "Charles yelled so in school they sent a boy in from first grade to tell the teacher she had to make Charles keep quiet, and so Charles had to stay after school. And so all the children stayed to watch him."

"What did he do?" I asked.

"He just sat there," Laurie said, climbing into his chair at the table. "Hi, Pop, y'old dust mop."

"Charles had to stay after school today," I told my husband. "Everybody stayed with him."

"What does this Charles look like?" my husband asked Laurie. "What's his other name."

"He's bigger than me," Laurie said. "And he doesn't have any rubbers and he doesn't ever wear a jacket."

Monday night was the first Parent-Teachers meeting, and only the fact that the baby had a cold kept me from going. I was dying to meet Charles's mother. On Tuesday Laurie remarked suddenly, "Our teacher had a friend come to see her today."

"Charles's mother?" my husband and I asked at the same time.

"Naaah," Laurie said scornfully. "It was a man who came and made us do exercises. We had to touch our toes. Look." He climbed down from his chair and squatted down and touched his toes. "Like this," he said. "Charles didn't even do exercises."

"That's fine," I said heartily. "Didn't Charles want to do the exercises?"

"Naaah," Laurie said, "Charles was so fresh to the teacher's friend he wasn't *let* do exercises."

"What are they going to do about Charles, do you suppose?" Laurie's father asked him.

Laurie shrugged. "Throw him out of school, I guess," he said.

By the third week of kindergarten, Charles was an institution in our family. The baby was being a Charles when she cried all afternoon; Laurie did a Charles when he filled his wagon full of mud and pulled it through the kitchen. Even my husband, when he caught his elbow in the telephone cord and pulled the telephone, ashtray, and a bowl of flowers off the table, said, "Looks like Charles."

During the third and fourth weeks it looked like Charles had reformed. Laurie reported grimly at lunch on Thursday of the third week, "Charles was so good today the teacher gave him an apple."

"What?" I said.

"He gave the crayons around and he picked up the books afterward and the teacher said he was her helper."

"What happened?" I asked in disbelief.

"He was her helper, that's all," Laurie said, and shrugged.

For over a week Charles was the teacher's helper. Each day he handed things out and he picked things up. No one had to stay after school.

"The PTA meeting's next week," I told my husband one evening. "I'm going to find Charles's mother there."

"Ask her what happened to Charles," my husband said. "I'd like to know."

"I'd like to know myself," I said.

On Friday that week things were back to normal. "You know what Charles did today?" Laurie demanded at the lunch table. "He told a little girl to say a word and she said it and the teacher washed her mouth out with soap and Charles laughed."

"What word?" his father asked unwisely, and Laurie said, "I'll have to whisper it to you, it's so bad." He got down off his chair and went around to his father. His father bent his head down and Laurie whispered joyfully. His father's eyes widened.

"Did Charles tell the little girl to say *that*?" he asked.

"She said it *twice*," Laurie said. "Charles told her to say it *twice*."

"What happened to Charles?" my husband asked.

"Nothing," Laurie said. "He was passing out the crayons."

My husband came to the door with me that Monday evening as I set out for the PTA meeting.

"Invite her over for a cup of tea after the meeting," he said. "I want to get a look at her."

"If only she's there," I said prayerfully.

"She'll be there," my husband said. "I don't see how they could hold a PTA meeting without Charles's mother."

At the meeting I sat restlessly, scanning each face, trying to determine which one hid the secret of Charles. None of them looked to me haggard enough. No one stood up in the meeting and apologized for the way her son had been acting. No one mentioned Charles.

After the meeting I identified and sought out Laurie's kindergarten teacher. She had a plate with a cup of tea and a piece of chocolate cake. I had a plate with a cup of tea and a piece of marshmallow cake. We approached each other cautiously and smiled.

"I've been so anxious to meet you," I said. "I'm Laurie's mother."

"We're all so interested in Laurie," she said.

"Well, he certainly likes kindergarten," I said. "He talks about it all the time."

"We had a little trouble adjusting, the first week or so," she said primly, "but now he's a fine little helper. With occasional lapses, of course."

"Laurie usually adjusts very quickly," I said. "I suppose this time it's Charles's influence."

"Charles?"

"Yes," I said laughing, "you must have your hands full in that kindergarten, with Charles."

"Charles?" she said. "We don't have any Charles in the kindergarten."

2 Understanding the Story. Answer the following questions in good sentence form.

1. Cite three clues Jackson gives you which indicate that Laurie—not Charles—is the problem in the kindergarten class.

   a. _____

   _____

   b. _____

   _____

   c. _____

   _____

2. What is the attitude of Laurie's mother toward Charles's mother?

   _____

   _____

3. Does Laurie's mother seem like the type of mother who thinks her child can do no wrong? Be sure to include details from the story to support your answer.

   _____

   _____

   _____

4. Experts in child behavior find that children often create imaginary people as a way of protecting themselves from pressure. Explain how this finding relates to the story "Charles."

   _____

   _____

3 What Might You Use if You Wanted to . . . Match each task below with the item you could use to complete it.

burlap	explosives	microscope	scissors	spectacles
cleaver	grid	plasma	scraper	stereo
compost	griddle	sauna	slogan	telescope

_____ **1.** blast a mountainside

_____ **2.** cut out items for a scrapbook

_____ **3.** butcher a hog

_____ **4.** listen to classical music

_____ **5.** examine bacteria on a slide

_____ **6.** fertilize your garden

_____ **7.** locate a point on a map

_____ **8.** manufacture bags for seeds and feed

_____ **9.** observe Mars

_____ **10.** perform a transfusion

_____ **11.** prepare to repaint the front porch

_____ **12.** read the fine print on a mortgage

_____ **13.** catch consumers' attention

_____ **14.** ease the tensions of a stressful day

_____ **15.** treat yourself to a pancake breakfast

4 Spelling. Change the *y* to *i* before adding *–ly* to these words. Study the example before you begin.

1. shaky   _shakily_____

2. hungry _____

3. bossy _____

4. fancy _____

5. thrifty _____

6. sturdy _____

7. stocky _____

8. naughty _____

9. nasty _____

10. hasty _____

11. ordinary _____

12. extraordinary _____

5 The Suffix -ly. Use both words in each set to complete these sentences.

evident
evidently

1. After a lengthy cross-examination, it was _____ to the foreman of the jury that the witness was _____ lying in order to protect the defendant.

responsible
responsibly

2. As the cleaning woman _____ finished the last chore on the list her employer had left with her, she hoped she would not be held _____ for the expensive china vase she had accidentally dropped.

probable
probably

3. Convinced that it was highly _____ he would win the election by a landslide, the Republican candidate dismissed the polls that had predicted he would _____ be badly defeated.

furious
furiously

4. Dennis _____ devoured the last of the lemon chiffon pie, knowing full well that he would be _____ with himself the next morning for having broken his strict diet.

spiritual
spiritually

5. Even among those who usually sneered at _____ people, the local pastor was highly respected for being so _____ concerned with the welfare of everyone he encountered.

indignant
indignantly

6. "How can you sit there and say I'm being _____," said Alfred _____ to his assistant, "when you know perfectly well I never lose my temper at the office!"

earnest
earnestly

7. "If you make an _____ attempt to explain your financial predicament to the creditors, I'm sure they will try to work out another payment plan with you," Johnny _____ told his brother.

physical
physically

8. None of her friends could understand how Betsy could be so _____ fit when it was a well-known fact that she shunned all _____ exercise as if it were the plague.

casual
casually

9. The _____ conversations among the players in the locker room came to an immediate halt when the coach _____ announced that he intended to resign his position right after the game.

smug
smugly

10. With a _____ look on his face, the imp sprawled out on the couch to watch the late movie, _____ ignoring the screams from the babysitter whom he had locked in the hall closet.

6 Find the Quote. The first kindergarten was opened by Friedrich Frobel in Germany in 1837. Can you find this quote by the founder, which describes what he thought kindergarten should be?

A. Each of the fourteen descriptions defines or gives a clue for a certain word. Write that word on the lines to the left of each description.

B. Put the letters of those words in the blanks on the next page. The quote, when all the blanks are filled in, will be Frobel's description of kindergarten.

C. The first one has been done for you. Study it before you begin.

F O O T N O T E
<u>84</u> <u>31</u> <u>46</u> <u>13</u> <u>4</u> <u>40</u> <u>74</u> <u>53</u>

1. a note placed at the bottom of a page of a book

___ ___ ___ ___
94 56 3 68

2. the residence of the old woman who had so many children that she didn't know what to do

___ ___ ___ ___ ___ ___ ___ ___
20 89 60 43 71 7 38 78

3. an explosive used to blast mines, foundations, etc.

___ ___ ___ ___ ___ ___ ___ ___ ___
75 27 33 57 83 17 25 51 42

4. invented in 1876 by Alexander Graham Bell

___ ___ ___ ___ ___ ___
36 82 66 9 62 48

5. a common glass container for liquids

___ ___ ___ ___ ___
1 70 29 30 89

6. how poison ivy makes you feel

___ ___ ___ ___ ___ ___ ___ ___ ___
76 11 86 – 65 14 18 85 35

7. the fraction that represents how much of our lives we spend sleeping

___ ___ ___ ___ ___ ___ ___
28 16 5 32 6 80 54

8. a vehicle that helps tots get around fast

___ ___ ___ ___ ___ ___ ___ ___ ___
44 1 24 39 10 21 26 50 58

9. a person who discards his trash carelessly in public areas

___ ___ ___
77 37 2

10. a slang synonym for *failure* or flop

$\overline{}_{23}\ \overline{}_{63}\ \overline{}_{47}\ \quad \overline{}_{15}\ \overline{}_{73}\ \overline{}_{58}\ \overline{}_{19}\ \overline{}_{69}\ \overline{}_{8}\ \overline{}_{52}$ **11.** the northeastern United States (2 words)

$\overline{}_{12}\ \overline{}_{72}\ \overline{}_{84}\ \overline{}_{45}\ \overline{}_{43}\ \overline{}_{55}\ \overline{}_{87}$ **12.** an antonym for *inflate*

$\overline{}_{61}\ \overline{}_{7}\ \overline{}_{71}\ \overline{}_{59}\ \overline{}_{66}\ \overline{}_{69}\ \overline{}_{41}\ \overline{}_{81}\ \overline{}_{22}$ **13.** what passengers at the bus station study to see when their bus leaves

$\overline{}_{26}\ \overline{}_{76}\ \overline{}_{50}\ \overline{}_{88}\ \overline{}_{34}\ \overline{}_{79}\ \overline{}_{43}\ \overline{}_{67}\ \overline{}_{49}$ **14.** a broad city street, often tree-lined and landscaped

Quote:

| 1 | | 2 | 3 | N 4 | 5 | 6 | | 7 | 8 | 9 | 10 | 11 | 12 | | T 13 | 14 | 15 |

| 16 | 17 | 18 | 19 | 20 | 21 | 22 | 23 | | 24 | 25 | | 26 | 27 | | 28 | 29 | 30 | O 31 | 32 | 33 | 34 | 35 , |

| 36 | 37 | 38 | | O 39 | 40 | | 41 | 42 | | 43 | 44 | 45 | O 46 | 47 | 48 | 49 | | 50 | 51 | 52 | E 53 | 54 |

| 55 | 56 | 57 | | 58 | 59 | 60 | 61 | 62 | 63 | 64 | 65 | | 66 | 67 | 68 | 69 | 70 | 71 | 72 | 73 | T 74 |

| 75 | 76 | | 77 | 78 | 79 | 80 | 81 | 82 | 83 | | F 84 | 85 | 86 | 87 | 88 | 89 . |

Review: Lessons 1-8

1 Word Review. Use the words listed below to fill in the blanks.

charity	fragment	memorial	nursery	schedule
decree	Iceland	mull	prejudice	scope
dignity	lapse	New Zealand	republic	stampede

_____ **1.** a minor slip or failure

_____ **2.** a negative judgment or opinion formed beforehand or without knowledge or examination of the facts

_____ **3.** a part broken off or detached from the whole; something incomplete

_____ **4.** a place where plants are grown for sale, transplanting, or experiments; a room or area set apart for children

_____ **5.** a program of upcoming events or appointments; a student's program of classes

_____ **6.** a sudden headlong rush of startled animals, especially cattle or horses, or of a crowd of people

_____ **7.** an island country that is a member of the Commonwealth of Nations and is located about 1,200 miles southeast of Australia

_____ **8.** an island republic located in the North Atlantic

_____ **9.** an order having the force of law

_____ **10.** a government that does not have a king or queen

_____ **11.** to consider or think over

_____ **12.** something, such as a monument or a holiday, designed or established to serve as a remembrance of a person or event

_____ **13.** the area covered by a given activity or subject; the range of one's thoughts or actions

_____ **14.** the presence of poise and self-respect in a person to a degree that inspires respect from others

_____ **15.** the provision of help or relief to the poor

2 Word Review. Put the letter of the best answer on the line.

1. Which animal's scent is its defense? _____
   a. skunk   **b.** gerbil   **c.** beaver   **d.** squirrel

2. Which of the following do you see least often during the Christmas season? _____
   a. holly   **b.** mistletoe   **c.** orchids   **d.** poinsettias

3. Which prices usually offer the consumer the best deal? _____
   a. advertised   **b.** inflated   **c.** retail   **d.** wholesale

4. Whose favorite pastime is eavesdropping? _____
   a. sniper   **b.** snoop   **c.** snob   **d.** snip

5. What would you purchase if you wanted to swab the deck of your boat? _____
   a. broom   **b.** dishwasher   **c.** hoe   **d.** mop

6. A candidate's interests are usually _____.
   a. cultural   **b.** political   **c.** religious   **d.** social

7. If you had trouble breathing because you had a bad cold, you would probably _____.
   a. sniffle   **b.** murmur   **c.** howl   **d.** whimper

8. What kind of meals might a person on a diet eat? _____
   a. hasty   **b.** ordinary   **c.** skimpy   **d.** uninteresting

9. Which people do not live in Scandinavia? _____
   a. Danes   **b.** Norwegians   **c.** Russians   **d.** Swedes

10. Drinking more orange juice than usual when you feel a cold coming on is an example of a _____.
    a. precaution   **b.** schedule   **c.** symptom   **d.** theory

11. If the sight of blood makes you feel queasy, you are probably a(n) _____ person.
    a. cowardly   **b.** dizzy   **c.** squeamish   **d.** unhealthy

12. When two friends who have been arguing decide to "bury the _____," they have declared a truce.
    a. cleaver   **b.** hatchet   **c.** machine gun   **d.** muzzle

13. An official car usually bears a(n) _____.
    a. aide   **b.** deputy   **c.** microphone   **d.** insignia

14. The country that is traditionally neutral in world affairs is _____.
    a. Switzerland   **b.** Russia   **c.** Greece   **d.** United States

3 Sound Review. On the line to the right, write the word in which the underlined sound is different from the other words.

1. <u>e</u>qual   r<u>e</u>cip<u>e</u>   r<u>e</u>gional   s<u>e</u>nator   th<u>e</u>ater   _____

2. d<u>ai</u>ly   f<u>ai</u>thful   pl<u>ai</u>d   unafr<u>ai</u>d   w<u>ai</u>tress   _____

3. an<u>ch</u>or   <u>ch</u>rome   dis<u>ch</u>arge   me<u>ch</u>anically   or<u>ch</u>estra   _____

4. <u>th</u>icken   <u>th</u>orough   <u>th</u>yroid   <u>th</u>yself   <u>Th</u>anksgiving   _____

5. di<u>sc</u>   <u>sc</u>andal   <u>sc</u>ience   <u>sc</u>our   <u>sc</u>ulpture   _____

6. <u>ch</u>apter   <u>ch</u>andelier   <u>ch</u>auffeur   <u>Ch</u>eyenne   para<u>ch</u>ute   _____

7. br<u>oa</u>dcast   c<u>oa</u>ster   g<u>oa</u>d   <u>oa</u>tmeal   p<u>oa</u>ch   _____

8. <u>au</u>dience   <u>au</u>thorize   h<u>au</u>nted   l<u>au</u>ghter   n<u>au</u>ghtily   _____

4 Word Families. Use the words in each set at the left to complete these sentences.

apologize
apology
apologetic

1. While offering his _____ for his absence, Albert was so _____ that his boss, who had been thinking of firing him on the spot, experienced a change of heart and said kindly, "It's all right; there's no need to _____."

disloyal
disloyally
disloyalty

2. Astonished that Charlotte suspected him of behaving _____, Dwight said, "If _____ means simply disagreeing with you, then probably every person you've ever known has been _____ at one time or another."

competent
incompetent
competence

3. If you tell a person he's _____ often enough, even the most _____ person will suffer a decline in his _____.

official
officially
unofficial

4. Firmly but politely, the _____ explained to the press that the accident report was still _____, but that he would tell them everything as soon as the information was _____ released.

acquaint
unacquainted
acquaintance

5. _____ with the new equipment that had been ordered for the shop, Earl was so eager to _____ himself with its operation that he rushed up to the special instructor as soon as she arrived as if she were a long lost _____.

observed
observer
observations

6. Gene was highly regarded as an _____ of human nature because he limited his written _____ to what he actually _____.

residence
resident
residential

7. When asked to state his place of _____, the hobo cheerfully replied, "You might say my _____ quarters are everywhere; for, I, sir, am a _____ of the entire universe."

familiar
unfamiliar
familiarity

8. When her English professor asked if she was _____ with the old saying, "_____ breeds contempt," Christine responded, "No, and I'm glad I'm _____ with it because it's the most negative expression I've ever heard."

respect
respectful
respectable
disrespect

9. Mrs. Sands always seemed _____ to the caseworkers at the welfare department, but, inwardly, she felt no _____ toward those who treated her with _____ even if others claimed they were highly _____ employees.

determine
determined
undetermined
determination

10. The _____ look in the chief investigator's eye told everyone that he would continue trying to _____ who had murdered wealthy Aunt Sylvia. But the guilty chauffeur was filled with _____ that no new evidence would come to light, and the cause of her death remained _____.

5 Standard English: A Review. Each of the following sentences has four underlined sections. Choose the number of the section that is incorrect. Then circle that number in the answer row. If there are no incorrect sections, circle number 5.

1 2 3 4 5   **1.** <u>About</u> fifteen minutes before bedtime every evening, Johnny would come <u>in</u> the
                        1   2
                      den and plead, "<u>May</u> I please have just five cookies before I brush my teeth <u>since</u>
                                   3   4
                      I've been such a good boy all day?"

1 2 3 4 5   **2.** "For me, being single is <u>hardly any</u> <u>different from</u> being married," responded the
                                                 1   2
                      movie star in answer to the interviewer's question, "and <u>being that</u> I've been both
                                                                    3
                      many times, I don't think I'm far <u>off</u> the mark."
                                                4

1 2 3 4 5   **3.** Having <u>all ready</u> called the police, Jerry decided to sit in his car parked <u>beside</u>
                                     1   2
                      the hardware store—no matter how <u>stupid</u> he looked—until the police told him
                                                         3
                      that everything in the store was <u>all right</u>.
                                                4

1 2 3 4 5   **4.** Mr. Madison tried to <u>teach</u> his children that <u>borrowing</u> their friends' possessions
                                        1   2
                      was a bad habit, but his words of wisdom had <u>scarcely any</u> <u>affect</u> on them.
                                                               3   4

1 2 3 4 5   **5.** When the woman at the employment agency sat down <u>beside</u> Mr. Weaver to
                                                       1
                      tell him that he had <u>scarcely any</u> mistakes on his test, he was so <u>affected</u> that he
                                            2   3
                      looked at her as if he had been struck <u>dumb</u>.
                                              4

1 2 3 4 5   **6.** "You may think you're healthy," cried Mrs. Jefferson to her husband in alarm,
                      "but I think <u>this here</u> jogging <u>around</u> the block could cause another heart attack,
                                       1   2
                      and I can <u>can hardly</u> <u>sit</u> in peace until you consult our physician."
                                     3   4

6 A Poet's Thoughts. Study this poem by English poet Christina Rossetti (1830–1894), and then answer the questions which follow in complete sentence form.

Uphill
by Christina Rossetti

Does the road wind uphill all the way?
  Yes, to the very end.
Will the day's journey take the whole long day?
  From morn to night, my friend.

But is there for the night a resting-place?
  A roof for when the slow, dark hours begin.
May not the darkness hide it from my face?
  You cannot miss that inn.

Shall I meet other wayfarers at night?
  Those who have gone before.
Then must I knock, or call when just in sight?
  They will not keep you waiting at that door.

Shall I find comfort, travel-sore and weak?
  Of labor you shall find the sum.
Will there be beds for me and all who seek?
  Yes, beds for all who come.

1. Does Rossetti seem to think that pressures and problems are common or uncommon in life? Cite evidence from the poem to support your answer.

_____

_____

_____

_____

2. Rossetti says the difficulties that one confronts in life continue until night. But she probably is using night to represent something else. What do you think night represents?

_____

_____

3. According to Rossetti, there will be an inn and beds waiting at the end of the journey. What do you think the inn and the beds represent?

_____

_____

4. There are two speakers in this poem. One speaker asks the questions in the odd lines in the poem. The other speaker answers them in the even lines in the poem.

   a. What kind of person do you think is asking the questions?

   _____

   _____

   b. Who do you think is giving the answers?

   _____

   _____

UNIT 3
Fantasy vs. Reality

Sometimes, the differences between fantasy and reality can become blurred. We hear a sound in the middle of the night that we can't identify. Is it a leaking pipe or the creaking of the house? Or is it something more threatening? Our minds tell us one thing, our fears and imagination another. At that moment, how do we know what is real and what is not? It can be very hard to tell the difference. The stories that follow explore this place where fantasy and reality meet.

"The Open Window" is the story in Lesson 9. In it, a young man pays a visit to the home of a respectable family. Unexpectedly, fantasy creeps into this visit. What is real takes on new meaning. Imaginations run wild.

"Down the Rabbit-Hole," the story in Lesson 10, provides a different look at fantasy and reality. The author, Lewis Carroll, invites readers to follow him into a fantasy world. If we think about it, that world is not so different from ones we may have visited ourselves once upon a time.

We have all awakened in the middle of the night in a cold sweat. We've been dreaming so vividly that we cannot shake the feeling it was somehow more than a dream. In Lesson 11, you'll read "Sleep Disorder," a story that examines the possibility that dreams are not just dreams.

Finally, in Lesson 12, "The Boarded Window" shocks us into questioning what we think we know. And in the end, we're left wondering if we have it figured out.

Review of Vowel Combinations: Part 2

ei	**ei**	**ie**	**oo**
perceive	freighter	achieve	hoop
deceive	reindeer	hygiene	zoom
conceive	reign	grievance	kangaroo
conceited	neigh	wield	raccoon
seize	beige	siege	typhoon
ou	**ou**	**ue**	**ui**
oust	coupon	pursue	bruiser
vouch	roulette	subdue	pursuit
douse	rouge	residue	recruit
spouse	souvenir	revenue	nuisance
arouse	bayou	virtue	suitable

1 Definitions. Match the words listed below with the correct definitions.

grievance	oust	residue	siege	typhoon	vouch
hygiene	reign	revenue	spouse	virtue	

_____ **1.** a complaint based on an actual or supposed circumstance

_____ **2.** a strong hurricane occurring in the western Pacific or China Sea

_____ **3.** goodness; the quality of moral excellence

_____ **4.** one's marriage partner; a husband or wife

_____ **5.** the exercise of power by a king or queen

_____ **6.** the income of a government from money set aside for the payment of public expenses

_____ **7.** the remainder of something after removal of a part

_____ **8.** the science of health and the prevention of disease

_____ **9.** the surrounding and blockading of a town or fortress by an army bent on capturing it

_____ **10.** to force out; to remove from a position

_____ **11.** to serve as a guarantee; to furnish supporting evidence

Words for Study

Framton	widowed	Bertie	hoarse
endeavored	tragedy	scarcity	headlong
rectory	engulfed	prospects	cemetery
distinct	spaniel	horrible	Ganges
Sappleton	Ronnie	sympathetic	specialty

The Open Window
by Saki

"My aunt will be down presently, Mr. Framton," said a very confident young lady of fifteen; "in the meantime you must try and put up with me."

Framton endeavored to say the correct something which should properly flatter the niece without ignoring the aunt that was to come. . . .

"Do you know many of the people round here?" asked the niece. . . .

"Hardly a soul," said Framton. "My sister was staying here, at the rectory, you know, some four years ago, and she gave me letters of introduction to some of the people here."

He made the last statement in a tone of distinct regret.

"Then you know practically nothing about my aunt?" asked the self-possessed young lady.

"Only her name and address," admitted the caller. He was wondering whether Mrs. Sappleton was in the married or widowed state. An undefinable something about the room seemed to suggest a masculine presence.

"Her great tragedy happened just three years ago," said the child; "that would be since your sister's time."

"Her tragedy?" asked Framton; somehow in this restful country spot tragedies seemed out of place.

"You may wonder why we keep that window wide open on an October afternoon," said the niece, indicating a large French window that opened on to a lawn.

"It is quite warm for the time of the year," said Framton; "but has that window got anything to do with the tragedy?"

"Out through that window, three years ago to a day, her husband and her two young brothers went off for their day's shooting. They never came back. In crossing the moor to their favorite snipe-shooting ground they were all three engulfed in a treacherous swamp. It had been that dreadful wet summer, you know, and places that were safe in other years gave way suddenly without warning. Their bodies were never recovered. That was the dreadful part of it." Here the child's voice lost its self-possessed note and became weakly human. "Poor aunt always thinks that they will come back someday. They and the little brown spaniel that was lost with them will walk in at that window just as they used to do. That is why the window is kept open every evening till it is quite dusk. Poor dear aunt, she has often told me how they went out, her husband with his white waterproof coat over his arm, and Ronnie, her youngest brother, singing 'Bertie, why do you bound?' as he always did to tease her, because she said it got on

her nerves. Do you know, sometimes on still, quiet evenings like this, I almost get a creepy feeling that they will all walk in through that window—"

She broke off with a little shudder. It was a relief to Framton when the aunt walked swiftly into the room with a whirl of apologies. . . .

"I hope you don't mind the open window," said Mrs. Sappleton briskly; "my husband and brothers will be home directly from shooting, and they always come in this way. They've been out for snipe in the marshes today, so they'll make a fine mess over my poor carpets. So like you men-folk, isn't it?"

She rattled on cheerfully about the shooting and the scarcity of birds, and the prospects for duck in the winter. To Framton it was all purely horrible. . . . Mrs. Sappleton . . . suddenly brightened into alert attention—but not to what Framton was saying.

"Here they are at last!" she cried. "Just in time for tea, and don't they look as if they were muddy up to the eyes!"

Framton shivered slightly and turned towards the niece with a look intended to suggest sympathetic understanding. The child was staring out through the open window with dazed horror in her eyes. In a chill shock of nameless fear Framton swung round in his seat and looked in the same direction.

In the deepening twilight three figures were walking across the lawn towards the window. They all carried guns under their arms, and one of them was additionally burdened with a white coat hung over his shoulders. A tired brown spaniel kept close at their heels. Noiselessly they neared the house, and then a hoarse young voice chanted out of the dusk: "I said, Bertie, why do you bound?"

Framton grabbed wildly at his stick and hat; the hall-door, the gravel-drive, and the front gate were dimly-noted stages in his headlong retreat. A cyclist coming along the road had to run into the bushes to avoid crashing into him.

"Here we are, my dear," said the bearer of the white raincoat, coming in through the window; "fairly muddy, but most of it's dry. Who was that who bolted out as we came up?"

"A most extraordinary man, a Mr. Framton," said Mrs. Sappleton; "could only talk about his illnesses. He dashed off without a word of good-bye or apology when you arrived. One would think he had seen a ghost."

"I expect it was the spaniel," said the niece calmly; "he told me he had a horror of dogs. He was once hunted into a cemetery somewhere on the banks of the Ganges by a pack of wild dogs. He had to spend the night in a newly dug grave with the creatures snarling and grinning and foaming just above him. Enough to make anyone lose their nerve."

Romance at short notice was her specialty.

2 Understanding the Story. Put the letter of the correct answer on the line.

1. The niece greets Framton all by herself because _____.
   a. her aunt has been delayed
   b. her aunt is out looking for her husband
   c. her aunt refused to meet with Framton
   d. her aunt wanted to play a joke on Framton

2. Why has Framton come to visit Mrs. Sappleton? _____
   a. When he met her at the rectory, she invited him to visit.
   b. Framton's sister knows her and arranged for him to meet her.
   c. He has come to hear about the tragedy she experienced.
   d. She is an old friend of the family and he wanted to see her again.

3. According to the niece, Mrs. Sappleton's husband and two brothers _____ three years before.
   a. were killed in a war
   b. have been out shooting all day
   c. are expected home at any moment
   d. died by stumbling into a treacherous swamp

4. According to the niece, Mrs. Sappleton leaves the window open because _____.
   a. she likes the fresh autumn air
   b. she refuses to change the room since her husband and brothers were lost
   c. she keeps expecting her husband and brothers to return
   d. since the tragedy, Mrs. Sappleton feels too closed in when the window is closed

5. When Mrs. Sappleton sees her husband and brothers, she calls out "Just in time for tea." Framton looks at the niece with sympathy because _____.
   a. he feels sorry for the niece because her aunt is imagining that the men are still alive
   b. he sees that the men are all muddy and will track up the house
   c. he thinks the niece will be embarrassed for telling the story of their deaths
   d. the men are coming home without any birds for dinner

6. Framton bolts for the door when _____.
   a. he hears the niece describe the tragedy from three years before
   b. he sees the three men and their dog walking toward the house
   c. he hears one of the men sing out, "I said, Bertie, why do you bound?"
   d. the three men step in through the open window

7. According to the niece, why has Framton left so suddenly? _____
   a. He is afraid of ghosts.   c. He is afraid of the men's guns.
   b. He is afraid of dogs.   d. He was suddenly feeling sick.

8. The word that best describes the niece is _____.
   a. cautious   b. clever   c. sorrowful   d. trusting

3 What Do You Think?

1. How does the niece learn that Framton doesn't know her aunt or anything about the "tragedy" she describes?

_____

_____

_____

2. Are Mrs. Sappleton's husband and brothers and their spaniel really ghosts? How do you know?

_____

_____

_____

_____

3. Would any other person be as easily fooled as Framton by the niece's story? Why do you think so?

_____

_____

_____

_____

4. What does the narrator mean at the end when she says of the niece that "romance at short notice was her specialty"?

_____

_____

4 Word Relationships. On the line, write the letter of the phrase that best completes each statement.

1. Whale is to mammal as _____.
   a. bug is to insect
   b. cobra is to reptile
   c. skeleton is to human being
   d. wings are to bird

2. Sailor is to navy as _____.
   a. colonel is to rank
   b. informer is to treason
   c. soldier is to army
   d. troop is to combat

3. Humble is to conceited as _____.
   a. stable is to unsteady
   b. probable is to likely
   c. aroused is to alert
   d. subdued is to rapid

4. Kindle is to douse as _____.
   a. distinct is to vague
   b. loiter is to trespass
   c. parole is to pardon
   d. scrimp is to save

5. Ordinary is to common as _____.
   a. goal is to achievement
   b. truth is to lie
   c. usual is to normal
   d. scarce is to rare

6. Rectory is to pastor _____.
   a. church is to sermon
   b. cemetery is to grave
   c. hymn is to chapel
   d. pastor is to religion

7. Erect is to upright as _____.
   a. apologetic is to guilty
   b. haggard is to stubborn
   c. parched is to dry
   d. slender is to slippery

8. Offense is to defense as _____.
   a. contradict is to agree
   b. moat is to castle
   c. siege is to blockade
   d. tackle is to quarterback

9. Reign is to rain as _____.
   a. kingdom is to weather
   b. king is to forecaster
   c. dough is to doe
   d. rule is to downpour

10. Yen is to Japan as _____.
    a. dollar is to England
    b. peso is to New Mexico
    c. pound is to Canada
    d. euro is to Europe

5 More about Standard Usage. Study each rule below, and then underline the correct word in the sentences that follow it.

1. *All together* and *Altogether*

All together means just what the two words indicate—all the persons in a group. *Altogether* means completely or entirely.

   a. Gene felt (all together, altogether) bewildered when Mrs. Bacchus chose him to chair the safety committee at the plant.

   b. The students were making (all together, altogether) too much noise, so the teacher told them to discuss their answers more quietly.

c. The family was (all together, altogether) when Donald announced that he intended to marry Wendy in the spring.

d. The first thing the foreman told his crew when they were (all together, altogether) was that they were (all together, altogether) wrong in thinking that he did not respect their skills.

2. *Last* and *Latest*

Last means final. *Latest* means the most recent in a series.

a. Jenny, a great fan of "As the World Squirms," didn't learn of the leading lady's (last, latest) scheme until she returned from her trip to Austria.

b. Television stations sometimes break into the regular programs to bring viewers the (last, latest) news.

c. The scatterbrain promised himself that this was the (last, latest) time he would act without thinking.

d. "You may call these slacks the (last, latest) fashion," the woman said to the clerk, "but I call them the (last, latest) straw. I wouldn't wear them to do my gardening."

3. *Between* and *Among*

Between is used when only two persons or things are involved. *Among* is used when more than two persons or things are involved.

a. Whenever the Monroe twins had to share a dessert (between, among) them, one did the cutting and the other got to choose the piece he wanted.

b. Only two students (between, among) the five hundred in the class failed to graduate.

c. The manager had a tough time deciding (between, among) the applicants for the job because many of them seemed able to handle the work.

d. When the first student walked into the classroom, the English professor said, "Just (between, among) us, (between, among) all the lectures I give in this course, today's is my favorite."

4. *Proceed* and *Precede*

Proceed means to go on. *Precede* means to come before.

a. John Quincy Adams (proceeded, preceded) Andrew Jackson as president of the United States.

b. After Gloria finished practicing her clarinet, she (proceeded, preceded) to do her homework.

c. In a restaurant, the salad course generally (proceeds, precedes) the main course.

d. Dick (proceeded, preceded) Jane into the lobby of the movie theater and then (proceeded, preceded) to comment on how ill-mannered people were acting as they waited for the next show to begin.

Review of *r*-Controlled Vowels

ar	**ar**	**are**	**er**
ark	Gary	beware	verdict
Arkansas	various	carefree	persuade
artistic	wary	Delaware	convert
garment	apparent	threadbare	inert
sardine	comparison	day care	proverb
narcotic	imaginary		eternal

ere	**ir**	**or**	**ur**
mere	irk	adore	lurk
sincere	irksome	corridor	furnace
severe	virgin	torture	urban
severely	Virginia	Oregon	rural
sphere	circuit	fortunate	purgatory
hemisphere		endorse	

1 Definitions. Match the words listed below with the correct definitions.

convert	inert	lurk	proverb	rural	urban
garment	irksome	narcotic	purgatory	threadbare	wary

_____ **1.** a place or state of suffering

_____ **2.** a saying expressing a well-known truth or fact

_____ **3.** any drug that dulls the senses and with prolonged use can become an addiction

_____ **4.** causing annoyance or bother; boring

_____ **5.** characteristic of the city or city life

_____ **6.** related to the country as opposed to the city

_____ **7.** on one's guard; cautious; watchful

_____ **8.** shabby; wearing old, shabby clothing

_____ **9.** to change from one form or belief to another

_____ **10.** unmoving or very slow to move

_____ **11.** to lie in wait, as in ambush; to sneak or slink

_____ **12.** an article of clothing

Words for Study

Alice	latitude	curtsey	alas
hedge	longitude	ignorant	occupied
marmalade	Antipathies	Dinah	illustrated

Down the Rabbit-Hole (from *Alice in Wonderland*)
by Lewis Carroll

Alice was beginning to get very tired of sitting by her sister on the bank, and of having nothing to do . . . when suddenly a White Rabbit with pink eyes ran close by her.

There was nothing so *very* remarkable in that; nor did Alice think it so *very* much out of the way to hear the Rabbit say to itself, 'Oh dear! Oh dear! I shall be late!' . . . but when the Rabbit actually *took a watch out of its waistcoat-pocket*, and looked at it, and then hurried on, Alice started to her feet, for it flashed across her mind that she had never before seen a rabbit with either a waistcoat-pocket, or a watch to take out of it, and burning with curiosity, she ran across the field after it, and fortunately was just in time to see it pop down a large rabbit-hole under the hedge.

In another moment down went Alice after it, never once considering how in the world she was to get out again.

The rabbit-hole went straight on like a tunnel for some way, and then dipped suddenly down, so suddenly that Alice had not a moment to think about stopping herself before she found herself falling down a very deep well.

Either the well was very deep, or she fell very slowly, for she had plenty of time as she went down to look about her and to wonder what was going to happen next. First, she tried to look down and make out what she was coming to, but it was too dark to see anything; then she looked at the sides of the well, and noticed that they were filled with cupboards and bookshelves; here and there she saw maps and pictures hung upon pegs. She took down a jar from one of the shelves as she passed; it was labeled 'ORANGE MARMALADE', but to her great disappointment it was empty: she did not like to drop the jar for fear of killing somebody, so she managed to put it into one of the cupboards as she fell past it.

'Well!' thought Alice to herself, 'after such a fall as this, I shall think nothing of tumbling down stairs! How brave they'll all think me at home! Why, I wouldn't say anything about it, even if I fell off the top of the house!' (Which was very likely true.)

Down, down, down. Would the fall *never* come to an end! 'I wonder how many miles I've fallen by this time?' she said aloud. 'I must be getting somewhere near the center of the earth. Let me see: that would be four thousand miles down, I think—' (for, you see, Alice had learnt several things of this sort in her lessons in the schoolroom, and though this was not a *very* good opportunity for showing off her knowledge, as there was no one to listen to her, still it was good practice to say it over) '—yes, that's about the right distance—but then I wonder what latitude or longitude I've got to?' (Alice had no idea what latitude was, or longitude either, but thought they were nice grand words to say.)

Presently she began again. 'I wonder if I shall fall right *through* the earth! How funny it'll seem to come out among the people that walk with their heads downward! The Antipathies, I think—' (she was rather glad there *was* no one listening, this time, as it didn't sound at all the right word) '—but I shall have to ask them what the name of the country is, you know. Please, Ma'am, is this New Zealand or Australia?' (and she tried to curtsey as she spoke— fancy *curtseying* as you're falling through the air! Do you think you could manage it?) 'And what an ignorant little girl she'll think me for asking! No, it'll never do to ask: perhaps I shall see it written up somewhere.'

Down, down, down. There was nothing else to do, so Alice soon began talking again. 'Dinah'll miss me very much tonight, I should think!' (Dinah was the cat.) 'I hope they'll remember her saucer of milk at tea-time. Dinah my dear! I wish you were down here with me! There are no mice in the air, I'm afraid, but you might catch a bat, and that's very like a mouse, you know. . . . Now, Dinah, tell me the truth: did you ever eat a bat?' when suddenly, thump! thump! down she came upon a heap of sticks and dry leaves, and the fall was over.

Alice was not a bit hurt, and she jumped up on to her feet in a moment: she looked up, but it was all dark overhead; before her was another long passage, and the White Rabbit was still in sight, hurrying

down it. There was not a moment to be lost: away went Alice like the wind, and was just in time to hear it say, as it turned a corner, 'Oh my ears and whiskers, how late it's getting!' She was close behind it when she turned the corner, but the Rabbit was no longer to be seen: she found herself in a long, low hall, which was lit up by a row of lamps hanging from the roof.

There were doors all round the hall, but they were all locked; and when Alice had been all the way down one side and up the other, trying every door, she walked sadly down the middle, wondering how she was ever to get out again.

Suddenly she came upon a little three-legged table, all made of solid glass; there was nothing on it except a tiny golden key, and Alice's first thought was that it might belong to one of the doors of the hall; but, alas! either the locks were too large, or the key was too small, but at any rate it would not open any of them. However, on the second time round, she came upon a low curtain she had not noticed before, and behind it was a little door about fifteen inches high: she tried the little golden key in the lock, and to her great delight it fitted!

Alice opened the door and found that it led into a small passage, not much larger than a rat-hole: she knelt down and looked along the passage into the loveliest garden you ever saw. How she longed to get out of that dark hall, and wander about among those beds of bright flowers and those cool fountains, but she could not even get her head though the doorway; 'and even if my head *would* go through,' thought poor Alice, 'it would be of very little use without my shoulders. Oh, how I wish I could shut up like a telescope! I think I could, if I only know how to begin.' For, you see, so many out-of-the-way things had happened lately, that Alice had begun to think that very few things indeed were really impossible.

2 Understanding the Story. Write the letter of the correct answer on the line.

1. What surprises Alice most about the White Rabbit when she sees it while sitting on the bank? _____
   a. its pink eyes
   b. that it says "Oh dear! Oh Dear! I shall be late!"
   c. that it has a waistcoat-pocket and a watch
   d. that it disappears down a rabbit-hole

2. When Alice sees the White Rabbit run down the rabbit-hole, she _____.
   a. crawls in after him without a thought
   b. discovers she's too big to follow him
   c. worries that she may not be able to get out
   d. runs back to tell her sister where she's going

3. Which words best describe Alice? _____
   a. curious and adventurous
   b. humorous and careless
   c. unpleasant and brave
   d. thoughtful and far-sighted

4. Alice tumbles down a well and thinks to herself that _____.
   a. her family will worry and they'll never find her
   b. she will never get out of the rabbit-hole
   c. she is falling very slowly or the well is very deep
   d. she will be hurt badly when she lands

5. As she falls down the well, Alice _____.
   a. discovers that she likes orange marmalade
   b. sees a brightly lit garden below
   c. sees the rabbit tumbling below her
   d. grabs a marmalade jar off a shelf

6. After falling a long time, Alice lands _____.

    a. in a beautiful garden

    b. on a pile of sticks and leaves

    c. in a comfortable old chair

    d. on a little three-legged table

7. Alice races down a long passage, turns a corner and finds herself _____.

    a. face to face with the White Rabbit

    b. standing before a low curtain

    c. in a long passage with doors on either side

    d. looking into a rat-hole

8. Alice finds a golden key _____.

    a. lying on the floor before the tiny door

    b. on a little three-legged table

    c. that unlocks each door that enters the long passage

    d. hidden in a marmalade jar

9. Alice wishes she could shut up like a telescope because _____.

    a. she could see to the top of the rabbit-hole

    b. she would like to fit through the tiny door

    c. she wouldn't be seen by the White Rabbit

    d. she could see to Australia

10. Because so many odd things have happened to Alice, she _____.

    a. has learned to expect the worse

    b. hopes no more strange things will happen

    c. believes she has no control over events

    d. believes few things are impossible

3 What Do You Think? Answer these questions in good sentence form.

1. Why does Alice think that if she falls right through the earth, she'll see people walking "with their heads downward"?

_____

_____

_____

_____

2. The passage ends with Alice unable to get through a small doorway. If you were the author, how would you solve Alice's problem?

_____

_____

_____

_____

_____

4 Alice in Wonderland. Use the words listed at the left to complete these statements about the book
Alice in Wonderland.

outing
occupied
including
daughters
casually
rowed

1. The story of *Alice in Wonderland* began _____ on a warm summer
day back in 1862. Lewis Carroll was on a day _____ with
some friends, _____ three young _____
of his friend Henry Liddell. The group _____ a small boat
down the Thames River in England. While resting on a river bank, Carroll
_____ the girls' time by telling them a story.

version
expanded
pestered
eventually
originally
basis

2. The story Carroll told the girls was the _____ for the story
that became known as *Alice in Wonderland.* Carroll _____
called it *Alice's Adventures Under Ground.* After hearing the story, ten-year-old
Alice Liddell _____ Carroll to write down the story.
_____, Carroll did write an _____
_____ of the tale he had told on the river.

assumed
actual
author
profession
mathematics
instructor

3. The real name of the _____ of *Alice in Wonderland* was not
Lewis Carroll. His _____ name was Charles Dodgson. Carroll
was a name Dodgson _____ as a writer. Writing, moreover,
was not his main _____. He was a _____
_____ at Oxford University.

encouraged
illustrated
handwritten
popular
publish
edition

4. The first _____ of the book was a _____
copy. Dodgson _____ it himself with drawings. The book
was _____ among his friends and others who read it. They
_____ Dodgson to _____ it.

immediate
success
novel
famous
continuous
expense

5. In 1865, Dodgson published the book at his own _____. It
was an _____ _____, and Dodgson became
_____. In 1871, he published another _____
about Alice called *Alice Through the Looking-Glass and What Alice Found There.* The two
Alice books have been in _____ print ever since.

5 Spelling Check. Charles Dodgson first told the story of Alice in Wonderland to the three daughters of a close friend. The middle daughter, Alice, was 10 years old at the time. Who were the other two girls? Solve this spelling puzzle to discover the answer.

- Use each syllable in the box only once. The number next to each clue tells you how many syllables are in the answer.

- When you have finished, the first letter of each answer, reading down, should spell the name of each of the two girls.

- Study the example before you begin.

al	ber	cent	✓dro	ful	i	light	✓mat	oc	spec	ti
ance	ble	de	dur	fy	in	lip	neigh	pi	ta	to
ance	bor	den	en	hos	✓laun	low	no	re	tal	tu

First Daughter's Name

<u>laundromat</u>

_____

_____

_____

_____

_____

1. a place to wash dirty clothing (3)

2. the tenth month of the year (3)

3. a word used to describe a person who does the right thing and acts properly (4)

4. to recognize someone or something (4)

5. someone who lives near where you live (2)

6. money that parents often regularly give their children (3)

Second Daughter's Name

_____

_____

_____

_____

_____

7. the ability to do an activity for a very long time without tiring (3)

8. what you might call an experience that was very pleasant and enjoyable (3)

9. a word used to describe someone who has very little world experience (3)

10. a bright flower with a pleasant smell that is widely grown in Holland (2)

11. a place you might go if you are injured or very sick (3)

First Daughter's Name: _____

Second Daughter's Name: _____

Review of *r*-Controlled Vowel Combinations

air	ear	ear	eer
fair-haired	shears	earthy	veer
millionaire	endear	yearn	leer
lair	endearment	hearse	eerie
prairie	weary	rehearse	pioneer
impair	bleary	rehearsal	auctioneer

oar	our	our	our
boar	journal	mourn	tour
coarse	courtesy	mournful	tourist
coarsely	nourish	courtship	tournament
hoarse	flourish	gourd	tourniquet
hoarsely	adjourn	outpouring	gourmet

1 Definitions. Match the words listed below with the correct definitions.

> bleary   coarse   endearment   gourmet   lair   veer   yearn
> boar   eerie   gourd   impair   tourniquet   weary

_____ **1.** a wild pig with dense, dark bristles

_____ **2.** an expression of affection; a loving word

_____ **3.** any device, such as a band or strip of cloth, used to stop temporarily the flow of blood through a large artery

_____ **4.** a vine related to the pumpkin and squash; a drinking vessel or utensil made from the shell of one of these fruits

_____ **5.** blurred or dimmed by tears

_____ **6.** mysterious; inspiring fear without being openly threatening; unsettling

_____ **7.** one who knows about and enjoys fine food and drink

_____ **8.** the den or dwelling of a wild animal

_____ **9.** tired

_____ **10.** to have a strong or deep desire

_____ **11.** to injure; to lessen in strength or value

_____ **12.** to turn aside from a course, direction, or purpose; to shift or swerve

_____ **13.** inferior or common; crude

Words for Study

Anika	clients	aspect	dedicated
Moka	vital	rhythms	satisfaction
antelope	electrodes	dispense	dimension
erratic	Webster	illusion	valid
receptionist	transition	fantasized	vice versa

Sleep Disorder
by S. Dean Wooten

Anika raced through the forest. She had just joined the chase, replacing two other tired runners. Now it was just her and Moka, her brother. He was exhausted and only a few steps ahead of her. Her clan was in pursuit of an antelope and had been taking turns running it down. Her breathing was steady but rapid as she sprinted up the steep slope after Moka; her legs screamed with the effort. She saw light up ahead, a meadow. She and Moka broke into the light and saw the antelope stumble. Moka threw his spear, but missed. Anika ran forward several more paces and hurled her spear directly on the mark. . . . Her family would have food for several days now. . . .

Anika's eyes opened with a start. Her forehead and face were damp from the exertion of her dream and her breaths came quickly. "I did my part," she said quietly to herself with a smile.

Anika sat up in bed and began pulling wires loose from her head and chest. She was participating in a sleep study at a university lab. She'd signed up for it because she'd always had trouble sleeping. She'd fall asleep quickly and then awaken four hours later, still tired but unable to sleep. Her dreams were erratic. Now, she had long nights of restful sleep packed with dreams that seemed to go on and on. Sometimes, she lived for weeks inside her dream only to awaken

in the morning to find only one night had passed. It was all due to one little blue capsule that she was given before going to bed each night.

Finished at the lab and fully rested, Anika went to work, a not very glamorous job as a receptionist in an insurance office.

"Good morning, Anika," John McCormick, the agent, said as she walked in. "How's your sleep lab going?" Before she could answer, the phone rang, and McCormick disappeared into his office.

"Good morning, McCormick Insurance Agency." Anika answered. "How can I direct your call?" Anika labored to get through the day, trying to sound interested in the concerns of clients and to remain pleasant despite their complaints. The boredom of it all brought tears to Anika's eyes. She kept going by remembering what she was accomplishing at the lab and the fulfilling life she lived in her dreams.

When Anika got to the lab each night, her vital signs were taken and electrodes and leads were attached to her skull and chest so her sleep patterns could be recorded. When all was ready, the nurse dispensed the blue capsule that helped Anika sleep. Usually, a nurse performed these duties, but this evening one of the physicians overseeing the study examined her.

medicines for an upcoming experiment has been received. "Yes," *she says to herself,* "*we're all set to begin the study.*"

On Friday evening, the last evening of the study, Anika sat in the examination room. The nurse had been called away to assist a doctor. While Anika sat there, she found herself staring at the door to a storage closet. She realized that it was the one in her dream. Anika entered the closet, glanced around, and walked directly to a locked cabinet. She swiftly dialed in the combination from her dream. The tumblers rolled into place and the cabinet snapped open crisply. Anika knew exactly what she was searching for and quickly emptied a box of blue capsules into her purse. When the nurse returned a few minutes later, Anika was waiting patiently on the examination table.

Anika went home calmly the next morning, having finished up her part of the sleep study. Her purse bulged with a year's supply of blue capsules. She didn't know what she'd do when the supply was exhausted, but for now at least, her sleep and the dreams would continue.

Anika opened her eyes and stared out the window. It was fall, and the leaves outside her window were bright yellow. She rose quickly and was soon off to the lab. She was beginning an important sleep study that day. Thirty volunteer patients would be checked in and prepped for the experiment. But when she arrived, a nurse, Ms. Kim, met her, a worried look on her face. "Doctor Webster," Ms. Kim began, "the medicine cabinet has been broken into; the meds for the new study have been stolen!"

2 Understanding the Story. Put the letter of the best answer on the line.

1. Anika goes to the laboratory because _____.
   a. she has trouble sleeping
   b. she doesn't like her job
   c. she wants to understand why she dreams
   d. she is afraid to go to sleep because of her dreams

2. Anika's forehead and face are damp when she awakens because _____.
   a. she is worried and restless because the sleep study is ending
   b. the blue capsules cause her to sweat
   c. the sleep laboratory is very warm
   d. in her dream, she was running after an antelope and was sweating

3. In one of Anika's dreams, she _____.
   a. works as a receptionist in an insurance agency
   b. asks the doctor to give her a prescription for blue capsules
   c. takes blue capsules out of the medicine cabinet
   d. learns the combination to the medicine cabinet in the lab

"I want to let you know, Anika," Doctor Webster said as she began hooking up the electrodes, "that our study is coming to an end. We've gathered a lot of really good data and had some surprising results. Thanks for your participation. We'll be wrapping up the study this Friday night."

"The study is ending?" Anika said, surprised. "I knew, of course, that it wouldn't go on forever, but Friday, that's so soon. What'll I do?"

"Well, you'll go back to your usual life," Doctor Webster said matter-of-factly. "You may see some residual benefits from the study and the drugs for a while that will help you transition back to normal."

"But, I won't sleep. I'll lose the dreams."

"I hope that you will sleep better than you used to. You've formed some excellent sleep habits here that should carry over when you get home. And you'll still dream. You just won't remember them as well as you do now. And actually, that's one aspect of the study that has us a little puzzled . . . why you have such vivid and memorable dreams. No one else reports that experience, even those using the same drugs. It's interesting, but everyone responds differently to drugs as well as to changes in their sleep situation. Perhaps you'll be able to hold onto them for a while."

"Maybe you can prescribe the drug for me, Doctor Webster, so I can continue taking it. It would be so helpful!"

"I'm sorry, Anika," she said. "You know these drugs are experimental. We don't know what the long-term effects could be. Who knows what might happen if you stayed on these drugs for an extended period of time? It might upset your nervous system or alter your sleep rhythms, or worse. Besides, we're not approved to dispense them except during the study."

"But the dreams are so real, Doctor. They're more real than my life. When I dream, it's like a different life I'm living, one where time almost stands still and events that can never happen in my life do happen. I really can't give them up."

"It's only an illusion, Anika. The dreams are only dreams. We've discussed this before. These dreams you're having, like all dreams, exist only in the mind. It only seems like they're real and that they last for days. In reality, dreams only last a few minutes, perhaps as much as 90 minutes, not any longer. Please, try not to imagine they are more than they are; they're just dreams. And I promise, you will still have the dreams; you just won't remember them as well." And with that not very reassuring advice, Doctor Webster left a shaken Anika to deal with the news of the study's end.

As Anika lay down that night, her mind was on her predicament. She worried over her sleep and fantasized about how she could obtain a supply of blue capsules.

As the doctor walks into the new laboratory dedicated to sleep studies, she feels a great sense of satisfaction. Her hard work has paid off. As one of a group of doctors and researchers working in this laboratory, Dr. Anika Webster will now be able to test many of her theories about sleep and dreams. She has been preparing for this opportunity all of her life. Now, she'll be able to learn for sure if her theory that dreams can actually take us into another dimension is valid. She believed, but has never been able to prove, that dreams are as real as the lives we live every day; they're simply lived in another dimension, or plane of existence. When we live in one dimension, our lives in the other seem like a dream, and vice versa. In a sense, she thought, all of life is a dream. How it appears to us depends upon the dimension we're occupying at the time. Anika walks into a storage closet and spins the dial of a combination lock on one of the cabinets. She wants to check whether the supply of

4. The electrodes and leads that are hooked to Anika's head are used to _____.

   a. keep her from sleeping
   b. record her sleep patterns
   c. record her dreams
   d. record her thoughts

5. When Anika learns the study is ending, she _____.

   a. hopes she will be able to keep her job at the insurance agency
   b. is sad that she won't see her brother Moka again
   c. worries she won't have her dreams anymore
   d. is satisfied that she will sleep better in the future

6. Anika thinks her dreams _____.

   a. are enjoyable   c. help her sleep
   b. are real   d. are frightening

7. Why doesn't the doctor give Anika a prescription for the blue capsules? _____

   a. She doesn't think Anika needs them.
   b. She doesn't have the capsules because they've been stolen.
   c. The capsules can only be used during the study.
   d. There are no capsules; they are only in Anika's dreams.

3 What Do You Think? Think about the story. Then answer the questions.

1. Reread the opening scene describing Anika's hunt for the antelope, and then think about how the story ends. Is the antelope chase a dream or reality? Explain your answer.

   _____

   _____

   _____

   _____

2. Explain the connection between Anika, the woman with the sleep problems, and Dr. Anika Webster, the lab scientist.

   _____

   _____

   _____

   _____

4 Word Review. Fill in the blanks in each sentence with the best pair of words. Study the example first.

1. Graham had a(n) _____ **eerie** _____ feeling that his boss's avoiding him in the workers' lounge

   was a(n) _____ **omen** _____ that he was about to be ousted from his position.

   a. constant — omission   c. eerie — omen

   b. earthy — establishment   d. mere — persuasion

2. "I don't know why we're _____ over whether to buy sirloin steak or shrimp for

   dinner when we really don't have the _____ for either," exclaimed Virginia.

   a. wavering — resources   c. contending — fondness

   b. bickering — profit   d. yearning — patience

3. A _____ home is referred to as a _____.

   a. boar's — cave   c. swan's — stable

   b. crocodile's — sty   d. lion's — lair

4. The king found it _____ that his public duties demanded so much of his time that

   he had little opportunity to pursue the _____ of his sweetheart.

   a. sickening — courthouse   c. irksome — courtship

   b. evident — courtrooms   d. disagreeable — courtyards

5. Sylvia had always wanted to photograph _____, so she purchased an airline ticket

   to _____.

   a. the Grand Canyon — Europe   c. the Eiffel Tower — China

   b. Pearl Harbor — Hawaii   d. the Okefenokee — Delaware

6. In writing her report on state capitals for history class, Jackie discovered that _____

   was not the capital of _____.

   a. Salt Lake City — Utah   c. New York City — New York

   b. Atlanta — Georgia   d. Columbia — South Carolina

7. Many students think that the _____ were a(n) _____ group
   of people because they are often pictured with dark clothes and grim expressions.

   a. forty-niners — coarse

   b. Founding Fathers — earthy

   c. frontiersmen — reckless

   d. Pilgrims — dull

8. Howard thought he had spoken _____ to the woman standing ahead of him in
   the line, but the _____ of her response made him wish he had kept quiet.

   a. courteously — bluntness

   b. encouragingly — drowsiness

   c. jokingly — graciousness

   d. mysteriously — feebleness

9. After having _____ a perfect swan dive, Glen _____ his
   hidden tension by furiously biting his fingernails as he awaited the judges' decision.

   a. achieved — bemoaned

   b. attempted — repressed

   c. completed — betrayed

   d. created — subdued

10. Kate found the working conditions at the plant _____, but she felt
    _____ because of the limited opportunities for advancement.

    a. agreeable — frustrated

    b. convenient — unsuitable

    c. fulfilling — privileged

    d. specialized — unskilled

11. A(n) _____ may be _____ with people who are not reserved
    in their behavior.

    a. actress — unintentional

    b. hostess — unbearable

    c. housewife — uncertain

    d. prude — displeased

12. At halftime, Coach McCormick tried to _____ confidence in his players by
    reminding them how _____ they had played the last time the two teams met,
    but the final score revealed that his effort was fruitless.

    a. incite — responsibly

    b. inflict — smugly

    c. insert — generously

    d. instill — boldly

5 Words That Describe. Use the words listed below to complete the sentences. Use each word only once.

beige	dismal	feeble	romantic	severe	steadfast
classified	eerie	hoarse	scarlet	sincere	treacherous

1. A harsh scolding is _____.

2. Secret government papers are _____.

3. An icy road is _____.

4. A dreary winter day is _____.

5. A male cardinal is _____.

6. A honeymoon is _____.

7. A lame excuse is _____.

8. A loyal companion is _____.

9. A haunted house is _____.

10. A light brown suit is _____.

11. An exhausted auctioneer is _____.

12. An earnest apology is _____.

6 Words That *Don't* Describe. Use the words listed below to complete the sentences. Use each word only once.

apparent	distinct	generous	heartfelt	persistent	savage
deafening	frizzy	hasty	nourishing	relaxed	unintentional

1. Smooth, straight hair is not _____.

2. A deliberate action is not _____.

3. A gentle lamb is not _____.

4. A hidden motive is not _____.

5. A phony compliment is not _____.

6. A quitter is not _____.

7. A slowpoke is not _____.

8. A tightwad is not _____.

9. A frustrated person is not _____.

10. Junk food is not _____.

11. Slurred speech is not _____.

12. The sound of one hand clapping is not _____.

Vowels Followed by the Letters *w* and *l*

aw	ew	ow	ow	al	al
awe	dew	fowl	widower	halter	valve
awkward	hew	browse	bellow	alternate	Alps
brawl	steward	trowel	tow	almanac	caliber
tomahawk	stewardess	nowadays	stowaway		

el	il	ol	ol	ul	ul
elevator	jilt	jolt	trolley	bulldozer	pulpy
relish	kilt	enfold	polish	pull-up	pulpit
delicatessen	mildew	voltage	volume	full-fledged	culprit
cello	villain	bolster	solitaire	impulse	cultivate

1 Definitions. Match the words listed below with the correct definitions.

almanac	brawl	cultivate	hew	jolt	pulpit	widower
bolster	culprit	fowl	jilt	kilt	stowaway	

_____ **1.** a pleated skirt reaching to the knees, especially the skirt worn sometimes by men of the Scottish Highlands

_____ **2.** a book-like calendar that contains information about the weather, sun, moon, stars, tides, church days, and other facts

_____ **3.** a long narrow pillow or cushion

_____ **4.** a man who outlives the woman to whom he was married

_____ **5.** a noisy fight or quarrel

_____ **6.** a person accused of a crime, or a person who is guilty of a crime

_____ **7.** a person who hides aboard a ship, airplane, etc., to get free passage or hide from port officials

_____ **8.** a platform from which a clergyman preaches in church

_____ **9.** to prepare the soil for planting; to help something grow

_____ **10.** any bird uscd as food or hunted as game

_____ **11.** to cut down with an ax

_____ **12.** to bump into; to shake or knock about; to jiggle

_____ **13.** to deceive or cast aside a lover

Words for Study

sparsely	voluntarily	Murlock	ventured
habitable	forsaken	lusterless	abundant
abandoned	barter	coroners	delirious
perils	zeal	preceded	sacred
meager	expiring	penetrated	enormous

The Boarded Window

by Ambrose Bierce

In 1830, only a few miles away from what is now the great city of Cincinnati, lay an immense and almost unbroken forest. The whole region was sparsely settled by people of the frontier. They were restless souls who no sooner had hewn fairly habitable homes out of the wilderness . . . then driven by some mysterious impulse of

their nature they abandoned all and pushed farther westward. There they would begin again—running into new perils and hardships in the effort to regain the meager comforts which they had voluntarily renounced. Many of them had already forsaken that region for the remoter settlements, but among those remaining was one who had been of those first arriving. He lived alone in a house of logs surrounded on all sides by the great forest, of whose gloom and silence he seemed a part. No one had ever known him to smile nor speak a needless word. His simple wants were supplied by the sale or barter of skins of wild animals in the river town. There were evidences of "improvement"—a few acres of ground immediately about the house had once been cleared of its trees, the decayed stumps of which were half concealed by the new growth that had been suffered to repair the damage from the ax. Apparently the man's zeal for agriculture had burned with a failing flame, expiring in sorrowful ashes.

The little log house, with its chimney of sticks, its roof of warping clapboards weighted with crossing poles and its "chinking" of clay, had a single door and, directly opposite, a window. The latter, however, was boarded up—nobody could remember a time when it was not. And none knew why it was so closed. It was certainly not because of the occupant's dislike of light and air, for on those rare occasions when a hunter had passed that lonely spot the loner had commonly been seen sunning himself on his doorstep if heaven had provided sunshine for his need. I fancy there are few persons living today who ever knew the secret of that window, but I am one, as you shall see.

The man's name was said to be Murlock. He looked like he was seventy years old, actually about fifty. Something besides years had had a hand in his aging. His hair and long, full beard were white, his gray, lusterless eyes sunken, his face singularly seamed with wrinkles which appeared to belong to two intersecting systems. In figure he was tall and spare, with a stoop of the shoulders—a burden bearer. I never saw him; these particulars I learned from my grandfather, from whom also I got the man's story when I was a lad. He had known him when living nearby in that early day.

One day Murlock was found in his cabin, dead. It was not a time and place for coroners and newspapers, and I suppose it was agreed that he had died from natural causes or I should have been told, and should remember. I know only that with what was probably a sense of the fitness of things, the body was buried near the cabin, alongside the grave of his wife. She had preceded him by so many years that local tradition had retained hardly a hint of her existence. That closes the final chapter of this true story—excepting, indeed, that many years afterward, in company with an equally fearless spirit, I penetrated to the place and ventured near enough to the ruined cabin to throw a stone against it. Then I quickly ran away to avoid the ghost which every well-informed boy thereabout knew haunted the spot. But there is an earlier chapter—that supplied by my grandfather.

When Murlock built his cabin and began laying sturdily about with his ax to hew out a farm—the rifle, meanwhile, his means of support—he was young, strong and full of hope. In that eastern country where he had come from and had married, as was the fashion, a young woman in all ways worthy of his honest devotion, who shared the dangers and hardships of his lot with a willing spirit and light heart. There is no known record of her name. Of her charms of mind and person, tradition is silent and the doubter is at liberty to entertain his doubt; but God forbid that I should share it! Of their affection and happiness there is abundant assurance in every added day of the man's widowed life; for what but the charm of a blessed memory could have chained that adventurous spirit to a lot like that?

One day Murlock returned from gunning in a distant part of the forest to find his wife lying sick with fever, and delirious. There was no physician within miles, no neighbor; nor was she in a condition to be left, to go get help. So he set about the task of nursing her back to health. But at the end of the third day she fell into unconsciousness and so passed away, apparently, with never a gleam of returning reason.

From what we know of a nature like his, we may venture to sketch in some of the details of the outline picture drawn by my grandfather. When convinced that she was dead, Murlock had sense enough to remember that the dead must be prepared for burial. In performance of this sacred duty he blundered now and again, did certain things incorrectly, and others which he did correctly were done over and over. His occasional failures to accomplish some simple and ordinary act filled him with astonishment. He was surprised, too, that he did not weep—surprised and a little ashamed; surely it is unkind not to weep for the dead. "Tomorrow," he said aloud, "I shall have to make the coffin and dig the grave; and then I shall miss her, when she is no longer in sight. But now—she is dead, of course, but it is all right—it *must* be all right, somehow. Things cannot be so bad as they seem."

He stood over the body in the fading light, adjusting the hair and putting the finishing touches to the simple toilet, doing all mechanically, with soulless care. And still through his consciousness ran a sense of conviction that all was right—that he should have her again as before, and everything explained. He had had no experience in grief; his ability to grieve had not been enlarged by use. His heart could not contain it all, nor his imagination rightly conceive it. He did not know he was so hard struck; *that* knowledge would come later, and never go. Grief is an artist of powers as various as the instruments upon which he plays his hymns for the dead, prompting from some the sharpest, shrillest notes, from others the low, grave chords that throb over and over like the slow beating of a distant drum. Some natures it startles; some it stuns. To one it comes like the stroke of an arrow, stinging all the senses to a keener life; to another as the blow of a club, which in crushing benumbs. We may conceive Murlock to have been that way affected, for (and here we are not guessing) no sooner had he finished his holy work than, sinking into a chair by the side of the table upon which the body lay, and noting how white the profile showed in the deepening gloom, he laid his arms upon the table's edge, and dropped his face into them, tearless yet and unutterably weary. At that moment came in through the open window a long, wailing sound like the cry of a lost child in the far deeps of the darkening wood! But the man did not move. Again, and nearer than before, sounded that unearthly cry upon his failing sense. Perhaps it was a wild beast; perhaps it was a dream. For Murlock was asleep.

Some hours later, as it afterward appeared, this unfaithful watcher awoke and lifting his head from his arms intently listened—he knew not why. There in the black darkness by the side of the dead, recalling all without a shock, he strained his eyes to see—he knew not what. His senses were all alert, his breath was halted, his blood had stilled its tides as if to assist the silence. Who—what had waked him, and where was it?

Suddenly the table shook beneath his arms, and at the same moment he heard, or fancied that he heard, a light, soft step—another—sounds as of bare feet upon the floor!

He was terrified beyond the power to cry out or move. He waited—waited there in the darkness through seeming centuries of such dread as one may know, yet live to tell. He tried vainly to speak the dead woman's name, vainly to stretch forth his hand across the table to learn if she were there. His throat was powerless, his arms and hands were like lead. Then occurred something most frightful. Some heavy body seemed hurled against the table with a force that pushed it against his breast so sharply as nearly to overthrow him. At the same instant he heard and felt the fall of something upon the floor with so violent a thump that the whole house was shaken by the impact. A scuffling followed, and a confusion of sounds impossible to describe. Murlock had risen to his feet. Fear had taken control of him. He flung his hands upon the table. Nothing was there!

There is a point at which terror may turn to madness; and madness incites to action. With no definite intent, from no motive but the wayward impulse of a madman, Murlock sprang to the wall, with a little groping seized his loaded rifle, and without aim discharged it. By the vivid flash which lit up the room, he saw an enormous panther dragging the dead woman toward the window, its teeth fixed in her throat! Then there were darkness blacker than before, and silence; and when he returned to consciousness the sun was high and the wood was filled with the songs of birds.

The body lay near the window, where the beast had left it when frightened away by the flash and report of the rifle. The clothing was disturbed, the long hair in disorder, the limbs lay anyhow. From the throat, dreadfully slashed, had issued a pool of blood not yet entirely dried. The ribbon with which he had bound the wrists was broken; the hands were tightly clenched. Between the teeth was a piece of the animal's ear.

2 Understanding the Story. Answer the following questions in good sentence form.

1. Who is the narrator and how does he know the secret of the boarded window?

_____

_____

_____

2. How does Murlock change due to the events told about in the story?

_____

_____

_____

_____

3. How does Murlock light up the cabin, and what does he see happening?

_____

_____

_____

4. After seeing the panther, the narrator says there was "darkness blacker than before, and silence." What has happened to Murlock? Why might this have happened?

_____

5. Cite three details that may support the conclusion that the woman was not really dead when Murlock first prepared her for burial? Explain your answer.

a. _____

b. _____

c. _____

3 What Do You Think? Be sure to include reasons to support your point of view.

1. What does Murlock at first think is happening when he awakens from his sleep and before he sees the panther?

_____

_____

_____

_____

2. What did cause the woman's death? Why do you think so?

_____

_____

_____

_____

3. Why is the window boarded up?

_____

_____

_____

_____

4. Should Murlock feel guilty about his wife's death? Why or why not?

_____

_____

_____

_____

4 Proverbs. A proverb is a short saying that expresses a well-known truth or fact. Choose the best meaning for the following proverbs, and write its letter on the line to the left.

1. "You can't teach an old dog new tricks" means about the same as: _____
   a. Be kind to animals.
   b. Learn from nature.
   c. Lightning never strikes twice in the same place.
   d. People become set in their ways.
   e. Time does not stand still.

2. "All that glitters is not gold" means about the same as: _____
   a. Beware of false appearances.
   b. Chase a rainbow, catch a cold.
   c. Gold is where you find it.
   d. Out of the frying pan, into the fire.
   e. Waste not, want not.

3. "People who live in glass houses shouldn't throw stones" means about the same as: _____
   a. Do unto others as you would have them do unto you.
   b. People who have faults shouldn't criticize others.
   c. If you live a stone's throw away, don't throw stones.
   d. Soft heart, hard head.
   e. Your mirror never lies.

4. "Don't look a gift horse in the mouth" means about the same as: _____
   a. As the pony trots, the horse gallops.
   b. Beware of Greeks bearing gifts.
   c. Don't be too critical of a gift.
   d. If you get a horse for a gift, feed it.
   e. One man's horse is another man's headache.

5. "Don't judge a book by its cover" means about the same as: _____
   a. Appearances can be deceiving.
   b. Beware of strangers.
   c. Books make the best friends.
   d. Don't judge others unless you want to be judged yourself.
   e. The early bird gets the worm.

6. "Too many cooks spoil the broth" means about the same as: _____
   a. All roads lead to Rome.
   b. It doesn't pay to work too hard.
   c. The more people in charge, the less gets done.
   d. There's safety in numbers.
   e. Two is company; three's a crowd.

7. "Hitch your wagon to a star" means about the same as: _____
   a. A good cart needs a good horse.
   b. It's good to have great goals.
   c. If you live in the space age, ride a missile.
   d. Great haste wears out horseshoes.
   e. Wish upon a star for good luck.

8. "A stitch in time saves nine" means about the same as: _____
   a. Cheap clothes have a short life.
   b. Opportunity only knocks once.
   c. Sewing is an important skill.
   d. Take care of small problems before they become large.
   e. Waste not, want not.

9. "When in Rome, do as the Romans do" means about the same as: _____
   a. Do unto others as you would have them do unto you.
   b. Italian laws are strict.
   c. Make love, not war.
   d. Adjust to your surroundings.
   e. Traveling is educational.

10. "A bird in the hand is worth two in the bush" means about the same as: _____
    a. Birds require man's protection.
    b. Most hunters are greedy.
    c. Don't risk what you have to go after something you want.
    d. Respect nature's creatures.
    e. This exercise is for the birds.

5 **The Suffix *-ness*.** Use the words listed below to complete these sentences.

bluntness	earnestness	idleness	skimpiness
casualness	feebleness	queasiness	sturdiness
cleanliness	godliness	scornfulness	suddenness
drowsiness	graciousness	scrawniness	thriftiness

1. Paul knew from the _____ with which his girlfriend stormed out of the living room that the _____ of his remarks had hurt her deeply.

2. As _____ overcame Grandfather and he began to snore softly in his favorite armchair, Christina was saddened to see that his _____ was increasing daily and he would soon require almost constant care.

3. From the _____ of the meals his wife had been serving lately, Alex could tell that she was on another one of her _____ campaigns and was probably squirreling away money like crazy.

4. Although Mr. and Mrs. Kelly were impressed with the _____ of the service in the charming little French restaurant, their stomachs filled with _____ as they warily watched the waiter approach with a platter of sizzling snails swimming in garlic butter.

5. The _____ of the teenagers who hung out at the game room all hours of the day and night prompted much sneering and _____ from the town's older residents who spent all their spare time hanging out at the coffee shop next door.

6. Even her aides didn't fully realize the _____ with which Mrs. Alexander pursued the Republican nomination because she delivered her speeches with such _____ that no one took her campaign seriously.

7. When Mrs. Porter compared the _____ of her neighbor's sick child with the _____ of her own healthy baby, she realized how much she had to be grateful for.

8. In an effort to cheer up her sister-in-law, who resented the fact that most of her day seemed to be spent mopping and sweeping and scouring and scrubbing, Carol said, "Now just remember, dear, '_____ is next to _____.'"

6 More about Standard English. Study the following rules, and then correct the mistakes in the sentences at the end of the exercise by crossing out and/or adding words as necessary.

1. **Use *have*, not *of*, after *could*, *should*, *would*, and *might*.**

   Right: I could have worked longer.

   She should have gone to bed earlier.

   It would have been better to save our money.

   He might have enjoyed this movie.

   Wrong: I could of worked longer.

   She should of gone to bed earlier.

   It would of been better to save our money.

   He might of enjoyed this movie.

2. **Use *doesn't*, not *don't*, after *he*, *she*, and *it*.**

   Right: He doesn't want to stay home.

   She doesn't like raw rhubarb.

   It doesn't matter to me when we leave.

   Wrong: He don't want to stay home.

   She don't like raw rhubarb.

   It don't matter to me when we leave.

3. **Use *ought*, not *had ought*.** *Ought* alone expresses duty or obligation without the need for any other word.

   Right: We ought to call home.

   Wrong: We had ought to call home.

4. **Use *the reason . . . is that*, not *the reason . . . is because*.**

   Right: The reason I didn't go to the party was that I was sick.

   Wrong: The reason I didn't go to the party was because I was sick.

5. **Don't use *a* or *an* after the expressions *a kind of* or *the kind of* and *a sort of* or *the sort of*.**

   Right: This is the kind of party I enjoy.

   Charles is the sort of friend everyone would like.

   Wrong: This is the kind of a party I enjoy.

   Charles is the sort of a friend everyone would like.

1. Bierce was born in Ohio in 1842. When he was seventeen, Bierce enrolled in the Kentucky Military Institute and studied history, Latin, architecture, and other subjects. He could of continued in school, but chose to begin a wandering life.

2. The American Civil War broke out in 1861, and Bierce decided he had ought to join the Union Army. Many of his ancestors had been in the military, so his choice was natural.

3. Bierce fought in many of the most famous battles of the Civil War. He might of stayed in the army, but he was wounded and resigned in 1865.

4. After the war, Bierce went to San Francisco where he began writing. He wrote for newspapers and also began writing short stories. In time, he became known as "Bitter Bierce." The reason for the nickname is because he had a biting wit.

5. Bierce was the kind of a writer who enjoyed pointing out the greed, selfishness, and self-importance he saw in people. He often made fun of writers, politicians, and just about anyone else that caught his attention.

6. Bierce often wrote about war. The reason, of course, is because he had seen so much of the Civil War.

7. In 1913, when Bierce was 71, he decided to travel south to Mexico. It don't seem possible, but no one knows for sure what happened to Bierce in Mexico. All we know for certain is that he disappeared.

8. He could of died in the Mexican Civil War, but no one really knows. Some people say he never went there at all. Some say he committed suicide in the Grand Canyon. Others say he went to South America and was held captive in Brazil.

7 Word Families. Use the words in each set at the left to complete these sentences correctly.

rehearsed
unrehearsed
rehearsal

1. On opening night, the _____ skits turned out to be far more

entertaining than those the performers had _____ repeatedly

during the eight-hour _____ on Saturday.

achieved
achievements
unachieved

2. Thor believed he had not _____ as much as he might have in

life because he spent more time bemoaning his _____ goals

than he did striving for new _____.

nourishing
nourishment
unnourishing

3. The three glazed doughnuts Francis gobbled down each morning during his coffee

break were _____ as far as the nutrition books were concerned.

But as far as he was concerned, they were _____ to his spirits,

and that was the only kind of _____ he wanted.

mourning
mournful
mournfully

4. Hearing a _____ song on the radio that brought back

memories of her youth, Martha began to weep _____,

_____the passing of those days which were gone forever.

apparent
unapparent
apparently

5. "If it is _____ to you that this home is falling apart

while you're off with your friends," shrieked the shrew shrilly at her husband,

"then it's _____ to me that you've lost your mind and

_____ need a psychiatrist!"

courtesy
courteous
courteously

6. Even though she feared her stomach would burst, Mrs. Court was so eager

to appear _____ that she _____

accepted a third helping of roast beef and mashed potatoes because she thought

_____ meant always saying "yes" to your hostess.

sincere
sincerely
sincerity

7. At the retirement dinner given in his honor, the clergyman arose from his seat and said with astonished _____, "I _____ want to thank you for your many generous gifts, and it is my _____ wish that you welcome your next pastor with the same warmth with which you're saying good-bye to me."

suitable
unsuitable
suitably

8. Luke thought he was _____ dressed for the Garfields' party until his spouse told him that a tuxedo was completely_____ for watching the Super Bowl and that the clothes he normally wore on Sunday afternoon would be more _____.

persuade
persuasion
persuasive

9. Anthony had such confidence in his _____ abilities that he knew, with just a little _____, he could _____ his friends to invest in his latest business adventure.

unfortunate
unfortunately
fortune
misfortune

10. In spite of her recent _____, Rosella believed she was not nearly so _____ as her neighbor whose entire _____ had mysteriously disappeared from the family safe which, _____, he had forgotten to lock.

1 Word Review. Use the words listed below to fill in the blanks.

awkward	erratic	prairie	verdict
bristle	kayak	receptionist	vice versa
circuit	marmalade	solitaire	volume
delicatessen	motive	tragedy	zeal

_____   **1.** a book; a large amount; the loudness of a sound

_____   **2.** a circular route or path; the path taken by an electric current

_____   **3.** the other way around

_____   **4.** a shop that sells cooked or prepared foods ready for serving

_____   **5.** a short, coarse, stiff hair

_____   **6.** a vast area of flat or rolling grassland, especially the plain of central North America

_____   **7.** clumsy or without grace

_____   **8.** a reason or cause that makes a person act

_____   **9.** irregular; without a fixed course

_____   **10.** a person employed to greet people and answer phones

_____   **11.** a very sad or terrible event

_____   **12.** eager desire

_____   **13.** the decision reached by a jury at the conclusion of a legal proceeding

_____   **14.** a single gem; a card game for one person

_____   **15.** a small boat made in the style of an Eskimo canoe

_____   **16.** sweetened preserves or jam made with fruit and pieces of the fruit peel

2 Which Word Does Not Fit? On the line to the right, write the word that doesn't fit with the other words.

1. checkers   chess   blackjack   poker   solitaire   _____

2. damage   impair   injure   jilt   wound   _____

3. exhausted   tired   sleepy   weary   withdrawn   _____

4. Australia   Austria   France   Holland   Switzerland   _____

5. loving   caring   endearing   marrying   charming   _____

6. earnest   qualified   serious   sincere   wholehearted   _____

7. alert   cautious   unsafe   wary   watchful   _____

8. spaniel   bloodhound   bulldog   antelope   mutt   _____

9. annoy   bother   disturb   grieve   irk   _____

10. clown   humorist   comic   entertainer   riddle   _____

11. hoe   scissors   shovel   spade   trowel   _____

12. diary   journal   blog   record   report   _____

13. flourish   increase   prosper   thrive   wield   _____

14. advertise   back   support   uphold   vouch   _____

3 A Review of Sounds. Choose the word in which the sound for the underlined letter or letters is the same as in the first word in each row. Write that word on the line.

1. **ch<u>o</u>rus:**   <u>Ch</u>inese   <u>ch</u>emistry   <u>ch</u>iefly   <u>ch</u>ute   _____

2. **l<u>ow</u>down:**   t<u>ow</u>   t<u>ow</u>el   t<u>ow</u>er   tr<u>ow</u>el   _____

3. **<u>pr</u>oceed:**   <u>pr</u>ophecy   <u>pr</u>overb   <u>pr</u>osper   <u>pr</u>ofile   _____

4. **re<u>g</u>ulate:**   avera<u>g</u>e   bei<u>g</u>e   <u>g</u>ourd   <u>g</u>ene   _____

5. **sp<u>ou</u>se:**   b<u>ou</u>t   d<u>ou</u>ble   res<u>ou</u>rce   s<u>ou</u>py   _____

6. **v<u>ei</u>n:**   conc<u>ei</u>ted   perc<u>ei</u>ve   sl<u>ei</u>gh   s<u>ei</u>zure   _____

7. **b<u>ear</u>d:**   h<u>ear</u>se   p<u>ear</u>l   w<u>ear</u>   w<u>ear</u>y   _____

8. **curt<u>ai</u>n:**   m<u>ai</u>nland   barg<u>ai</u>n   rem<u>ai</u>ns   str<u>ai</u>ner   _____

9. **d<u>ough</u>nut:**   th<u>ough</u>tless   thr<u>ough</u>   t<u>ough</u>   thor<u>ough</u>   _____

10. **arg<u>ue</u>:**   vag<u>ue</u>   iss<u>ue</u>   leag<u>ue</u>   plag<u>ue</u>   _____

4 Speaking in Idioms. An idiom is a phrase that means something different from just the sum of its words. Match these common idioms to the situations when someone might use them. You may need to use a dictionary or talk to your friends to figure out the meanings. On the line, fill in the best answer.

a dream come true	let sleeping dogs lie
die laughing	not on your life
I didn't sleep a wink	scared to death
I slept like a baby	takes your breath away
kick the bucket	the life of the party

1. When Rashid told the joke about the bartender, it was so funny that I thought I would

   _____.

2. Uncle Ernesto was so sick with the flu that he was sure that he was going to

   _____.

3. Alice was so afraid of heights that when her boyfriend suggested they go to the top of the Empire

   State Building, she replied, "_____!"

4. Mr. Framton was surely _____ when he thought that the

   ghosts of Mr. Sappleton and his brothers were coming through the window.

5. Mrs. Sappleton's niece tells such interesting stories that I'll bet she is

   _____.

6. Tuesday night I tossed and turned and _____, but last night

   I was so exhausted that _____.

7. Tran knew that if he brought up the subject of the loan his sister would become hysterical again so he

   decided to just _____.

8. The funny thing is that not only does climbing the mountain leave you breathless from the effort, but

   once you get to the top the incredible view _____.

9. Even though it was 50 years ago, Walt still remembered the day Maggie agreed to be his wife because it

   was _____ for him.

5 A Review of Standard Usage. Each of the following sentences has four underlined sections. Choose the number of the section that is incorrect, and then circle that number in the answer row. If there is no incorrect section, circle number 5.

1 2 3 4 5   **1.** When Tom wanted to <u>teach</u> his younger brother how to become a shoplifter, his

    1

    older brother <u>preceded</u> to explain that this <u>sort of</u> behavior was <u>altogether</u> wrong.

    2   3   4

1 2 3 4 5   **2.** "The reason I'm early," explained Mr. Washington to his bewildered boss, "<u>is that</u>

    1

    I had agreed to give my landlady a lift to her job; and, even though I <u>could of</u>

    2

    suggested the bus, I <u>proceeded</u> to offer her a ride to make her feel a little guilty

    3

    about the <u>latest</u> rent increase."

    4

1 2 3 4 5   **3.** <u>Being that</u> the detective knew there was no sense of loyalty <u>among</u> the three

    1   2

    brothers, he also knew that <u>hardly any</u> time would pass before they <u>proceeded</u> to

    3   4

    blame each other for the robbery.

1 2 3 4 5   **4.** As the school nurse cleaned the student's bruises, she scolded, "You <u>ought</u> to

    1

    know better than to jump <u>off</u> the top of the slide. You <u>could have</u> broken your

    2   3

    entire body. But you're very lucky—everything seems to be <u>alright</u>."

    4

1 2 3 4 5   **5.** "I don't think we <u>should have</u> bothered to go to that movie tonight," said Charles

    1

    to his wife. "<u>Since</u> we had <u>all ready</u> seen it once, we <u>ought</u> to have saved that

    2   3   4

    money for our vacation."

1 2 3 4 5   **6.** Realizing that her students were not <u>all ready</u> to take the test, Mrs. Peck

    1

    <u>preceded</u> it with a review of the material. Even so, Steven did poorly on it and

    2

    <u>proceeded</u> to blame Mrs. Peck for his low grade, claiming the test was <u>altogether</u>

    3   4

    too hard.

6 **"Life is real."** Study the poem below, and then answer the questions.

A Psalm of Life

by Henry Wadsworth Longfellow

Tell me not, in mournful numbers,
    "Life is but an empty dream!"
For the soul is dead that slumbers,
    And things are not what they seem.

Life is real! Life is earnest!
    And the grave is not its goal;
"Dust thou art, to dust returnest,"
    Was not spoken of the soul.

Not enjoyment, and not sorrow,
    Is our destined end or way;
But to act, that each to-morrow
    Find us farther than to-day.

Art is long, and Time is fleeting,
    And our hearts, though stout and brave,
Still, like muffled drums, are beating
    Funeral marches to the grave.

In the world's broad field of battle,
    In the bivouac of Life,
Be not like dumb, driven cattle!
    Be a hero in the strife!

Trust no Future, howe'er pleasant!
    Let the dead Past bury its dead!
Act,—act in the living Present!
    Heart within, and God o'erhead!

Lives of great men all remind us
    We can make our lives sublime,
And, departing, leave behind us
    Footprints on the sands of time;

Footprints, that perhaps another,
    Sailing o'er life's solemn main,
A forlorn and shipwrecked brother,
    Seeing, shall take heart again.

Let us, then, be up and doing,
    With a heart for any fate;
Still achieving, still pursuing,
    Learn to labor and to wait.

1. In the beginning of the poem, Longfellow states that "things are not what they seem." Describe a moment in each of these stories when things were not exactly as they seemed to be.

    a. "The Open Window"

        What was not as it seemed to be? _____

        _____

        What was the reality? _____

        _____

b. "The Boarded Window"

What was not as it seemed to be? _____

_____

What was the reality? _____

_____

c. "Sleep Disorder"

What was not as it seemed to be? _____

_____

What was the reality? _____

_____

2. When Longfellow says that "'dust thou art, to dust returnest,' was not spoken of the soul," he is saying that he believes that the soul continues on after the body dies. Write about a character in Unit 3 who believes in life after death.

What character in which story believes there is life after death? How do you know?

_____

_____

_____

3. When Longfellow says, "Act,—act in the living Present!" he is urging people to live life to the fullest. In "Down the Rabbit-Hole," does Alice live life to the fullest? Explain why you think she does or does not.

_____

_____

_____

4. Longfellow also encourages people to do something important with their lives in order to leave behind "footprints on the sands of time." Have you or has someone you know done something important enough to be remembered for a long time? Write about someone you know or a character you have read about that you believe will leave behind "footprints."

_____

_____

_____

UNIT 4
Brushes with Death

A German writer once wrote, "All interest in disease and death is only another expression of interest in life." This statement helps to explain why the subject of death is such a popular theme among writers. In this unit, you will read about the reactions of people who believe they are about to die and see how those close to them are affected.

The reading for Lesson 13 is taken from the last act of a well-known play entitled *On Golden Pond*. In the scene you will be reading, the elderly husband suffers an attack of severe heart pain, and his wife, for the first time, fears that he is about to die.

"The Execution," the reading for Lesson 14, is based on an actual experience that happened to the famous Russian writer, Fyodor Dostoyevsky. In 1849, Dostoyevsky was sentenced to death for his political activities. The reading describes his thoughts and feelings on the day he is to die in front of a firing squad.

In "A Day's Wait," the story in Lesson 15, a misunderstanding leads a young boy to believe that he is gravely ill. This story shows us that even those closest to us can sometimes be unaware of how we are feeling.

"The Last Leaf," the story for Lesson 16, is taken from an O. Henry story of the same title. Again, the main character—this time a woman—is certain that death is near at hand.

The Hard and Soft *g*

The hard *g* sounds like the *g* in *gasoline*, *gargle*, and *insignia*.
It is usually followed by the vowels *a*, *o*, or *u*.

gal	wag	eagle	marigold	mangle	morgue
galaxy	waggle	beagle	fungus	angle	vogue
guidance	haggle	spigot	penguin	triangle	fatigue
gangrene	straggle	bigot	jaguar	rectangle	dialogue

The soft *g* sounds like the *g* in *Georgia*, *clergy*, and *shrinkage*.
It is usually followed by the vowels *e* or *i*.

gel	logic	legend	bandage	image
gelatin	tragedy	agenda	mileage	sewage
genius	tragically	surgeon	postage	hostage
generator		pigeon	wreckage	beverage
genuine		margarine	savage	outrageous

1 Definitions. Match the words listed below with the correct definitions.

agenda	fatigue	gelatin	generator	haggle	legend	outrageous	tragedy	
bigot	fungus	gangrene	genuine	hostage	logic	spigot	vogue	

_____ **1.** a jelly formed by boiling the specially prepared skin, bones, and tissues of animals, and used in foods, drugs, and photographic film

_____ **2.** a list of things to be done, especially the program for a meeting

_____ **3.** a machine that converts mechanical energy into electrical energy

_____ **4.** a person held until certain terms have been fulfilled

_____ **5.** a story coming down from the past

_____ **6.** a system of reasoning

_____ **7.** another word for faucet

_____ **8.** a drama or story that has an unhappy ending

_____ **9.** any of certain plants which include yeasts, molds, and mushrooms

_____ **10.** cruel, rude, or insulting

_____ **11.** physical or mental weariness resulting from hard work

_____ **12.** real; not counterfeit

_____ **13.** a person who does not recognize or respect the rights or opinions of other races, religions, or political groups

_____ **14.** the current fashion, style, or practice

_____ **15.** the death and decay of tissue in a part of the body, usually a limb, due to failure of blood supply, injury, or disease

_____ **16.** to bargain over the price of something

Words for Study

Ethel	humiliated	grimaces	parlor
cottage	exits	angina	Monopoly
energetic	downstage	who'd	iodine
Parcheesi	Wilmington	moron	quaint

On Golden Pond
by Ernest Thompson

The setting is the living room of a summer home on Golden Pond in Maine. It is late morning in the middle of September. Norman and his wife Ethel are closing up the cottage and preparing to go home. Norman is 79. His hair is white. He wears glasses. He walks slowly but upright. Ethel, who is 69, is small but energetic beyond belief. They are best of friends, with a keen understanding of each other after 46 years of marriage.

Norman: Want to play a quick game of Parcheesi before we go? Loser drives.

Ethel: No. Haven't you been humiliated enough? You owe me four million dollars.

Norman: Double or nothing?

Ethel: When we get home, Norman. We've got the whole winter ahead of us.

Norman: Yes.

Ethel: Come on, let's get the other boxes, and be gone. (*She heads into the kitchen. Norman stays where he is, looking about. Ethel calls from offstage.*) Norman! Would you come here?

Norman: (*He crosses to the kitchen door.*) What is it? (*He exits.*)

Ethel: (*Offstage*) Get the last box if it's not too heavy. (*She enters.*)

Norman: (*Offstage*) Of course it's not too heavy. Good God, this is heavy!

Ethel: Tsk. Well, wait and I'll help you with it then.

Norman: (*Offstage*) You're trying to kill me.

Ethel: I've thought about it. (*She carries her box downstage as he comes out with his.*)

Norman: Good God! (*He crosses to the platform. She waits for him at the door. He moves slowly.*) Whatever have you got in here?

Ethel: My mother's china. I've decided to take it to Wilmington and use it there. (*Norman is feeling his way down the steps.*) We hardly ever eat off it here. Are you all right?

Norman: Your mother never liked me.

Ethel: Oh, stop. She loved you.

Norman: Then why did she have such heavy china? Oh, my God.

Ethel: Set it down if it's too much trouble. Norman! (*He is in pain. He leans against the couch, still holding the box.*) Norman! Put the box down!

Norman: (*He groans.*) Unh. I don't want to break your mother's china. Ouch.

Ethel: Norman! (*She drops her box with a tremendous crash. She runs to Norman. He drops his box.*)

Norman: Whoops. (*He sags against the couch, clutching his chest. She tries to hold him.*)

Ethel: Sit down, you fool. (*She helps him to the couch. He slumps.*) Where's your medicine?

Norman: I don't know. You packed.

Ethel: Oh, God! What did I do with it? I'm afraid it's in the car. (*She runs to the door and exits, her speech continuing outside.*) Which suitcase? Which suitcase? (*Norman grimaces and clutches his chest. He glances around the room, spots a book on the couch beside him. He reaches for it, opens it, grimaces again. Ethel runs back in with a little jar.*) What are you doing, you nitwit? Give me that book! (*She grabs it and throws it onto the floor.*)

Norman: What are you doing?

Ethel: I'm trying to save your life, damn you. Whoever designed these caps is a madman. There, take this and put it under your tongue.

Norman: What is it?

Ethel: Nitroglycerin. Put it under your tongue.

Norman: You must be mad. I'll blow up.

Ethel: Do it! (*Norman takes the pill. She kneels beside him, watching. He breathes deeply and leans his head back, his eyes closed. Ethel begins to weep.*) Oh, dear

God, don't take him now. You don't want him, he's a poop. Norman? Norman!

Norman: (*His eyes closed.*) Maybe you should call a doctor. We can afford it.

Ethel: Oh, yes! (*She jumps up.*) Of course. I should have done that. Dear God. (*She rushes to the phone and dials "O".*) Hello, hello. Dear God. How are you feeling, Norman?

Norman: Oh, pretty good. How are you?

Ethel: Norman, how's the angina?

Norman: The what?

Ethel: The pain, dammit!

Norman: Oh. It's pretty good, as pain goes.

Ethel: Is the medicine doing anything?

Norman: No.

Ethel: Why don't they answer the phone?

Norman: Who'd you call?

Ethel: The stupid operator. (*Into the receiver*) Hello? . . . Hello? (*getting frantic*) Hello, hello, hello, hello, hello, hello! Whatever is the matter with her?

Norman: She's slow.

Ethel: How do you feel now?

Norman: I don't know.

Ethel: Are you planning to die? Is that what you're up to? Well, while I'm waiting for this moron to answer the phone, let me just say something to you, Norman Thayer, Junior. I would rather you didn't.

Norman: Really?

Ethel: Yes! This stupid, stupid, woman. I'm going to have to call a hospital directly. (*She slams down the phone, and pulls out the phone book.*) Where do you look for hospitals? Yellow pages. Hospital, hospital. They're not listed. Oh, wait. . . .

Norman: Ethel.

Ethel: (*Fearing the worst*) Yes! What is it!?

Norman: Come here.

Ethel: Oh, God. (*She rushes over and kneels by his side.*) Yes, Norman. My darling.

Norman: Ethel.

Ethel: (*Crying*) Yes. I'm here. Oh, Norman.

Norman: Ethel. I think I feel all right now.

Ethel: Are you serious?

Norman: I think so. My heart's stopped hurting. Maybe I'm dead.

Ethel: It really doesn't hurt?

Norman: Really doesn't. Shall I dance to prove it?

Ethel: (*Falling against him*) Oh, Norman. Oh, thank God. I love you so much. (*A moment passes. She cries. Norman puts his arm around her.*)

Norman: Now my heart's starting to hurt again. (He holds her close.) Sorry about your mother's china. (He pulls himself forward to look at it.)

Ethel: You're such a poop. Sit still and don't move.

Norman: Are you mad at me?

Ethel: Yes. Why did you strain yourself? You know better.

Norman: I was showing off. Trying to turn you on.

Ethel: Well, you succeeded. There's no need for you to try that sort of thing again.

Norman: Good. (*For a long moment they sit without moving. She stares at him as though she's trying to memorize him. He smiles down at her. The moment passes and she glances away.*)

Ethel: (*After a pause*) Norman. This was the first time I've really felt we're going to die.

Norman: I've known it all along.

Ethel: Yes, I know. But when I looked at you across the room, I could really see you dead. I could see you in your blue suit and a white starched shirt, lying in Thomas's Funeral Parlor, your hands folded on your stomach, a little smile on your face.

Norman: How did I look?

Ethel: Not good, Norman.

Norman: Which tie was I wearing?

Ethel: I don't know.

Norman: How about the one with the picture of the man fishing?

Ethel: Shut up, Norman. (*Pause*) You've been talking about dying ever since I met you. It's been your favorite topic of conversation. And I've *had* to think about it. Our parents, my sister and brother, your brother, their wives, our dearest friends, practically everyone from the old days on Golden Pond, all dead. I've seen death, and touched death, and feared it. But today was the first time I've felt it.

Norman: How's it feel?

Ethel: It feels . . . odd. Cold, I guess. But not that bad, really. Almost comforting, not so frightening, not such a bad place to go. I don't know.

Norman: (*He holds her head for a moment.*) Want to see if you can find my book?

Ethel: Here it is. (*She picks it up from the floor.*) Going to take it?

Norman: Nope. It belongs here. Put it on the shelf. (*She crosses and returns the book to its place.*) I'll read it next year.

Ethel: Yes. Next year. (*She wanders around behind the couch.*) We'll have the whole summer to read and pick berries and play Monopoly, and Billy can come for as long as he likes, and you two can fish, and I'll make cookies, and life will go on, won't it?

Norman: I hope so.

Ethel: I guess I'll go down and say goodbye to the lake. Feel like coming?

Norman: Yes. (*He rises slowly.*)

Ethel: You sure you're strong enough?

Norman: I think so. If I fall over face first in the water you'll know I wasn't.

Ethel: (*Waiting for him*) Well, go easy, for God's sake. I'm only good for one near miss a day.

2 Understanding the Play. Answer the following questions in good sentence form.

1. What is the cause of Norman's angina attack?

   _____

   _____

2. What does Ethel offer as the reason for having thought about death in the past?

   _____

   _____

3. What action symbolizes Norman and Ethel's hope that they will be returning to Golden Pond next summer?

   _____

   _____

4. Write a brief but complete paragraph in which you describe Norman and Ethel's marriage. Include evidence from the dialogue and their actions to support your point of view.

   _____

   _____

   _____

   _____

   _____

   _____

3 What Do You Think? According to Ethel, she thinks about death only when she is forced to—when relatives or friends have died. Norman, on the other hand, thinks about death quite often. In a brief but complete paragraph, describe which of these two views you think is a better attitude toward death.

_____

_____

_____

_____

_____

_____

4 Tone of Voice. In a play, the actors and actresses use their voices to express feeling. In a story, the author must use words to describe how their characters speak. Decide which word best describes the tone of voice the characters would probably use in the following situations. Write the word on the line in each sentence.

1. "What chalk?" asked Lucy _____ when the teacher asked her who had thrown the

   chalk while he was writing the homework assignment on the blackboard.

   a. aimlessly   **b.** energetically   **c.** hopefully   **d.** innocently

2. Enjoying the puzzled look on her niece's face, Aunt Rose added _____.
   "This discussion will make perfect sense to you when you read the letter that's waiting for you at

   your apartment."

   a. automatically   **b.** fearfully   **c.** mysteriously   **d.** impatiently

3. "Come on, baby," the truck driver said _____ as he tried again and again to start the

   engine. "Just one more haul. I know you can do it."

   a. abruptly   **b.** coaxingly   **c.** negatively   **d.** resentfully

4. As the recruit fought back his tears, the veteran said _____, "Come on, son,

   it's not that bad. Before you know it, you'll be an old hand at all of this."

   a. bossily   **b.** encouragingly   **c.** jokingly   **d.** nastily

5. Mounting his horse, the sheriff _____ told his deputy, "I'll get that villain if it's the last thing I do."

    a. grimly   **b.** indifferently   **c.** thoughtfully   **d.** wishfully

6. "But why can't I try out for the hockey team?" asked the boy _____, even though his parents seemed to consider the issue closed.

    a. persistently   **b.** practically   **c.** precisely   **d.** privately

7. "Good afternoon, gentlemen," said the governor _____, because he didn't want to give the reporters the impression he was "just one of the boys."

    a. casually   **b.** impolitely   **c.** formally   **d.** traditionally

8. "All right! All right! You can use my stereo for the party," said Herbert's cousin _____. "But don't expect another favor from me for the rest of your life!"

    a. gleefully   **b.** grudgingly   **c.** tenderly   **d.** treacherously

9. "An ounce of prevention is worth a pound of cure," said Gary's grandmother _____ when the four-year-old demanded to know why she had put iodine on his cut.

    a. dreamily   **b.** foolishly   **c.** guiltily   **d.** wisely

10. "Yes, sweetheart, I heard every word you said," replied Annabel's spouse _____, as he patted her hand and continued reading the account of last night's basketball game in the *Tribune*.

    a. absent-mindedly   **b.** frankly   **c.** regretfully   **d.** spitefully

5 Vacations around the World. Norman and Ethel enjoyed vacationing at Golden Pond, Maine. Use the place names listed below to identify where other people want to spend their vacations. A good dictionary can help you find most, but not all, of the answers.

Amsterdam	Dead Sea	Las Vegas
Atlantic City	Greece	New York City
Austria	Hawaii	Philadelphia
Black Sea	Ireland	Utah
Boston	Jamestown	Washington, D.C.

1. The Joneses planned to visit _____ on the next three-day holiday weekend because, although they had lived in Massachusetts all their lives, they had never toured the state capital.

2. Mr. Beaumont decided to visit _____ on his way from Missouri to Seattle because he was curious to see what a casino was like.

3. Mr. Rogers decided a vacation in _____, the "City of Brotherly Love," was just the thing to lift his spirits and help him forget the strife he felt at work.

4. Grace's fond memories of Monopoly made her want to go to _____ to take a walk on the Boardwalk.

5. Adam bought an airline ticket to _____ so he could become better acquainted with Holland and enjoy the vast fields of tulips.

6. Dr. Miller made reservations at an inexpensive hotel in _____ so that he could do some research at the Library of Congress during winter recess.

7. Mr. Colt arranged a class field trip to _____, the first permanent English colony in the U.S., so that his students could get a better understanding of it.

8. The _____ is a popular vacation spot for beach-lovers in Russia

9. _____ was Phil's favorite place to vacation, mainly because of the quaint and lively pubs found there.

10. When Nancy told her brother that she was going to fly to _____, he asked her to send him a postcard of the Great Salt Lake.

11. Mrs. Monroe wanted to spend her vacation in _____, because she longed to ski in the scenic Alps.

12. When Helen won a one-week, all-expenses-paid trip to _____, she could hardly believe that she was, at last, going to visit the home of Aesop and Homer.

13. Having read books about the scrolls found near the _____ which shed light on Jewish customs in the first century AD, Mr. Isaacs hoped that by setting aside money from each paycheck, he could actually be there during Passover.

14. "All right! All right! We'll take a cruise to _____ to celebrate my retirement. But, just don't enroll me in any of those silly hula contests!" said Mr. Campbell to his wife at the end of a lengthy argument.

15. Rashid studied night and day to ace his exams because he was determined to graduate at the top of his class and get a job in a Wall Street financial firm in _____.

6 Synonyms and Antonyms. Choose a synonym to fill in the first blank in each sentence. Choose an antonym to fill in the second blank.

Synonyms

aimless

eternal

callous

fatigued

carefree

outrageous

counterfeit

swarthy

courteous

withdrawn

descendant

zesty

Antonyms

ancestor

outgoing

crude

sensible

deliberate

tasteless

energetic

temporary

fair

warmhearted

genuine

worried

1. Dark and _____ are antonyms for _____.

2. Everlasting and _____ are antonyms for

    _____.

3. Happy-go-lucky and _____ are antonyms for

    _____.

4. Offspring and _____ are antonyms for

    _____.

5. Phony and _____ are antonyms for _____.

6. Spicy and _____ are antonyms for _____.

7. Purposeless and _____ are antonyms for

    _____.

8. Shocking and _____ are antonyms for

    _____.

9. Shy and _____ are antonyms for _____.

10. Polite and _____ are antonyms for _____.

11. Unfeeling and _____ are antonyms for

    _____.

12. Weary and _____ are antonyms for _____.

The Hard and Soft c

The hard *c* sounds like the *c* in *cushion*, *comparison*, and *Arctic*.
It is usually followed by the vowels *a*, *o*, or *u*.

carnival	column	calculate	Jacob	encamp	fabric
canal	columnist	calculator	vacuum	encase	mimic
canary	coax	cuckoo	calculation	zinc	tonic
cavity	camera		macaroni	majestic	terrific
comedy	convert				
casualty					

The soft *c* sounds like the *c* in *cemetery*, *census*, and *incident*.
It is usually followed by the vowels *e* or *i*.

cement	celery	reception	icily	malice
ceremony	celebrity	receiver	Sicily	jaundice
cedar	citrus	discipline	larceny	noticeable
censor	civil	disciple	menace	precise
censorship	civilian			precision

1 Definitions. Match the words listed below with the correct definitions.

cavity	civilian	disciple	jaundice	majestic	menace	Sicily	vacuum
citrus	columnist	fabric	larceny	malice	mimic	tonic	zinc

_____ **1.** a bluish-white chemical element which is used as a protective coating for iron

_____ **2.** a condition in which the eyeballs, the skin, and the urine become abnormally yellow as a result of bile pigments in the blood

_____ **3.** a hole or hollow place; an area of decay in a tooth

_____ **4.** a material made from threads or fibers by weaving, knitting, felting, etc.

_____ **5.** anything, as certain medicines, supposed to make a person feel strong

_____ **6.** a space with nothing in it at all

_____ **7.** a student or follower of any teacher or religion; an early follower of Jesus

_____ **8.** a writer of a newspaper column

_____ **9.** an island off the southern tip of Italy

_____ **10.** any person who is not an active member of the armed forces

_____ **11.** any trees or shrubs that bear oranges, lemons, limes, or other such fruit

_____ **12.** a threat; a troublesome person

_____ **13.** grand; royal; having great dignity

_____ **14.** inclined to copy someone else; a person who does this

_____ **15.** the unlawful taking of another's goods; theft

_____ **16.** the desire to harm others or to see others suffer; ill will; spite

execution	tzar	Gospels	tempo
Fyodor	biography	proclaim	agony
Dostoyevsky	biographer	wart	charade
condemned	scaffold	crucifix	confrontation

The Execution

by Robert Payne

The famous Russian writer Fyodor Dostoyevsky confronted death in a way that was quite different from Norman's brush with death in the drama *On Golden Pond*. In 1849, Dostoyevsky was condemned to die for his involvement with a group that was accused of plotting against the tzar. The tzar was the absolute ruler of the Russian people.

In this reading, which is taken from a biography about Fyodor Dostoyevsky, the biographer describes the day appointed for the execution of Dostoyevsky and the other condemned men.

* * *

On that day which was the last of his youth, Fyodor was lying on his narrow cot when he heard steps in the corridor, whispers, the clanking of swords, sudden commands followed by the creaking of the key in the rusty lock. It was about half-past five in the morning and still dark. The door opened. In the light of a lantern, Fyodor saw an unknown officer standing there. Suddenly the officer announced that by orders of the Tzar the prisoner had been sentenced to death by shooting. The officer stepped back, the door was closed, and once more there was darkness in the cell.

Afterward, when Fyodor had recovered from the shock, he remembered that nothing had been said about when the sentence would be carried out.

About half an hour later one of the prison guards entered the cell, bringing with him a small package containing the clothes worn by the prisoner when he had entered prison eight months before. There was a thin overcoat, coat, trousers, shirt, tie, socks, heavy-soled boots. Fyodor put them on and was then led out into the courtyard. The first light was coming through the fog.

He shivered in the cold winter air. There was deep snow on the ground.

"What is happening?" he asked one of the guards.

"We are forbidden to tell you," the guard answered, and about this time Fyodor made out the shapes of five carriages. Mounted soldiers in light blue uniforms, with naked swords in their hands, came wheeling across the prison courtyard.

Slowly the courtyard was filling with prisoners. He could make out many with whom he had been arrested. They were not allowed to talk. Someone shouted that the prisoners were to get into the carriages—four to each carriage. A soldier jumped in after them. There was the crack of a whip, and soon all the carriages were rolling out of the courtyard. Fyodor said: "What are they going to do to us?"

"We have been told to tell you nothing," the soldier answered.

The glass in the carriage window was covered with a film of frost, and when Fyodor began to rub the frost away, the soldier stopped him. "Please don't do that," he said. "They'll have me flogged, if you do."

So the prisoners huddled together in silence, gazing straight in front of them or throwing secret glances at the window. It seemed an endless journey, but was in fact only three miles. At last the carriages came to a halt on the square overlooked by the Church of the Holy Virgin with its five golden domes, which could be seen dimly through the floating mist.

When Fyodor stepped out of the carriage, he realized he had come to the place of execution.

Already the crowds had gathered. In the middle of the square a small, sturdy platform had been built during the night. It was covered with black cloth which sparkled with snow. There were steps leading up to the platform. In front, a little to one side, were three thick oak stakes: to these the condemned men would be tied before they were shot.

Because the steps were narrow, the prisoners were led up to the platform in twos. Fyodor wanted to embrace the other prisoners and exchange words of comfort, but there was no time, and besides, as soon as they left the carriages they were marched to the scaffold. A priest ran before them, holding a cross and the Gospels.

The purpose of the Tzar was to instill fear in his prisoners and to torture them in such a way that they would become aware of the vastness of their crimes. Therefore, he prolonged the punishment.

Frozen, their faces turning blue, wearing only the clothes they were wearing on the spring day when they were arrested, they stood on the platform while an official proceeded to proclaim their names, their crimes, and the punishments which the Tzar in his mercy had chosen for them.

Fyodor could not believe he was going to die. He had the curious feeling that it was all a nightmare, and very soon he would wake up. Just at the moment when he heard the words: ". . . condemned to death by shooting" after his own name had been pronounced, the sun came out through the mist and lit the beautiful golden domes of the Church of the Holy Virgin. It occurred to him that this was a sign that he would not die, and none of the others would die.

But by the time the official had finished reading the list, Fyodor had lost all hope. In a dazed way he observed a wart on the cheek of one of the soldiers, and then he saw a copper button shining in the sun. The fog was clearing.

The official was replaced by a priest who invited the prisoners to make their confessions. Only one man confessed, but when the priest offered them the crucifix to kiss, they all knelt and kissed it. The priest went on to deliver a short sermon on the text: "The wages of sin is death." He spoke in a weak voice of the joys of Heaven, and the eternal joy which awaited them in the life to come.

When he had finished, two men climbed onto the platform and broke swords over the heads of all those who were noblemen, thus testifying that they no longer possessed any rights or privileges. This was the last act before the execution. In a sense the breaking of the swords was the worst punishment, removing the men from the world of honor; the actual shooting would be almost less tragic.

For a very long time the prisoners had remained on the platform, numbed and shivering, but the tempo was quickening. The men who had broken the swords left the platform, but the priest remained, muttering prayers. Another general rode up and shouted: "Father, you have done your work! There is no need to stay up there!" The priest walked down the steps.

Some soldiers then mounted the platform with the white robes in which the condemned were always clothed when they were led to their deaths. These robes took the form of white hooded shrouds with long sleeves trailing the ground.

Swords flashed, a trumpet sounded, and there was a roll of drums as three of the men were led down the steps and marched to the stakes where they were bound with ropes. Fifteen soldiers took up position. The command rang out: "Take aim!" and the soldiers lifted their rifles to their shoulders. In a moment the commanding general would shout: "Fire!" and then there would be wet bloodstains on the white shrouds.

Fyodor no longer had any hope that his life would be spared. He believed he had at most five minutes to live. In his agony he tried to imagine himself dead. It astonished him that a man could be full of life and consciousness one moment, the next moment nothing at all.

There was a strange stir on the platform. Everyone was turned and looking in the direction of an officer riding full-tilt across the square, waving a white handkerchief. The rider rode straight up to the general and handed him a sealed letter. The soldiers still had their rifles at their shoulders.

"Lower arms!" the general shouted, and then he began to read the letter he had just received, signed by the Tzar in his own hand.

The letter was very long. Fyodor listened, but he heard very little of it. Just as when he was told for the first time that he was condemned to death by shooting and could not believe it, so now, learning that he was about to be pardoned or at least to suffer a punishment less than death, he could not believe that he would be spared.

Everyone knew that the Tzar had deliberately arranged this charade to punish and torture the prisoners. Fyodor, who was tenth on the list, was sentenced to four years hard labor. Only one of the men, whose name was Palm, received a full pardon. Palm fell to his knees and began praying and exclaiming: "How good the Tzar is! Oh, how grateful I am to the Tzar!" Another of the prisoners shouted bitterly: "It would have been better if they had shot us!" but no one paid any attention to him.

For a few more minutes the prisoners remained on the platform. Some were already suffering from frostbite. All in their different ways were suffering from the fever of joy now that death had been lifted from them. They embraced one another and wept. Only one prisoner seemed indifferent, but he had in fact gone mad while he was being tied to the stake.

At last, some clothes were given to them. Having reduced the prisoners to quivering fear and shown his power over them, it pleased the Tzar to show his mercy and generosity; and he gave them new felt boots, new sheepskin overcoats, and new fur hats. Soon the prisoners were being ordered off the platform to the waiting carriages.

They walked through the snow like men walking through a nightmare. None of the prisoners recovered from the experience; they all bore the scars to the end of their days.

2 Understanding the Reading. Put the letter of the correct answer on the line.

1. Dostoyevsky was condemned to die because he was accused of _____.
   a. stealing food to feed his family
   b. staying home to write books rather than going to work
   c. plotting against the Tzar
   d. failing to vote in an election

2. Which of the following is described as being worse than death? _____
   a. insanity   b. loss of noble rights   c. prison sentence   d. torture and fear

3. Dostoyevsky temporarily believed he was not going to be executed _____.
   a. after he had kissed the crucifix
   b. after the official finished reading the list of crimes
   c. after he observed the sun's rays shining on the church
   d. after he was taken from the prison cell and entered the carriage

4. Later, having lost all hope that his life would be spared, Dostoyevsky began to _____.
   a. curse the day he was born   c. prepare for confession
   b. think about the meaning of life   d. notice unimportant details

5. When Dostoyevsky learned that he had been pardoned, his first reaction was _____.
   a. disbelief   b. anger   c. indifference   d. joy

6. One of the prisoners was indifferent to the Tzar's pardon because _____.
   a. he considered execution a better fate than a sentence to hard labor
   b. he had been considering suicide anyway
   c. he was no longer sane
   d. he no longer valued life since he had lost the privileges of a nobleman

7. Ordered off the platform, the prisoners _____.
   a. joked about their confrontation with death
   b. were anxious about what the future held for them
   c. were grateful to the Tzar for his mercy
   d. would always remember this experience

8. Which of the following symbolized the condemned men? _____
   a. the white robes   b. the Gospels   c. the white handkerchief   d. the broken swords

9. Which of the following symbolized the Tzar's mercy? _____
   a. the carriages   c. new clothing the Tzar gave the condemned men
   b. the crucifix   d. the Church of the Holy Virgin

10. The Tzar had prolonged the punishment of the prisoners because _____.
    a. he loved charades
    b. he wanted to heighten their fear and awareness of their wrongdoing
    c. he wanted to show the public what happened to men who committed crimes against the state
    d. they were noblemen who deserved greater attention than common criminals

3 Which Word Does Not Fit? On the line to the right, write the word that does not fit with the others.

1. ignorant	stupid	unaware	knowledge	dumb	_____
2. bellow	howl	roar	scream	whimper	_____
3. scarce	certain	rare	unusual	uncommon	_____
4. courteously	earnestly	frankly	honestly	sincerely	_____
5. cube	rectangle	sphere	square	triangle	_____
6. announce	broadcast	proclaim	propose	publish	_____
7. enfold	founder	submerge	swamp	sink	_____
8. almond	chestnut	coconut	pecan	walnut	_____
9. agony	folly	grief	suffering	woe	_____
10. constant	steady	regular	dependable	erratic	_____
11. cultivate	frustrate	hinder	impede	restrain	_____
12. reality	dream	vision	image	fantasy	_____
13. agony	pain	suffering	mourn	grief	_____
14. earthquake	flood	hurricane	plague	typhoon	_____
15. absolute	distinct	pure	total	utter	_____
16. age	century	era	period	vast	_____

4 Look It Up. To find out more about tzars, use a dictionary, an encyclopedia, or the Internet to help you answer the following questions.

1. What are the two other spellings listed in the dictionary for the word *tzar*?

_____

2. What is a *tzar*? _____

_____

3. The last tzar of Russia was Nicholas II. What were the dates of his life? _____

4. In what year was Nicholas II crowned tzar? _____

5. What were the dates of Nicholas II's reign? _____

6. What was the fate of Nicholas II? _____

_____

© New Readers Press. All rights reserved.

5 Who Might Know Most about . . . ? Match each person below with what he or she might know most about.

artist	columnist	motorist	psychiatrist	receptionist
chemist	florist	pharmacist	naturalist	tourist
colonist	humorist	pianist	nutritionist	violinist

_____ **1.** appointments and switchboards

_____ **2.** chords and keys

_____ **3.** editors and publishers

_____ **4.** easels and charcoal

_____ **5.** frontiers and settlements

_____ **6.** gags and punch lines

_____ **7.** good places for vacations

_____ **8.** strings and bows

_____ **9.** the cost of gasoline

_____ **10.** flower arrangements

_____ **11.** nervous breakdowns

_____ **12.** plants and animals

_____ **13.** prescriptions and pills

_____ **14.** the composition of matter

_____ **15.** vitamins and diets

Question: Having completed this exercise, what do you think the suffix -_ist_ means?_____

_____

6 The Mystery Tzar. The letters of the word in each box can be used to form another word. Use the clues to help you figure out what that other word is. Then, put the number of the clue into the circle. The circled numbers in each row—both across and down—will add up to 34. Write the first letter of each rewritten word on the correct lines at the end of the puzzle and you will discover the name of the tzar who ruled during "The Execution." To get you off to a good start, the first and last clues have been answered for you.

CRATE ⑯ TRACE	ASIDE ◯ ___	THERE ◯ ___	CANOE ◯ ___	= 34
BLEAT ◯ ___	ANGLE ◯ ___	STALE ◯ ___	LEAFS ◯ ___	= 34
WEEPS ◯ ___	SHORE ◯ ___	CAROB ◯ ___	SLIDE ◯ ___	= 34
TONES ① NOTES	CAUSE ◯ ___	FLIER ◯ ___	SHORN ◯ ___	= 34
= 34	= 34	= 34	= 34	

✓**1.** Reminders to yourself

2. Thoughts or opinions

3. A poisonous snake of Asia and Africa

4. Goats butt you with these if you irk them.

5. The Atlantic or Pacific

6. The opposite of *most*

7. This heavenly being wears a halo.

8. What brooms do

9. This has four legs, but it's not an animal.

10. This has four legs, and it's an animal ridden by cowboys.

11. This knocks people out during an operation.

12. These cause a dog to scratch.

13. Wastes time

14. A gun fired from the shoulder

15. Thanksgiving favorite: cranberry _____

✓**16.** To outline

The Mystery Tzar:

N __ __ __ __ __ __ __   __ __ __   __ __ __ __ **T**
  1 2 3 4 5 6 7 8   9 10 11   12 13 14 15 16

waylay	balcony	bygone	cymbal	sycamore	cylinder	paralyze
bayonet	sentry	bylaw	Cynthia	synagogue	syringe	paralysis
heyday	majesty	cypress	cynical	sympathy	Syria	analyze
	pansy	hydrogen	typical	gymnastic	pyramid	analysis
	ebony	hyena	hysteria	homonym	crystal	
		python	hysterical			hypnotize
			hypocrite		Floyd	hypnosis
	pygmy				Lloyd	hypnotist
	Sydney				foyer	
	dynasty					

1 Definitions. Match the words listed below with the correct definitions.

analyze	cypress	foyer	hypocrite	Sydney	Syria	waylay
cynical	ebony	hydrogen	sentry	synagogue	syringe	

_____ **1.** a building used for Jewish worship and religious instruction

_____ **2.** a colorless, odorless chemical element and the most plentiful element in the universe; its symbol is H

_____ **3.** an Arab country on the eastern Mediterranean Sea

_____ **4.** a guard, especially a soldier posted at some spot to prevent the passage of unauthorized persons

_____ **5.** a medical instrument used to inject fluids into the body or draw them from it

_____ **6.** a person who pretends to have certain beliefs, feelings, or moral values that he really doesn't have

_____ **7.** an evergreen tree growing in a warm climate

_____ **8.** a tree of southern Asia having a dark wood; the wood of these trees is used in cabinetwork and for piano keys

_____ **9.** sneering; bitterly mocking; scornful of the goals or good qualities of others

_____ **10.** the capital of New South Wales, Australia

_____ **11.** the lobby or entrance room of a public building

_____ **12.** to break something down into its parts in order to examine it

_____ **13.** to lie in wait for and attack; to delay the progress or movement of

A Day's Wait

by Ernest Hemingway

He came into the room to shut the windows while we were still in bed and I saw he looked ill. He was shivering, his face was white, and he walked slowly as though it ached to move.

"What's the matter, Schatz?"

"I've got a headache."

"You better go back to bed."

"No. I'm all right."

"You go to bed. I'll see you when I'm dressed."

But when I came downstairs he was dressed, sitting by the fire, looking a very sick and miserable boy of nine years. When I put my hand on his forehead, I knew he had a fever.

"You go up to bed," I said, "you're sick."

"I'm all right," he said.

When the doctor came, he took the boy's temperature.

"What is it?" I asked him.

"One hundred and two."

Downstairs, the doctor left three different medicines in different colored capsules with instructions for giving them. One was to bring down the fever, another a purgative, the third to overcome an acid condition. The germs of influenza can only exist in an acid condition, he explained. He seemed to

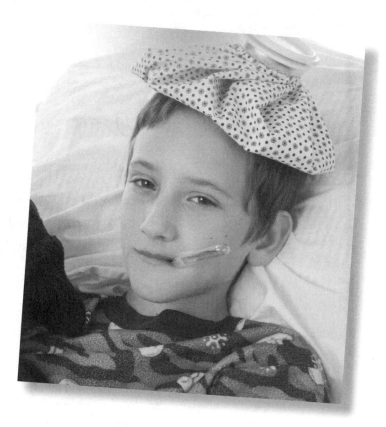

know all about influenza and said there was nothing to worry about if the fever did not go above one hundred and four degrees. This was a light epidemic of flu, and there was no danger if you avoided pneumonia.

Back in the room I wrote the boy's temperature down and made a note of the times to give the various capsules.

"Do you want me to read to you?"

"All right. If you want to," said the boy. His face was very white, and there were dark areas under his eyes.

He lay still in the bed and seemed very detached from what was going on.

I read aloud from Howard Pyle's *Book of Pirates*; but I could see he was not following what I was reading.

"How do you feel, Schatz?" I asked him.

"Just the same, so far," he said.

I sat at the foot of the bed and read to myself while I waited for it to be time to give another capsule. It would have been natural for him to go to sleep, but when I looked up he was looking at the foot of the bed, looking very strangely.

"Why don't you try to go to sleep? I'll wake you up for the medicine."

"I'd rather stay awake."

After a while he said to me, "You don't have to stay in here with me, Papa, if it bothers you."

"It doesn't bother me."

"No, I mean you don't have to stay if it's going to bother you."

I thought perhaps he was a little lightheaded and after giving him the prescribed capsules at eleven o'clock I went out for a while.

It was a bright, cold day, the ground covered with a sleet that had frozen so that it seemed as if all the bare trees, the bushes, the cut brush and all the grass and the bare ground had been varnished with ice. I took the young Irish setter for a little walk up the road and along a frozen creek, but it was difficult to stand or walk on the glassy surface, and the red dog slipped and slithered and I fell twice, hard, once dropping my gun and having it slide away over the ice.

We flushed a covey of quail under a high clay bank with overhanging brush, and I killed two as they went out of sight over the top of the bank. Some

of the covey lit in trees, but most of them scattered into brush piles, and it was necessary to jump on the ice-coated mounds of brush several times before they would flush. Coming out while you were poised unsteadily on the icy, springy brush they made difficult shooting and I killed two, missed five, and started back pleased to have found a covey close to the house and happy there were so many left to find on another day.

At the house they said the boy had refused to let anyone come into the room.

"You can't come in," he said. "You mustn't get what I have."

I went up to him and found him in exactly the position I had left him, white-faced, but with the tops of his cheeks flushed by the fever, staring still, as he had stared, at the foot of the bed.

I took his temperature.

"What is it?"

"Something like a hundred," I said. It was one hundred and two and four tenths.

"It was a hundred and two," he said.

"Who said so?"

"The doctor."

"Your temperature is all right," I said. "It's nothing to worry about."

"I don't worry," he said, "but I can't keep from thinking."

"Don't think," I said. "Just take it easy."

"I'm taking it easy," he said and looked straight ahead. He was evidently holding tight onto himself about something.

"Take this with water."

"Do you think it will do any good?"

"Of course it will."

I sat down and opened the pirate book and commenced to read, but I could see he was not following, so I stopped.

"About what time do you think I'm going to die?" he asked.

"What?"

"About how long will it be before I die?"

"You aren't going to die. What's the matter with you?"

"Oh, yes, I am. I heard him say a hundred and two."

"People don't die with a fever of one hundred and two. That's a silly way to talk."

"I know they do. At school in France the boys told me you can't live with forty-four degrees. I've got a hundred and two."

He had been waiting to die all day, ever since nine o'clock in the morning.

"You poor Schatz," I said. "Poor old Schatz. It's like miles and kilometers. You aren't going to die. That's a different thermometer. On that thermometer, thirty-seven is normal. On this kind, it's ninety-eight."

"Are you sure?"

"Absolutely," I said. "It's like miles and kilometers. You know, like how many kilometers we make when we do seventy miles in the car?"

"Oh," he said.

But his gaze at the foot of the bed relaxed slowly. The hold over himself relaxed too, finally, and the next day it was very slack and he cried very easily at little things that were of no importance.

2 Understanding the Story. You may need to use a dictionary to help you answer some of these questions.

1. *Fahrenheit* is the name of the temperature scale Americans use. What is the boiling point on a *Fahrenheit* temperature scale? _____

2. Which two characters in "A Day's Wait" think in terms of the Fahrenheit temperature scale? _____

   _____

3. *Celsius* is the name of the temperature scale most Europeans use. What is the boiling point on a *Celsius* temperature scale? _____

4. Which character in "A Day's Wait" thinks in terms of the Celsius temperature scale? _____

5. Which character is waiting in "A Day's Wait" and what is he waiting for? _____

   _____

6. Why does Schatz think he is going to die? _____

_____

_____

7. Why do you think the father goes out hunting instead of staying with his son?

_____

_____

8. How does Schatz come to realize that he is not going to die?

_____

_____

_____

9. How do you know that Schatz was feeling a great deal of tension during "A Day's Wait"?

_____

_____

_____

3 Working with Measurements. Use a dictionary to help you answer the questions below.

1. If you drove 50 miles to visit a friend, how many kilometers would you have traveled?

_____

2. How many meters are in one kilometer? _____

3. If a parking meter were a meter high, how many inches high would it be? _____

4. What is the freezing point on a Celsius temperature scale? _____

5. What is the freezing point on a Fahrenheit temperature scale? _____

6. What is the full name of the person for whom the Fahrenheit temperature scale is named?

_____

7. In what country did this man live? _____

8. What were the dates of his life? _____

4 Word Relationships. Choose the answer which best completes each statement, and write it on the line.

1. Beverage is to dessert as _____.
   a. cider is to pudding
   b. glass is to plate
   c. hot is to cold
   d. shortcake is to lemonade

2. Microphone is to newscaster as _____.
   a. auction is to auctioneer
   b. gossip is to columnist
   c. nightstick is to patrolman
   d. tourniquet is to surgeon

3. Cobra is to slither as _____.
   a. bulldozer is to swerve
   b. hostage is to kidnap
   c. prowler is to lurk
   d. stowaway is to stalk

4. Severe is to serious as _____.
   a. fragment is to piece
   b. resident is to citizen
   c. condemn is to die
   d. almond is to nut

5. Unite is to divorce as _____.
   a. adapt is to conform
   b. advise is to listen
   c. adore is to yearn
   d. alternate is to vary

6. Stalk is to celery as _____.
   a. batch is to fudge
   b. wheat is to grain
   c. clove is to garlic
   d. quart is to milk

7. Little Rock is to Arkansas as _____.
   a. Chicago is to Illinois
   b. Denver is to Colorado
   c. Detroit is to Michigan
   d. Wilmington is to Delaware

8. Shabby is to threadbare as _____.
   a. permanent is to repaired
   b. photographic is to glamorous
   c. respectable is to famous
   d. ordinary is to everyday

9. Ebony is to black as _____.
   a. tree is to wood
   b. piano is to key
   c. ruby is to gem
   d. ivory is to white

10. Cowardly is to chicken as _____.
    a. bald is to eagle
    b. friendly is to robin
    c. graceful is to peacock
    d. nutty is to cuckoo

5 Multiple Meanings. As you know, a word can have many meanings. In this exercise, only one dictionary definition has been given for each word. This is followed by four sentences in which the underlined word is used correctly. Find the sentence in each set in which the underlined word means the same as the given dictionary definition. Write the letter of that sentence in the blank on the left.

_____ 1. **flush:** to glow, especially with a reddish color

    a. At first, the burglar did not see the iron safe, which was <u>flush</u> against the wall.

    b. ". . . but with the tops of his cheeks <u>flushed</u> by fever . . ."

    c. Each time you <u>flush</u> a toilet, five to seven gallons of water are used.

    d. "We <u>flushed</u> a covey of quail under a high clay bank . . ."

_____ 2. **angle:** a scheme

    a. Gail wanted to belong to the most popular clique in school so badly that she <u>angled</u> for their approval by treating them to sodas at the local ice cream parlor.

    b. It was apparent from the way the shortstop <u>angled</u> his bat that he intended to bunt.

    c. Terry would have had a perfect score on the math test if only he had recalled the number of degrees in a right <u>angle</u>.

    d. When Phyllis told Walt that they could be rolling in money by the end of the week, he eyed her warily and said, "Okay, what's the <u>angle</u>?"

_____ 3. **credit:** a source of honor or praise

    a. Angry that the family schedule seemed to revolve around her brother's sports activities, Joyce shouted, "You may be a <u>credit</u> to the high school wrestling team, but as far as I'm concerned, you're just a big nuisance!"

    b. Steven realized that if he flunked chemistry, he would be one <u>credit</u> short of graduating.

    c. When Mrs. Hunter asked her boss who had told him that they could leave work early, he confidently replied, "One of no less <u>credit</u> than the general manager."

    d. When Gary saw the blazers displayed in Franklin's Men's Clothing Shop, he wished he hadn't lost his <u>credit</u> rating.

_____ 4. **blunt:** extremely frank and outspoken

    a. "Don't use my good sewing scissors to clip your coupons, or they'll be too <u>blunt</u> for me to use," warned Elizabeth.

    b. Mr. Martin had never thought of his intelligence as <u>blunt</u>, but he truly couldn't make heads nor tails out of what the radio announcer was saying.

    c. So <u>blunt</u> were the professor's judgments that Brady was frightened to ask her opinion of a poem he had just written.

    d. The many arguments about strategy <u>blunted</u> the commanders' spirits at the weekly staff meeting.

_____ 5. **provision:** a measure of preparation

    a. After making <u>provisions</u> for the care of his pets, Floyd drove to the bank to purchase traveler's checks for his trip.

    b. Because there was no <u>provision</u> in the rental agreement for the upkeep of the furnace and water heater, Mrs. Scott had to pay for the repairs herself.

    c. Mr. Van Buck told his son that he would give him a Rolls-Royce as a graduation present on the <u>provision</u> that he never smoke again.

    d. The pioneers waited anxiously for the supply wagon to arrive, for their <u>provisions</u> were running very low.

_____ 6. **labor:** a group of workers

    a. After four hours in <u>labor</u>, Polly gave birth to a healthy ten-pound, four-ounce boy.

    b. Disheartened, Karen was convinced that even if she <u>labored</u> at the gym for two hours each evening, she still wouldn't be able to shed those extra five pounds.

    c. During his press conference, the governor proudly pointed out that his state's <u>labor</u> enjoyed more benefits than ever before.

    d. Noting that the foreman had talked about his grievance for at least twenty minutes, the worker finally said, "Uh, I think you're <u>laboring</u> the point, sir."

6 Homonyms. *Homonyms* are words that sound alike but are different in both spelling and meaning. Complete the following sentences with the correct homonyms.

ad add	**1.** "I might _____," said Mrs. Ford icily to her spendthrift husband, "that _____ is merely a come-on, and if you fall for it, you'll just be spending more money than we already don't have."
lessen lesson	**2.** "If you scholars could _____ the horseplay a bit, we might be able to get through today's _____," growled the exasperated professor.
chute shoot	**3.** "_____ me if I'm wrong," said Harry to his outraged wife, "but I didn't throw your favorite velvet gown down the laundry _____."
aid aide	**4.** "How do you expect me to _____ you with this project when you refuse to show me what you want?" said the _____ helplessly.
hoarse horse	**5.** "If you kids continue to _____ around," said Bob in a _____ voice, "I'm going to be minus my vocal cords, and your mother's going to be minus a babysitter."

foul fowl	**6.** "I thought that _____ smelled _____," shrugged the cook as she watched her employer being carried out of the mansion on a stretcher.
but butt	**7.** "I don't mind being the _____ of your cynical remarks, _____ don't expect any sympathy from me when the shoe's on the other foot," Troy told his girlfriend.
vary very	**8.** "If you can't _____ the menu," complained the _____ disagreeable diner, "could you at least try using a few spices to disguise the taste of this lousy stuff you call gourmet food?"
ball bawl	**9.** "You can't stand there and _____ your eyes out every time you hit a foul _____," the manager explained to the rookie third baseman.
weakly weekly	**10.** "Well, you won't have me to kick around any more at our _____ meetings," said the principal _____, "because I've just been fired."
fir fur	**11.** "How can you accuse me of not conserving our natural resources just because I bought a _____ tree? You want an outrageously expensive _____ coat under it on Christmas morning," fumed Mr. Carpenter.
shear sheer	**12.** "It's _____ madness to go out to _____ sheep when you're just beginning to recover from pneumonia," fretted the rancher's wife.
plum plumb	**13.** "The reason I'm home early," Daniel explained to his mother, "is that the teacher wanted us to learn a silly verse about a little boy who stuck in his thumb and pulled out a _____ and when I told her she must be _____ crazy, they expelled me from kindergarten."
cents scents sense	**14.** "It doesn't make any _____ to consider buying perfume when we have only fifty _____ between us, so why don't we just spray the _____ on us and then we'll be ready for our dates," reasoned Jill.
cite sight site	**15.** "I don't have to _____ all the reasons you shouldn't be hanging around our peace-loving town," the sheriff grimly told the gang. "But if you're not out of my _____ by sunset, this _____ will mark your last stop before the morgue."

The Sound for *ph*

phooey	graphite	Adolphe	sophomore	lymph
pheasant	graphic	Randolph	dolphin	nymph
Philippines	autograph	Rudolph	asphalt	triumph
philosophy	biographical	Joseph	pamphlet	triumphant
philosopher	autobiography	Josephine	prophecy	triumphantly
physicist	autobiographical	Humphrey	amphibian	
phosphorus	hyphen	Sophie	cipher	
phobia	hyphenate	saxophone	decipher	
Phoenix	orphan	xylophone		
	orphanage	symphony		

1 Definitions. Match the words listed below with the correct definitions.

amphibian	decipher	lymph	philosophy	prophecy
asphalt	dolphin	pamphlet	phobia	saxophone
autobiography	graphic	pheasant	phosphorus	triumph

_____ 1. a watery, yellowish liquid that contains white blood cells and removes bacteria from the tissues

_____ 2. a poisonous element used in safety matches, fertilizers, glass, steel, etc.

_____ 3. a mixture used in paving, roofing, and waterproofing

_____ 4. an illogical fear of a particular thing or situation; any strong fear or dislike

_____ 5. a prediction; the inspired speech of a prophet

_____ 6. a wind instrument having a single-reed mouthpiece, finger keys, and made in a variety of sizes (invented in 1846 by Adolphe Sax)

_____ 7. an unbound printed work, usually with a paper cover

_____ 8. any of various cold-blooded, smooth-skinned animals, such as a frog, toad, or salamander; a vehicle that can travel on land or water

_____ 9. a long-tailed bird with brilliant feathers, often hunted for sport

_____ 10. a sea mammal related to whales and having a beaklike snout

_____ 11. described in colorful detail; clearly outlined

_____ 12. a system of thought that concerns itself with truth and wisdom

_____ 13. the story of a person's life written by himself

_____ 14. to convert from a code to plain text; to decode

_____ 15. victory; success; to win

Words for Study

Greenwich	cafeteria	Naples	stricken
Johnsy	trod	ragtime	Behrman
studio	moss	literature	mingled
Joanna	bedstead	Idaho	janitor

The Last Leaf

by O. Henry

In a little district west of Washington Square, the streets have run crazy and broken themselves into small strips called "places." These "places" make strange angles and curves. One street crosses itself a time or two. An artist once discovered a valuable possibility in this street. Suppose a collector with a bill for paints, paper, and canvas should, in traveling this route, suddenly meet himself coming back, without a cent having been paid on account!

So, to quaint old Greenwich Village the art people soon came prowling, hunting for north windows and Dutch attics and low rents. Then they became an artists' "colony."

At the top of a squat, three-story brick building, Sue and Johnsy had their studio. "Johnsy" was the nickname for Joanna. One was from Maine; the other from California. They had met at an Eighth Street cafeteria and found their tastes in art so similar that they decided to share a studio.

That was in May. In November a cold, unseen stranger whom the doctors called Pneumonia stalked about the colony touching one here and there with his icy fingers. Over on the East Side, he walked boldly, striking his victims by scores. But, his feet trod slowly through the maze of the narrow and moss-grown "places."

Mr. Pneumonia was not what you would call a kindly old gentleman. A small, weak woman was hardly fair game for him. He struck Johnsy; and she lay, scarcely moving, on her painted iron bedstead, looking through the small Dutch window-panes at the blank side of the next brick house.

One morning the busy doctor invited Sue into the hallway with a shaggy, gray eyebrow.

"She has one chance in—let us say, ten," he said, as he shook down the mercury in his thermometer. "And that chance is for her to want to live. This way people have of lining up on the side of the undertaker makes the entire medical profession look silly. Your little lady has made up her mind that she's not going to get well. Has she anything on her mind?"

"She—she wanted to paint the Bay of Naples someday," said Sue.

"Paint? Bosh! Has she anything on her mind worth thinking about twice—a man, for instance?"

"A man?" said Sue, with a jew's harp twang in her voice. "Is a man worth—but, no, doctor; there is nothing of the kind."

"Well, it's the illness, then," said the doctor. "I will do all that science can accomplish. But whenever my patient begins to count the carriages in her funeral procession, I subtract 50 percent from the healing power of medicine. If you will get her to ask one question about the new winter styles in cloak sleeves, I will promise you a one-in-five chance for her, instead of one in ten."

After the doctor had gone, Sue went into the workroom and cried a Japanese napkin to a pulp. Then she swaggered into Johnsy's room with her drawing board, whistling ragtime.

Johnsy lay, scarcely making a ripple under the bedclothes, with her face toward the window. Sue stopped whistling, thinking she was asleep.

She arranged her board and began a pen-and-ink drawing to illustrate a magazine story. Young artists must pave their way to Art by drawing pictures for magazine stories that young authors write to pave their way to Literature.

As Sue was sketching a pair of fancy horseshow riding trousers for the figure of the hero, an Idaho cowboy, she heard a low sound, several times repeated. She went quickly to the bedside.

Johnsy's eyes were open wide. She was looking out the window and counting—counting backward.

"Twelve," she said, and a little later "eleven;" and then "ten" and "nine;" and then "eight" and "seven" almost together.

Concerned, Sue looked out the window. What was there to count? There was only a bare, dreary yard to be seen, and the blank side of the brick house forty feet away. An old, old ivy vine, twisted and decayed at the roots, climbed half-way up the brick wall. The cold breath of autumn had stricken its leaves from the vine until its skeleton branches clung, almost bare, to the crumbling bricks.

"What is it, Johnsy?" asked Sue.

"Six," said Johnsy, in almost a whisper. "They're falling faster now. Three days ago there were almost a hundred. It made my head ache to count them. But now it's easy. There goes another one. There are only five left now."

"Five what, dear? Tell me."

"Leaves. On the ivy vine. When the last one falls, I must go, too. I've known that for three days. Didn't the doctor tell you?"

"Oh, I never heard of such nonsense!" scorned Sue. "What have old ivy leaves to do with your getting well? You used to love that vine so, you naughty girl. Why, the doctor told me this morning that you had a good chance of getting well real soon. Try to take some broth now, and let me get back to my drawing, so I can sell it, and buy port wine for you and pork chops for my greedy self."

"You needn't get any wine for me," said Johnsy, keeping her eyes fixed out the window. "There goes another. No, I don't want any broth. That leaves just four. I want to see the last one fall before it gets dark. Then I'll go, too."

"Johnsy, dear," said Sue, bending over her, "will you promise me to keep your eyes closed, and not look out the window until I am done working? I must hand those drawings in by tomorrow. I need the light, or I would pull the shade down."

"I'm tired of waiting. I'm tired of thinking. I want to turn loose my hold on everything and go sailing down, down, just like one of those poor leaves."

"Try to sleep," said Sue. "I must call Behrman up to be my model for the old hermit miner. I'll not be gone a minute. Don't try to move until I come back."

Old Behrman was a painter who lived on the ground floor beneath them. He was past sixty and a failure at art. He had been always about to paint a masterpiece, but had never yet begun it. He earned a little by serving as a model to those young artists who could not pay the price of a professional. He drank a great deal of gin and still talked of his coming masterpiece. For the rest he was a fierce little old man, who scorned softness in anyone, and who regarded himself as the protector of the two young artists in the studio above.

Sue found Behrman smelling strongly of gin in his dimly lighted den below. In one corner was a blank canvas on an easel that had been waiting there for twenty-five years to receive the first line of the masterpiece. She told him about Johnsy, and how she feared she would, indeed, float away when her slight hold upon the world grew weaker.

Old Behrman, with his red eyes plainly streaming, cried, "Vass! Is dere people in de world mit der foolishness to die because leafs dey drop off from a stupid vine? Gott! Some day I vill baint a masterpiece, and ve shall all go away. Gott! yes."

Johnsy was sleeping when they went upstairs. Sue pulled the shade down to the window sill and motioned Behrman into the other room. In there they peered out the window fearfully at the ivy vine. Then they looked at each other for a moment without speaking. A persistent, cold rain was falling, mingled with snow. Behrman, in his old blue shirt, took his seat as the hermit-miner on an upturned kettle for a rock.

When Sue awoke from an hour's sleep the next morning, she found Johnsy with dull, wide-open eyes staring at the drawn green shade.

"Pull it up," she ordered, in a whisper. "I want to see."

Wearily, Sue obeyed.

After the beating rain and fierce gusts of wind throughout the night, there yet stood out against the brick wall one ivy leaf. It was the last on the vine. Still dark green near its stem, it hung bravely from a branch some twenty feet above the ground.

"It's the last one," said Johnsy. "I thought it would surely fall during the night. I heard the wind. It will fall today, and I shall die at the same time."

"Dear, dear!" cried Sue, leaning down to the pillow. "Think of me, if you won't think of yourself. What would I do?"

But Johnsy did not answer. The most lonesome thing in all the world is a soul when it is making ready to go on its mysterious far journey. One by one the ties that bound her to friendship and to earth were loosed.

The day wore away, and even through the twilight they could see the lone ivy leaf clinging to its stem against the wall. And then, with the coming of the night the north wind was again loosed, while the rain still beat against the windows and pattered down from the low Dutch roofs.

When it was light enough Johnsy, the merciless, commanded that the shade be raised.

The ivy leaf was still there.

Johnsy lay for a long time looking at it. And then she called to Sue, who was stirring her chicken broth over the gas stove.

"I've been a bad girl, Sue," said Johnsy. "Something has made the last leaf stay there to show me how wicked I was. It is a sin to want to die. Bring me a little broth now and then pack some pillows about me. I will sit up and watch you cook."

An hour later she said, "Some day I hope to paint the Bay of Naples."

The doctor came in the afternoon, and Sue had an excuse to go into the hallway as he left.

"Even chances," said the doctor. "With good nursing, you'll win. And now I must see another case I have downstairs. Behrman, his name is—some kind of artist, I believe. Pneumonia, too. He is an old, weak man, and the attack is severe. There is no hope for him, but he's going to the hospital today."

The next afternoon Sue came to the bed where Johnsy lay. "I have something to tell you," she said. "Mr. Behrman died of pneumonia today in the hospital. He was ill only two days. The janitor found him on the morning of the first day in his room downstairs, helpless with pain. His shoes and clothing were wet through and icy cold. They couldn't imagine where he had been on such a dreadful night. And then they found a lantern, still lighted, and a ladder that had been dragged from its place and some scattered brushes. Look out the window, Johnsy, at the last ivy leaf on the wall. Didn't you wonder why it never moved or fell when the wind blew? Ah, it's Behrman's masterpiece—he painted it there the night the last leaf fell."

2 Understanding the Story. Put the letter of the correct answer on the line.

1. Johnsy is seriously ill with _____.
   a. a digestive disorder   b. gangrene   c. pneumonia   d. smallpox

2. The doctor's attitude toward women artists is _____.
   a. encouraging   b. realistic   c. respectful   d. scornful

3. At first, the doctor predicts Johnsy will not get better because _____.
   a. her symptoms are so alarming
   b. she has lost her will to live
   c. she has waited too long to seek professional care
   d. the epidemic has resulted in so many deaths

4. Mr. Behrman is probably from _____.
   a. eastern Europe   b. India   c. northern Africa   d. southern Italy

5. Mr. Behrman's major source of income is _____.
   a. painting   c. modeling
   b. begging   d. keeping the apartment building clean

6. Which of the following symbolizes Johnsy's desire to live? _____ .

    a. port wine   **b.** the Bay of Naples   **c.** the last leaf   **d.** the raised shade

7. Which of the following symbolizes Johnsy's desire to live—according to the doctor? _____ .

    a. a lower temperature   **c.** sipping chicken broth

    b. an interest in fashions   **d.** Sue's tender care

8. At the end of the story, Johnsy _____ her earlier behavior.

    a. condemns   **b.** defends   **c.** excuses   **d.** ignores

9. Which of the following indicates that "The Last Leaf" was not written recently? _____ .

    a. the artists' studios   **c.** the ivy vine

    b. the doctor's house calls   **d.** the narrow streets

3 What Do You Think? Answer these questions in good sentence form. Be sure to include details that support your point of view.

1. If "The Last Leaf" had continued for another sentence or two, how do you think Johnsy would have reacted upon learning that Behrman had given his life for her?

    _____

    _____

2. Describe the difference between Schatz in "A Day's Wait" and Johnsy in "The Last Leaf" regarding their attitude toward approaching death.

    _____

    _____

    _____

3. Describe the difference between Schatz's and Johnsy's reactions when they realize they are not going to die.

    _____

    _____

    _____

    _____

4 Hyphenated Words. Fill in each blank with the best answer. Don't forget the hyphens!

1. The _____ technical training Ted had received in his night school course resulted in his finding a job almost immediately.
   a. all-out
   b. all-round
   c. all-star
   d. all-time

2. The doctor was such a(n) _____ fellow that he could explain the most complicated symptoms in a way his patients could understand.
   a. down-to-earth
   b. good-for-nothing
   c. happy-go-lucky
   d. out-and-out

3. Daily exercises helped Jack become a _____ he-man.
   a. well-balanced
   b. well-built
   c. well-fed
   d. well-mannered

4. A coward is not usually described as _____.
   a. chicken-hearted
   b. lily-livered
   c. thick-skinned
   d. yellow-bellied

5. Mr. Garfield had a _____ view of the accident because he happened to be raising the shades in the living room of his thirtieth-floor apartment when the two cars collided.
   a. bird's-eye
   b. cold-eyed
   c. dry-eyed
   d. starry-eyed

6. Mrs. McDonald was so _____ that she seemed to spend as much time poking about her desk and looking in the drawers for her glasses as she did working.
   a. open-minded
   b. high-minded
   c. absent-minded
   d. single-minded

7. During the interview, the interviewer's gaze made Linda feel so _____ that she wished she could crawl into a hole and disappear.
   a. self-conscious
   b. self-important
   c. self-interested
   d. self-taught

8. By the time Adolphe became a _____ lawyer, he was so tired of reading small print that he began to wish he had chosen another profession.
   a. full-bodied
   b. full-dress
   c. full-fashioned
   d. full-fledged

9. You are speaking _____ when you say something in a serious tone of voice but mean it as a humorous remark.

   a. hand-to-mouth

   b. matter-of-fact

   c. off-the-record

   d. tongue-in-cheek

10. Being very _____, Josephine didn't know how to accept compliments on her fine performance graciously.

    a. self-addressed

    b. self-critical

    c. self-evident

    d. self-seeking

11. A nervous person might be described as _____.

    a. high-pitched

    b. high-priced

    c. high-sounding

    d. high-strung

12. "How can you plead 'not guilty' when the police caught you _____?" the judge asked the defendant.

    a. cold-blooded

    b. head-on

    c. red-handed

    d. thin-skinned

13. The behavior of a hypocrite is best described as _____.

    a. mealy-mouthed

    b. two-faced

    c. up-and-down

    d. wishy-washy

14. "We're all just fine. Everything is _____ now," Sophie replied when her mother asked if she and the children had recovered from their colds.

    a. hanky-panky

    b. helter-skelter

    c. hunky-dory

    d. hurdy-gurdy

15. As he read a biography of Thomas Edison, Lloyd wondered if the inventor ever fully realized that his creations would have such _____ consequences.

    a. far-off

    b. far-out

    c. far-reaching

    d. far-sighted

5 The $24 Swindle. "The Last Leaf" is set in Greenwich Village, which is a section of Manhattan. To learn more about how the Indians sold Manhattan to the Dutch in 1626, fill in the blanks with the words listed below.

absolutely	colonies	outright	rival
betrayed	colony	particularly	settled
chuckling	intelligent	purchase	situation
claim	official	quibble	unsettling

Peter Minuit with the Indians

By now it is probably too late to do anything about it, but the _____ fact remains that the so-called sale of Manhattan Island to the Dutch in 1626 was a totally illegal deal. This is how it happened.

On May 4, 1626, Peter Minuit was sent by the Dutch West India Company to be the _____ director-general of what is now known as Manhattan. Now the Dutch knew that the British, who had established _____ at Plymouth and Jamestown, would not be _____ pleased at the establishment of a Dutch _____. Neither would the French.

So, the Dutch decided to make their _____ of Manhattan as legal as possible, hoping that if the Indians backed up their _____, the British or French would not attack.

Minuit did what seemed like the _____ thing: he asked the first Indians he saw if he could see their chief. Now the chief wasn't sure what it meant to sell land. The land was, after all, Mother Earth to the Indians, and they felt you could no more sell it _____ than you could sell the sky.

What the chief did know was that a(n) _____ tribe controlled the upper three quarters of Manhattan, but the chief wasn't one to _____ over small points. He took the sixty guilders' worth of knives, axes, clothing, and beads and went _____ back to Brooklyn.

Everybody _____ down and was happy except the rival tribe who could do _____ nothing. Even if they had wanted to fight, the Dutch had guns and they didn't. The only thing the _____ tribe could do was try to make the best of an impossible _____.

1 Word Review. Put the letter of the best answer on the line.

1. _____ is known for its fragrant odor.
   a. Cedar   b. Ebony   c. Maple   d. Walnut

2. Which "ship" is frequently engaged in business transactions? _____.
   a. censorship   b. courtship   c. dealership   d. leadership

3. A _____ is an example of a fungus.
   a. crystal   b. gel   c. narcotic   d. mushroom

4. A place where someone might go to visit a grave is a _____.
   a. corridor   b. cemetery   c. coroner   d. ceremony

5. A mallet is part of the equipment used in _____.
   a. badminton   b. polo   c. soccer   d. tennis

6. Another word for pasta is _____.
   a. rice   b. marmalade   c. macaroni   d. strudel

7. A _____ is an example of an artificial waterway.
   a. bay   b. canal   c. channel   d. cove

8. A synonym for *foyer* is _____.
   a. basement   b. parlor   c. pantry   d. lobby

9. A synonym for *humiliate* is _____.
   a. debate   b. degrade   c. deprive   d. derive

10. In the North, a _____ is a warmly welcomed prelude to spring.
    a. cardinal   b. pheasant   c. robin   d. woodpecker

11. _____ is the largest island in the Mediterranean Sea.
    a. Sicily   b. Sydney   c. Syracuse   d. Syria

12. To the gossip columnist, a _____ person is usually someone of consequence.
    a. noteworthy   b. praiseworthy   c. seaworthy   d. trustworthy

13. Taxpayers are a basic source of _____ for the government.

    a. civilization   **b.** legends   **c.** mourning   **d.** revenue

14. If you _____ someone's progress, it might be said that you are putting up a roadblock.

    a. impede   **b.** encourage   **c.** recruit   **d.** prolong

15. A grimace is often a sign of _____.

    a. contempt   **b.** genius   **c.** hysteria   **d.** triumph

16. A _____ would most likely attempt to hide his or her malice toward others.

    a. bigot   **b.** disciple   **c.** hypocrite   **d.** prude

2 Find the Homonym. Next to each word listed below write its homonym. Then, match each homonym you have written with the correct description. Study the example before you begin.

aisle   _isle_   dough _____   tense _____

beat _____   genes _____   vain _____

coax _____   seen _____   weed _____

cord _____   sore _____   yoke _____

_____   **1.** a combination of musical notes

_____   **2.** a common contraction

_____   **3.** a female deer

_____   **4.** a section of a play

_____   **5.** a red vegetable

isle   **6.** a small island

_____   **7.** a blood vessel

_____   **8.** pants made from a strong cotton

_____   **9.** popular soft drinks

_____   **10.** things campers sleep in

_____   **11.** the most nutritious part of an egg

_____   **12.** to rise high in the air

3 Word Review. Fill in the blanks with the set of words that makes the best sense in each sentence.

1. A _____ is an example of a _____.
   a. geyser—vacuum
   b. penguin—bird
   c. sergeant—civilian
   d. stereo—generator

2. The _____ _____ the audience with his prejudiced statements.
   a. bigot—enraged
   b. genius—hypnotized
   c. hostage—paralyzed
   d. humorist—flustered

3. A generator converts _____ energy into _____ energy.
   a. electrical—mechanical
   b. manmade—electrical
   c. manmade—mechanical
   d. mechanical—electrical

4. A(n) _____ is an example of a _____.
   a. agenda—meeting
   b. beagle—hound
   c. bayonet—sword
   d. saxophone—stringed instrument

5. The Congresswoman's _____ throughout the television interview _____ not only her campaign manager but also her loyal supporters.
   a. abruptness—unified
   b. coarseness—embarrassed
   c. dignity—blemished
   d. malice—endeared

6. The fortune-teller gazed into her crystal ball and advised Floyd not to be so _____ about his career because in time it would be marked with _____.
   a. burdened—misery
   b. cynical—execution
   c. jaundiced—brilliance
   d. shortsighted—hysteria

7. Many citizens consider the widespread abuse of _____ to be a(n) _____ to the well-being of our society.
   a. computers—embarrassment
   b. hypnosis—humiliation
   c. narcotics—menace
   d. plastic—encouragement

8. As she prepared her husband's breakfast, Mrs. Olson observed, "I cannot _____ of a more _____ way to begin such a beautiful day than by reading that dreadful newspaper."
   a. analyze—instructive
   b. assume—logical
   c. conceive—unpleasant
   d. identify—embarrassing

9. The traffic commission discussed _____ measures that could be taken to avoid the possibility of future _____ occurring at the treacherous intersection.

    a. airtight—brawls   **c.** protective—tragedies

    b. guaranteed—failures   **d.** temporary—breakdowns

10. Marching proudly in the Labor Day _____, the high school band looked _____ in their royal blue uniforms.

    a. auditorium—confined   **c.** procession—outrageous

    b. parade—majestic   **d.** stadium—noticeable

11. "My niece is so _____ that you'd think her brains were made out of _____," sighed Uncle Edward sadly.

    a. awkward—overshoes   **c.** intelligent—gelatin

    b. hardheaded—cement   **d.** understandable—galaxies

12. After the plumber's helpful _____ of the problem with his disposal, Frank realized that his attitude toward repairmen was much too _____.

    a. analysis—cynical   **c.** guidance—traditional

    b. discipline—hysterical   **d.** logic—probable

4 Word Sound Review. Choose the word in each line that has the same sound as the underlined letter or letters in the first word, and write your choice on the line.

1. **dignity:**	gel	gospel	legend	magician	_____
2. **alternate:**	alcohol	calendar	halter	palace	_____
3. **voltage:**	golf	jolly	polish	Polish	_____
4. **chow:**	billow	elbow	powder	tow	_____
5. **theft:**	thaw	thereafter	thine	thou	_____
6. **hydrogen:**	hyena	hymnbook	hypnosis	hysteria	_____
7. **terrific:**	ceremony	disciple	larceny	vocal	_____
8. **beagle:**	agenda	jaguar	tragedy	genius	_____
9. **balance:**	balcony	cavity	reception	vacuum	_____
10. **subdue:**	league	residue	morgue	vogue	_____
11. **obey:**	eyelid	geyser	heyday	volley	_____
12. **mystery:**	analyze	python	rhyme	symbol	_____

5 A Poet's View of Dying. Read the following excerpt from a poem by Edna St. Vincent Millay (1892–1950), and then answer the questions that follow.

Excerpt from **Moriturus**

by Edna St. Vincent Millay

Withstanding Death
   Till Life be gone,
I shall treasure my breath,
   I shall linger on.

I shall bolt my door
   With a bolt and a cable;
I shall block my door
   With a bureau and a table;

With all my might
   My door shall be barred.
I shall put up a fight,
   I shall take it hard.

With his hand on my mouth
   He shall drag me forth,
Shrieking to the south
   And clutching at the north.

1. What is the speaker's view of dying in this poem? Be sure to include evidence from the poem to support your point of view.

_____

_____

_____

2. How do you think each of the following people would react to the view of dying presented in this poem? Be sure to support your answer with evidence from the stories.

   a. Norman in *On Golden Pond*:

_____

_____

   b. Dostoyevsky in "The Execution":

_____

_____

   c. Schatz in "A Day's Wait":

_____

_____

   d. Johnsy in "The Last Leaf":

_____

_____

UNIT 5
Giving

The last unit in this book deals with the theme of giving. Sometimes the best way to begin exploring a topic is to take a look at a situation in which just the opposite is described. This unit begins just this way.

The reading for Lesson 17 is a short story by Irish author James Joyce. The boy who narrates the story wants to give a gift to a girl he likes. But buying a gift for her turns out to be a lot more complicated than he realizes.

"To Have or to Be," the reading for Lesson 18, is from the writings of Erich Fromm, a German-born philosopher who came to the United States in 1934 and taught at various universities in addition to writing many books. As the title suggests, Dr. Fromm believed that *having* and *being* represent two very different approaches to life—one that is selfish and one that is giving.

The reading for Lessons 19 and 20 is a play called "The Woman Who Willed a Miracle." The title character in this play is a woman who is very giving and unselfish. Based on actual events, the play tells the story of a couple whose main concern is the happiness of someone other than themselves.

LESSON 17
Silent Letters

hedge	nestle	know-it-all	rhinestone	wriggle	ghostly
wedge	trestle	Knoxville	Rhode Island	Wright	ghastly
fidget	jostle	knoll	rhinoceros	playwright	ghetto
widget	bustle	knighthood	rhythmic	wrangle	ghoul
gadget	rustle	knave	rhythmical	wreath	gherkin
cartridge	rustler		rhapsody	wretched	
porridge	hustler				lasagna
abridge				salve	yacht
badger				salmon	khaki

1 Definitions. Match the words listed below with the correct definitions.

abridge	ghastly	ghoul	khaki	porridge	salve	wrangle	wretched
bustle	gherkin	jostle	knoll	rhinestone	widget	wreath	Wright

_____ 1. a light olive or light yellowish brown color; a sturdy cloth of this color

_____ 2. a colorless, manmade gem that often sparkles like a diamond

_____ 3. a ring of flowers or leaves worn on the head or used as a decoration

_____ 4. a small cucumber, especially one used for pickling

_____ 5. a small rounded hill or mound

_____ 6. an evil spirit or demon in folklore that is said to rob graves and feed on corpses; one who delights in anything that is disgusting or revolting

_____ 7. an ointment

_____ 8. boiled oatmeal, usually eaten with milk at breakfast

_____ 9. miserable; sad; very unpleasant

_____ 10. terrifying; dreadful; having a deathlike color; extremely unpleasant or bad

_____ 11. the last name of the brothers who invented and flew the first heavier-than-air craft in 1903

_____ 12. to hurry about busily and with energy; excited activity; commotion

_____ 13. to knock or push together; collide

_____ 14. to quarrel or bicker noisily or angrily

_____ 15. to reduce the length of a short story, book, etc.; to condense

_____ 16. an unnamed object; a device that displays information on a web page

Words for Study

somber	hostile	Araby	prolonged
Mangan	amid	bazaar	interpret
diverged	converged	convent	Buckingham
summons	adoration	luxuriated	lingered
accompanied	gestures	liberated	vanity

Araby (from *The Dubliners*)
by James Joyce

When the short days of winter came dusk fell before we had well eaten our dinners. When we met in the street the houses had grown somber. The space of sky above us was the color of ever-changing violet and towards it the lamps of the street lifted their feeble lanterns. The cold air stung us and we played till our bodies glowed. . . . If my uncle was seen turning the corner we hid in the shadow until we had seen him safely housed. Or if Mangan's sister came out on the doorstep to call her brother in to his tea we watched her from our shadow peer up and down the street. We waited to see whether she would remain or go in and, if she remained, we left our shadow and walked up to Mangan's steps wearily. She was waiting for us, her figure defined by the light from the half-opened door. Her brother always teased her before he obeyed and I stood by the railings looking at her. Her dress swung as she moved her body and the soft rope of her hair tossed from side to side.

Every morning I lay on the floor in the front parlor watching her door. The blind was pulled down to within an inch of the sash so that I could not be seen. When she came out on the doorstep my heart leaped. I ran to the hall, seized my books and followed her. I kept her brown figure always in my eye and, when we came near the point at which our ways diverged, I quickened my pace and passed her. This happened morning after morning. I had never spoken to her, except for a few casual words, and yet her name was like a summons to all my foolish blood.

Her image accompanied me even in places the most hostile to romance. On Saturday evenings when my aunt went marketing I had to go to carry some of the parcels. We walked through the flaring streets, elbowed by drunken men and bargaining women, amid the curses of laborers. We heard the shrill chorus of shop-boys who stood on guard by the barrels of pigs' cheeks and the nasal chanting of street-singers, who sang about the troubles in our native land. These noises converged in a single sensation of life for me: I imagined that I bore my trophy safely through a throng of foes. Her name sprang to my lips at moments in strange prayers and praises which I myself did not understand. My eyes were often full of tears (I could not tell why) and at times a flood from my heart seemed to pour itself out into my chest. I thought little of the future. I did not know whether I would ever speak to her or not or, if I spoke to her, how I could tell her of my confused adoration. But my body was like a harp and her words and gestures were like fingers running upon the wires....

At last she spoke to me. When she addressed the first words to me I was so confused that I did not know what to answer. She asked me was I going to Araby. I forgot whether I answered yes or no. It would be a splendid bazaar, she said she would love to go.

"And why can't you?" I asked.

While she spoke she turned a silver bracelet round and round her wrist. She could not go, she said, because there would be a retreat that week in her convent. Her brother and two other boys were fighting for their caps and I was alone at the railings. She held one of the spikes, bowing her head towards me. The light from the lamp opposite our door caught the white curve of her neck, lit up her hair that rested there and, falling, lit up the hand upon the railing. It fell over one side of her dress and caught the white border of a petticoat.

"It's well for you," she said.

"If I go," I said, "I will bring you something."

My waking and sleeping thoughts were filled with dreams after that evening! I wished to destroy the next few days. The work of school irritated me. At night in my bedroom and by day in the classroom her image came between me and the page I strove to read. The syllables of the word Araby were called to me through the silence in which my soul luxuriated and cast a spell over me. I asked my aunt for leave to go to the bazaar on Saturday night....

On Saturday morning I reminded my uncle that I wished to go to the bazaar in the evening. He was fussing at the hallstand, looking for the hat-brush, and answered me curtly:

"Yes, boy, I know."

As he was in the hall I could not go into the front parlor and lie at the window. I left the house in a bad mood and walked slowly towards the school. The air was raw and already my heart felt afraid.

When I came home to dinner my uncle had not yet been home. Still it was early. I sat staring at the clock for some time and, when its ticking began to irritate me, I left the room. I mounted the staircase and gained the upper part of the house. The high, cold, empty, gloomy rooms liberated me and I went from room to room singing....

When I came downstairs again I found Mrs. Mercer sitting at the fire. She was an old talkative woman, a pawnbroker's widow, who collected used stamps for some purpose. I had to endure the gossip of the tea-table. The meal was prolonged beyond an hour and still my uncle did not come.... My aunt said:

"I'm afraid you may put off your bazaar for this night of Our Lord."

At nine o'clock I heard my uncle's latchkey in the hall door. I heard him talking to himself and heard the hallstand rocking when it had received the weight of his overcoat. I could interpret these signs. When he was midway through his dinner I asked him to give me the money to go to the bazaar. He had forgotten.

"The people are in bed and after their first sleep now," he said.

I did not smile. My aunt plead:

"Can't you give him the money and let him go? You've kept him late enough as it is." . . .

I held a coin tightly in my hand as I strode down Buckingham Street towards the station. The sight of the streets crowded with buyers and glaring with gas recalled to me the purpose of my journey. I took my seat in a third-class carriage of a deserted train. . . . In a few minutes the train drew up beside a wooden platform. I passed out on to the road and saw by the lighted dial of a clock that it was ten minutes to ten. In front of me was a large building which displayed the magical name.

I could not find any sixpenny entrance and, fearing that the bazaar would be closed, I passed in quickly through a turnstile, handing a shilling to a weary-looking man. I found myself in a big hall circled by a gallery. Nearly all the stalls were closed and the greater part of the hall was in darkness. . . .

Remembering with difficulty why I had come I went over to one of the stalls and examined porcelain vases and flowered tea-sets. At the door of the stall a young lady was talking and laughing with two young gentlemen. I remarked their English accents and listened vaguely to their conversation. . . .

The young lady came over and asked me did I wish to buy anything. The tone of her voice was not encouraging. She seemed to have spoken to me out of a sense of duty. I looked humbly at the great jars that stood like eastern guards at either side of the dark entrance to the stall and murmured:

"No, thank you."

The young lady changed the position of one of the vases and went back to the two young men. They began to talk of the same subject. Once or twice the young lady glanced at me over her shoulder.

I lingered before her stall, though I knew my stay was useless, to make my interest in her wares seem the more real. Then I turned away slowly and walked down the middle of the bazaar. I allowed the two pennies to fall against the sixpence in my pocket. I heard a voice call from one end of the gallery that the light was out. The upper part of the hall was now completely dark.

Gazing up into the darkness I saw myself as a creature driven and mocked by vanity; and my eyes burned with anguish and anger.

2 **Understanding the Story.** Answer these questions in good sentence form.

1. Why do the narrator and his friends hide in the shadow if the narrator's uncle appears?

_____

_____

2. Why do the boys come "resignedly" out of the shadows if Mangan's sister remains on the doorstep?

_____

_____

3. What does the narrator do every morning before grabbing his books and going to school? Why?

_____

_____

_____

4. The narrator follows Mangan's sister when they go to school. Then he passes her just before their paths divide. What does this tell you about the narrator?

_____

_____

_____

5. Why does the narrator want to give Mangan's sister something from Araby?

_____

_____

_____

6. Why is the narrator late in leaving for Araby?

_____

_____

_____

7. When the young lady at Araby comes over to see if the narrator wants something, the narrator says "her voice was not encouraging." Why is she indifferent to helping him?

_____

_____

_____

8. Does the narrator give Mangan's sister something from Araby? Why or why not?

_____

_____

_____

3 Character Descriptions. Decide which word from the list below a writer might use to describe each of the characters below. Write the word in the blank. Use each word only once.

aimless	bustling	God-fearing	indifferent	solemn
bewitched	courageous	heartbroken	innocent	weary
boastful	ghastly	humble	sly	wrangling

_____ **1.** a bickering husband and wife

_____ **2.** an indecisive wanderer

_____ **3.** a daring soldier

_____ **4.** a serious scholar

_____ **5.** a ghoulish witch

_____ **6.** an exhausted athlete

_____ **7.** a disappointed lover

_____ **8.** a modest youth

_____ **9.** a busy housewife

_____ **10.** an uninterested clerk

_____ **11.** an inexperienced teen

_____ **12.** a religious pilgrim

_____ **13.** a scheming politician

_____ **14.** a smug know-it-all

_____ **15.** an enchanted princess

4 What Do You Think? Answer each of the following questions using complete sentences. Give reasons for your answers.

1. Will the narrator talk to Mangan's sister again?

_____

_____

_____

2. What will the narrator say to Mangan's sister about Araby?

_____

_____

_____

_____

3. Do you think Mangan's sister will expect the narrator to give her something from Araby? Why or why not?

_____

_____

_____

5 Occupations. Listed below are four occupations in which people write for a living. For instance, a person who writes a play is called a _playwright_. Match the words below with the occupations. Use each word only once.

acts	dialogue	play-offs	scores
casts	diaries	rhyme	stanzas
chapters	headlines	rhythm	trades
dates	personal letters	scenery	verse

Playwrights

1. _____

2. _____

3. _____

4. _____

Poets

1. _____

2. _____

3. _____

4. _____

Biographers

1. _____

2. _____

3. _____

4. _____

Sportswriters

1. _____

2. _____

3. _____

4. _____

6 More about Ireland. Use the words listed below to complete these sentences about Ireland.

missionaries	loyal	culture	compromise
scholars	✓prehistoric	conflict	warfare
numerous	invaders	attacked	established
flourished	vulnerable	conquered	civilization

Ireland is an ancient land that has been occupied since

___prehistoric___ times. About 300 BC, Celtic tribes

_____ the people of the island and established

their _____. During the next thousand years, the

Celts built an advanced _____. Art and literature

_____. The Celtic Catholic Church produced great

_____ who attracted students from around Europe.

The Church sent _____ to other parts of Europe to

spread the religion.

Ireland was ruled by a king or chief, but he was never able to

establish firm control of the island. There were many clans, or groups,

in Ireland, and _____ among them was common. This conflict among the people

of the island made them _____ to outside _____. The Norse

_____ the island in the 8th century and _____ settlements along

the shores. Then, in the 12th century, the English arrived.

The English ruled all of Ireland until the early 20th century, although the relationship was never easy.

Ireland rebelled _____ times. To help maintain control, the English began settling

English and Scottish Protestants in Ireland. These people were _____ to England.

The result gave England greater control of Ireland. However, it also increased _____

within Ireland as the Irish and the new settlers fought over religion and control of the state.

Finally, in 1922, a sort of _____ was reached. Ireland was divided into two parts.

Most of Ireland finally became independent. Northern Ireland, however, remained under British rule.

The division helped solved some problems, but the conflict in Northern Ireland continued for many years.

Double Consonants

To sound out a word with double consonants, divide the word between the two consonants. The first vowel is usually, but not always, short.

challenge	pebble	ripple	blossom	nugget
ballad	meddle	jitters	possum	rummage
asset	cheddar	jimmy	pollute	rubbish
dazzle	pennant	shimmy	fodder	hubbub
raffle	leggings	shimmer	holler	shuffle
waffle	eddy	minnow	motto	summit
narrate	essay	hiccups	horrid	Brussels
Sabbath	essence	giddy	collapse	burro
rabbi	session	missile	commerce	burrow

1 Definitions. Match the words listed below with the correct definitions.

asset	commerce	essay	fodder	jimmy	nugget	rubbish	shimmer
burrow	eddy	essence	giddy	motto	pollute	Sabbath	summit

_____ **1.** a brief sentence, phrase, or single word used to express a goal or ideal

_____ **2.** a current of water or air moving in circles; a whirlpool

_____ **3.** a hole or tunnel dug in the ground by a small animal, such as a rabbit or mole, for a place of safety or a home

_____ **4.** a short composition on a single subject

_____ **5.** a short crowbar with curved ends; to pry open with this tool

_____ **6.** a small lump, especially one of natural gold

_____ **7.** a useful or valuable quality or thing; a valuable item that is owned

_____ **8.** dizzy; having a reeling, lightheaded sensation

_____ **9.** feed for livestock, often consisting of coarsely chopped stalks and leaves of corn mixed with hay, straw, and other plants

_____ **10.** garbage; litter; worthless material

_____ **11.** the buying and selling of goods, especially on a large scale; business; trade

_____ **12.** the highest point or part; the top, especially of a mountain

_____ **13.** the most important part; the quality that gives a thing its identity

_____ **14.** the day of the week for rest and worship, usually Saturday or Sunday

_____ **15.** to dirty; to make impure

_____ **16.** to shine with a flickering light; a glimmer

Words for Study

versus	mode	opponent	sacrifice
contrary	acceptable	egos	superior
Latin	enriching	infant	conquer
Buddhism	stimulation	adolescent	intellectual

To Have or to Be
by Erich Fromm

The choice of *having* versus *being* does not appeal to common sense. *To have*, so it would seem, is a normal function of our life: in order to live we must have things. Moreover, we must have things in order to enjoy them. In a culture in which the highest goal is to have—and to have more and more—and in which one can speak of someone as "being worth a million dollars," how can there be a choice between having and being? On the contrary, it would seem that the very essence of being is having; that if one *has* nothing, one *is* nothing.

Having as a way of existence comes from the nature of private property. To acquire, to own, and to make a profit become the basic rights of the individual living in the *having* society. What the sources of property are does not matter; nor does possession impose any obligations on the property owners.

This kind of property may be called *private* property (from Latin *private*, "to deprive of"), because the person or persons who own it are its sole masters, with full power to deprive others of its use or enjoyment.

This desire for private property can be seen in our relationships also. People express it in speaking of "*my* doctor," "*my* dentist," "*my* workers," and so on. Also, people experience an unending number of objects, even feelings, as property. Take health and illness, for example. People who discuss their health do so with a feeling of ownership, referring to *their* sicknesses, *their* operations, *their* treatments, *their* diets, *their* medicines.

Ideas and beliefs can also become property, as can even habits. For instance, anyone who eats the same breakfast at the same time each morning can be disturbed by even a slight change in that routine, because his habit has become a property whose loss endangers his security.

Yet the great Masters of Living have made the choice between having and being a central issue of their teachings. Buddhism, for example, teaches that in order to arrive at the highest stage of human development, we must not crave possessions. Jesus teaches: "For whosoever will save his life shall lose it; but whosoever will lose his life for my sake, the same shall save it. For what is a man advantaged, if he gain the whole world, and lose himself, or be cast away?" (Luke 9:24–25).

"To have" seems to be a simple expression. Every human being *has* something: a body, clothes, shelter—on up to the modern man or woman who has a car, a television set, a washing machine, etc. Living without having something is practically impossible. Why, then, should having be a problem?

Because the society we live in is devoted to acquiring possessions and making a profit, we rarely see any evidence of the being mode of existence. Most people see the having mode as the most natural mode of existence, even the only acceptable way of life. This makes it especially difficult for people to understand that having is only one possible approach to life. The following simple examples of how having and being are demonstrated in everyday life may help you to understand these two different modes of existence.

Students in the having mode of existence will listen to a teacher's lecture, understand it as best they can, and take notes in their notebooks so that, later on, they can memorize their notes and thus pass an examination. But the content of the teacher's lecture does not become part of their own individual thought, enriching and widening it. The students and the content of the lectures remain strangers to each other.

Students in the having mode have but one aim: to hold onto what they "learned" either by entrusting it firmly to their memories or by carefully guarding their notes. They do not have to produce or create something new. In fact, the *having*-type individuals feel somewhat disturbed by new thoughts or ideas.

The process of learning has an entirely different quality for students in the being mode, What they listen to at a teacher's lecture stimulates their own thinking processes. New questions, new ideas, new ways of looking at situations arise in their minds. Their listening is an alive process. Of course, this type of learning can occur only if the lecture offers stimulation in the first place. Empty talk cannot be responded to.

Another example of the difference between having and being can be easily observed in conversations. Let us consider a typical conversation between two people in which A *has* opinion X and B *has* opinion Y. Each identifies with his own opinion. What matters to each is to find better arguments to defend his opinion. Neither expects to change his own opinion, or that his opponent's opinion will change. Each is afraid of changing his own opinion, precisely because it is one of his possessions and its loss would be too painful.

The situation is somewhat different in a conversation that is not meant to be a debate. In this type of conversation, the people forget about themselves, about their own knowledge and the positions they have. Their egos do not stand in the way. For this reason, they can fully respond to the other person and his ideas. They give birth to new ideas because they are not holding onto anything. Thus the conversation ceases to be an exchange of information or knowledge and becomes a dialogue in which it does not matter any more who is right.

The basic characteristic of the being mode is activity—not in the sense of outward activity, of busyness, but of inner activity. To be active means to give expression to our talents, to the wealth of human gifts which—though in varying degrees— every human being has. It means to grow, to flow out, to love, to rise above the prison of one's own ego, to be interested, to give.

Only to the extent that we decrease the having mode—that is, stop finding security and identity by clinging to what we have, by "sitting on it," by holding onto our ego and our possessions—can the being mode come forth. To be requires giving up selfishness and self-centeredness.

In our society the having mode of existing is thought to be rooted in human nature and, thus, unchangeable. The same idea is expressed in the belief that people are basically lazy and that they do not want to work or do anything else unless there is something in it for them. Hardly anyone doubts this negative concept. Yet, it is not true. In fact, to the members of many different societies of both past and present, the concept of natural human selfishness and laziness would seem as strange as their concepts seem to us.

The truth is that both the having and the being modes of existence are possibilities in human nature. Our desire to survive tends to further the having mode, but selfishness and laziness are not the only traits we have.

We human beings have an inner and deeply rooted desire to be: to express talents, to be active, to be related to others, to escape the prison cell of our selfishness. The truth of this statement is proven by so much evidence that a whole volume could easily be filled with it:

1. The data on animal behavior: experiments and direct observation show that many species undertake difficult tasks with pleasure, even when no material rewards are offered.

2. The data on infant behavior: recent studies show the ability and need of small infants to respond actively to complex stimulation.

3. The data on learning behavior: many studies show that the child and adolescent are lazy because learning material is presented to them in a dry and dead way that cannot arouse their genuine interest. If the pressure and boredom are removed and the material is presented in an alive way, remarkable activity and learning take place.

4. The data on work behavior: experiments have shown that if workers are allowed to be truly active, responsible, and knowledgeable in their work role, they find even the most boring work interesting and challenging.

5. The data on social and political life: history is filled with examples of how human beings have been willing to sacrifice "blood, sweat, and tears" for a meaningful cause.

Perhaps the goal of helping and sacrificing is given only lip service by many; yet the activity of a goodly number of people matches their stated values—values which are based on being rather than having.

The *having* mode of existence, an attitude which is centered on property and profit, produces the desire—indeed the need—for power. To control other living human beings we need to use power to break their resistance. To maintain control over private property we need to use power to protect it from those who would take it from us because they, like us, can never have enough. In the having mode, one's happiness lies in one's feeling superior to others, in one's power, and in the last analysis, in one's ability to conquer, rob, and kill. In the *being* mode, it lies in loving, sharing, and giving.

Having is based on something that weakens through use. For, indeed, whatever one has can be lost. On the contrary, in *being*, what is spent is not lost. The powers of the being mode grow through the process of being expressed—the power of reason, the power of intellectual and artistic creation, the power of love.

2 Understanding the Reading. Put the letter of the best answer on the line.

1. According to Erich Fromm, many other societies _____.
   a. are unsuccessful in attempting to perfect the *having* mode of existence
   b. have expressed envy toward our material wealth
   c. do not share our values and beliefs
   d. should strive to model themselves after our values

2. Fromm maintains that most of us have difficulty understanding the *being* mode of existence because _____.
   a. our society is not geared to this concept
   b. it is a complex concept
   c. we have no time to consider its value
   d. it is such a common function that we don't bother to give *being* much thought

3. According to Fromm, most of us find the *having* mode of existence _____.
   a. challenging   b. irksome   c. natural   d. stimulating

4. Fromm suggests that originally the word *private* had a _____ meaning.
   a. incorrect   b. negative   c. neutral   d. positive

5. Fromm uses the example *my doctor* to show that most of us _____.
   a. enjoy a close, personal relationship with our physicians
   b. feel more accepted if we use the same expressions as everyone else
   c. tend to think of our doctors as property
   d. want to believe our doctor is superior to our friends' doctors

6. Which activity would Fromm probably identify as most related to the being mode of existence? _____
   a. going to class   c. studying for an examination
   b. completing a homework assignment   d. thinking about the subject matter

7. Fromm cites data in order to support his claim that _____.
   a. human beings are more interested in having than in being
   b. modern research is on his side
   c. private property is the foundation of our civilization
   d. the essence of human beings is the soul

8. Fromm contends that the "Masters of Living" _____.
   a. taught the *being* mode of existence
   b. taught the *having* mode of existence
   c. were unconcerned with either *being* or *having*
   d. were widely appreciated by the people of their time

9. This reading is best described as a(n) _____.
   a. story   b. autobiography   c. biography   d. essay

3 What Do You Think? Answer these questions in good sentence form.

1. Would Erich Fromm see the narrator in Lesson 17 as pursuing the *having* or *being* mode of existence? Be sure to use examples from the story to support your viewpoint.

_____

_____

_____

_____

_____

2. Do you think Fromm is correct in describing *being* as a better way of life than *having*? Briefly develop reasons based on your experiences to support your viewpoint.

_____

_____

_____

_____

_____

3. Fromm describes our society as a *having* society. Assuming that he is correct, do you think we should or ever will become a *being* society? Again, develop reasons to support your point of view.

_____

_____

_____

_____

_____

_____

4 Word Relationships. Write the letter of the phrase that best completes each statement.

1. Paragraph is to essay as _____.
   a. graph is to textbook
   b. map is to geography
   c. postage is to envelope
   d. stanza is to ballad

2. Rhinoceros is to Africa as _____.
   a. tiger is to Asia
   b. penguin is to North Pole
   c. reindeer is to Central America
   d. kangaroo is to South America

3. Squishy is to squashy as _____.
   a. determined is to impatient
   b. entangled is to entwined
   c. glassy is to glittery
   d. mortal is to immortal

4. Knoxville is to Tennessee as _____.
   a. Cincinnati is to West Virginia
   b. Phoenix is to New Mexico
   c. Syracuse is to South Carolina
   d. Wilmington is to Delaware

5. Wealth is to poverty as _____.
   a. mansion is to shack
   b. shack is to mansion
   c. injustice is to prejudice
   d. prejudice is to injustice

6. Confuse is to bewilder as _____.
   a. erupt is to smolder
   b. censor is to enslave
   c. badger is to pester
   d. jostle is to shimmy

7. Lasagna is to pasta as _____.
   a. spaghetti is to noodle
   b. gherkin is to pickle
   c. chili is to spicy
   d. pastry is to flour

8. Narrator is to storyteller as _____.
   a. author is to book
   b. character is to plot
   c. illustrator is to artist
   d. play is to drama

9. Wreath is to decoration as _____.
   a. cheddar is to sandwich
   b. hiccups are to illness
   c. milk is to porridge
   d. salve is to medicine

10. Ghoul is to ghoulish as _____.
    a. busybody is to meddlesome
    b. companion is to lifelong
    c. demonstrator is to lawless
    d. hustler is to courageous

5 On Latin and Language. Use the word sets at the left to complete the following sentences correctly. For each sentence, you will have *one* word left over.

calculated consists influence persists roots	**1.** Although Latin is no longer spoken, its _____ _____; for it has been _____ that half the words in our dictionary have, either directly or indirectly, Latin _____.
ancient derived old-fashioned Romance tongue	**2.** The languages spoken by the people living in Italy, Spain, France, Portugal, and Romania are called _____ languages because they were _____ from Latin, the mother _____ of _____ Rome.
Hemisphere independent political two three	**3.** Latin America, a vast region in the Western _____ south of the United States, contains thirty-three _____ countries as well as several other _____ units; it gets its name from the fact that its _____ major languages are Spanish, French, and Portuguese.
AD BC buckle century inscription	**4.** The earliest Latin _____ we have found is on a belt _____ that was discovered near Rome and that experts believe dates back to the seventh _____ _____.
established grammar pore pour scholars	**5.** By 100 BC, a group of Roman _____ had _____ the _____ rules that have been passed on to the students who _____ over their Latin textbooks in high schools and universities today.

along
language
large
peak
throughout

6. Latin, at its _____, was the _____

spoken _____ North Africa, half of Europe, and

_____ parts of Western Asia.

conquer
conquerable
conquered
conquerors
unconquered

7. Even when Rome was _____, Latin remained

_____—an unusual occurrence in history; for usually, the

_____ impose their own language upon those whom they

_____.

despite
presence
presents
testify
traditional

8. Our own history is an example of the more _____ pattern; for,

_____ the fact that 26 states, hundreds of towns, lakes, rivers,

and streams _____ to the strength of the Native Americans'

_____, we have borrowed only a few hundred words from them

for use in everyday speech.

exceedingly
however
translator
translate
translation

9. It is thought, _____, that the main reason we did

not borrow more words from Native Americans was that their languages

were _____ difficult to _____

and pronounce. For example, the _____ of the word

nummatchekodtantamoonganunnonoas in one Indian language means _our loves_.

circumstances
importance
objects
phases
phrases

10. Recognizing the _____ of language in the growth

and development of a culture, Thomas Jefferson wrote in 1813, "The

new _____ under which we are placed call for new

_____, and for the transfer of old words to new

_____."

6 State Search. It was mentioned in the previous exercise that 26 states owe their names to North American Indian tribes. Can you find them all in the diagram? The words are formed in the diagram forwards, backwards, up, down, and diagonally, but they are always in a straight line and they are never formed by skipping over any letters. Letters may be used more than once and the words often overlap. You will not need to use all the letters. To get you off to a good start, the first one has been done for you.

✓Alabama	Iowa	Missouri	South Dakota
Alaska	Kansas	Nebraska	Tennessee
Arizona	Kentucky	North Dakota	Texas
Arkansas	Massachusetts	Ohio	Utah
Connecticut	Michigan	Oklahoma	Wisconsin
Idaho	Minnesota	Oregon	Wyoming
Illinois	Mississippi		

```
N A G I H C I M Y K C U T N E K W
E O P W U O I U A R I Z O N A A I
B A R O H L A K O B D G X W S N O
R R Q T C O B H R Y E E I Y I S W
A U T A H R A M E R L E P O O A A
S O U T H D A K O T A S P M N I T
K A N S I S A S I U W S I I I R O
A U T N E K B K H C A E S N L U S
S T L O S O H R O I R N S G L O E
S H E A M E A A S T O N I U I S N
I K L X V M P E A C A E S S R S N
M A S S A C H U S E T T S A T I I
A L A B A S M I N N E I I N I M M
I O A W A S W Y A N M W M O N T A
N L A M O H A L K O H A D A K O T
A R K A N S A S E C O N N E C T I
```

More Work with Two Consonants in the Middle of Words

magnet	stencil	pistol	goblin	jumble
mascot	textile	tidbit	bombard	musket
capsize	gremlin	tinsel	flounder	butler
campus	escort	tinder	chowder	utmost
atlas	elder	blister	ordeal	plunder
album	festive	crimson	morbid	surpass
pamper	kernel	dismal	porpoise	hurdle
drastic	verbal	Lisbon	corsage	nurture

1 Definitions. Match the words listed below with the correct definitions.

bombard	drastic	flounder	kernel	nurture	plunder	textile
crimson	festive	goblin	mascot	ordeal	surpass	verbal

_____ 1. any of several deep or bright reds or purplish reds

_____ 2. a grain or seed, as of a cereal grass, enclosed in a hard husk; a nucleus; essence; core

_____ 3. a haunting ghost; an ugly, elfin creature of folklore, thought to work evil

_____ 4. a person, animal, or object believed to bring good luck; especially, one kept as the symbol of an athletic team or other organization

_____ 5. a severely difficult or painful experience that tests character or endurance; a trying experience

_____ 6. fabric, especially one that is woven or knitted

_____ 7. especially severe; extreme; violently effective

_____ 8. associated with words

_____ 9. merry; joyous; relating to a feast or festival

_____ 10. to attack persistently; to attack with bombs, explosive shells, or missiles

_____ 11. to go beyond the limit or extent of; to exceed

_____ 12. to move clumsily, as to regain balance; a fish

_____ 13. to nourish; to educate or train; the act of promoting development

_____ 14. to rob of goods by force, especially in time of war

Words for Study

Lemke	cerebral palsy	Leslie	Perry
visible	retarded	hesitating	newborn
unaccustomed	vitality	formula	considerable
premature	crooning	Gladys	dangling

The Woman Who Willed a Miracle: Part I
by Arthur Heinemann

SCENE ONE

Narrator: Joe Lemke opens the porch door to admit a young nurse's aide. Joe is a quiet but caring man who peers curiously at the baby Jenny carries. With a blanket wrapped carefully around the infant's head, however, no face is visible.

Joe: Come in, Miss, we're ready.

Jenny: I'm Jenny Matthews, from the hospital. I have his things in this bag. Could you help me with him?

Narrator: Unaccustomed to holding babies, Joe grips the baby awkwardly. Then, as he pulls back the baby's blanket, Joe stops in shock.

Jenny: Didn't the hospital tell you?

Joe: Well, yes. But I didn't think—

Jenny: (*uncomfortable*) He was premature, you know. He has cerebral palsy and they say he's retarded—though how can they tell at six months?

May: (*shouting from another room*) What's keeping you, Joe?

Joe: Coming!

Jenny: Mrs. Lemke knows, doesn't she?

Joe: (*nodding*) Yes. The bedroom's this way.

Jenny: I was just wondering why the hospital chose her.

Joe: May's been nurse to a lot of babies. She's had training, both here and in England. She's British, you know.

Narrator: Just at that moment, May darts in from the bedroom. She's a tiny woman, but her energy and vitality make up for her size. She's about Joe's age—close to 50—and her speech is nonstop.

May: Good day to you, miss. I'll have a pot of tea up in a minute—soon's I look to the little one. Let's have him, Joe. (*crooning over the infant*) He doesn't weigh more than a feather! But we'll change that. We'll put flesh on him and roses in his cheeks, (*gently pushing the blanket from the child's face*) You've got him so bundled it's a wonder he can breathe. There, tad, Leslie—isn't that the name the hospital gave you? Let's have a look—

Narrator: May sees the baby's features and turns to Jenny in shock and fury.

May: What did they do to his eyes?

Jenny: (*stammering*) They had to operate.

May: They took them <u>out</u>???

Jenny: There was something wrong with them. I don't know what.

May: Ah, the poor little creature. As if there wasn't enough he suffered! And his mum—what did she say about it?

Jenny: She wasn't there. She left the hospital right after he was born and she never came back.

May: (*protectively*) Never mind, Leslie. We'll make you comfy now and see to your feeding, (*Cradling the baby in her arms, she goes into the bedroom.*) Come, baby, give us a smile. Just a little one. Don't you want to? You don't have to then. Would you rather cry a bit? (*to Jenny*) Not a move out of him. Is he always like that?

Jenny: Seems to be.

May: There's no strength in him, that's why. And no spirit. No wonder—the way they treated him.

Jenny: The hospital did all they could.

May: I'm not blaming you, miss. Are his things in that bag?

Narrator: Jenny nods, and May opens the bag. Its contents are few—a couple of bottles, some diapers, and a few undershirts.

May: Is that all they could spare?

Jenny: (*hesitating*) They said he wouldn't need much.

May: What kind of thinking is that?

Jenny: (*softly*) They didn't expect him to live long.

May: (*outraged*) Well, you go back and tell them I said they're wrong!

Narrator: After Jenny leaves, May attempts to feed the baby. She tries one formula and gets no response. Then she patiently returns to the sink to prepare a second formula.

May: (*testing the formula on her wrist*) Still a bit hot. (*settling into a rocking chair*) Ah, look at him lying so still—you'd think he was dead already. He holds himself so stiff, Joe—it's like he was frightened. (*kissing the baby's cheek*) Maybe you can't see me, but you can feel my lips. Feel that? That's what you have to do. Come now, drink.

Narrator: The baby does not respond.

Joe: Do you suppose he's deaf, too?

May: The hospital said no. Dear God, tell me what I have to do!

SCENE TWO

Narrator: Gladys, the Lemke's neighbor, stops by to see the new baby.

Gladys: He'll be dead before the week's out. You know it as well as I.

May: Nobody comes to my house to die. Ask Mr. Perry. (*She points to a crooked, stunted evergreen tree growing outside.*) Remember when the man was going to throw that tree away? I told him I'd feed it and put it in good soil and talk to it. Now if I could do that for a tree, I can do it for a babe.

Gladys: That baby is as weak as a newborn—and hardly any bigger. His heartbeat's just a flutter.

May: I'm not denying it, I told God about it, and He said—give it a try. And that's what I'm doing.

Gladys: I say, you and God have the strangest conversations!

Narrator: After Gladys leaves, May tries to feed the baby again. Joe watches with concern, fearing failure as much as May.

May: (*to the baby*) Don't pay attention to them that say you're going to die. I never let anyone die that wasn't ready for it. And you're not ready—or God wouldn't have sent you to me.

Joe: She knows what she's talking about, Leslie.

May: I've looked death in the face before and sent it packing!

Joe: It's a miracle you lived, May.

May: That was a long time ago. Not even fourteen and working in a factory. One day it just blew up and hundreds of people were blown to bits. They said I'd die—but I fooled them. And you, Leslie— you'll fool them too!

SCENE THREE

Narrator: Ten years have passed. May and Joe—nearing sixty now—still care for Leslie. In the bedroom, they watch closely as Dr. Edwards gives the boy an examination. Though Leslie is ten years old, his body is the size of a four-year-old's. He is slight, his muscles twitch from time to time, and he still wears diapers. His body is limp, and his face is forever expressionless.

May: What's the word, Doctor?

Dr. Edwards: The same. His lungs are clear, his heart sound.

May: Don't you think the palsy's not as bad?

Dr. Edwards: (*gently*) I think you're seeing what you want to see.

May: But when I exercise him—moving his arms and legs—the twitching's let up considerable.

Joe: She works over him morning and night.

Dr. Edwards: I've got to be blunt with you, May. He's no better than he was when you first brought him to me. He can't sit or stand. You have to feed him, diaper him, bathe him, dress him, carry him . . .

May: So?

Dr. Edwards: It's a miracle you've kept him alive this long. It's an even greater miracle that at your age, you can do so much. You're sixty years old, May—

May: Fifty-nine! I've managed so far—and Joe's a big help.

Joe: I'll be retiring soon and be able to do even more.

Dr. Edwards: You've both done all you can. (*pausing for a moment*) I've done some investigating, and I've got the name of a place that looks after children like Leslie.

The staff is good, and they know how to handle such cases—

May: He's not a case! He's a child! Why do you think I've kept him all these years? Institutions don't care for children like Leslie—or love them. And loving is what Leslie needs!

Dr. Edwards: Does he respond to your loving?

May: He does indeed!

Dr. Edwards: Does he smile? Does he even cry? He doesn't utter a sound, does he?

May: He knows when we're with him.

Joe: That's right. I can feel it.

Dr. Edwards: All I'm asking is that you be fair to yourselves.

May: We do what we want.

Dr. Edwards: All right, I won't argue with you. I've never seen anyone like you, May, for stubbornness!

Narrator: After the doctor leaves, May sits on the bed next to Leslie.

May: We'll manage, won't we, Leslie? Just like always. Maybe you are too much for me to carry about now, but we'll find a way, (raising her eyes) God, you'll tell me, won't you? And is it asking too much to let Leslie show me a little something? A wee sign that he hears me, and knows how I love him?

Narrator: Later that week, Joe sits at his worktable finishing up a leather belt. The belt is extra-wide, with two straps fastened in the back, made to hold a child's wrists.

Joe: Finished!

May: (*trying it on*) You could have been a leather worker, Joe. It's beautiful.

Joe: Does it fit?

May: Let's give it a try.

Narrator: Joe cinches the belt around May's waist, leaving the straps dangling in the back. Then he picks Leslie up and puts the boy's hands into the straps, tightening them about his wrists.

May: Not too tight, now. We don't want to hurt his little wrists. All right, let him go, Joe.

Narrator: Joe releases Leslie. His body sags, but he is held upright against May by the straps.

May: Do you think it'll support him? (*twisting around to see*) It doesn't upset him, does it?

Joe: I can't tell.

May: Does it feel strange, Leslie? It never dawned on me you couldn't know what it was to stand or walk—not seeing a thing. But now you'll feel my legs move, and maybe soon you'll move yours the same.

Joe: He's not too heavy for you?

May: No. Is he moving at all?

Joe: He just drags behind you.

May: Then I'll keep on walking till he moves. I'm walking, Leslie, just the way I want you to—and you <u>will</u>, someday. You'll stand, and then you'll take one step and another.

Narrator: During the next few weeks, May takes Leslie outdoors repeatedly. She props him up against the fence, clasping his fingers to the fence. Each time she releases the boy, his body sags to the ground as if there were no bones or muscles in it. But May doesn't give up—nor does Joe. During the summer months May and Joe even take Leslie swimming. And one day, to May's astonishment, she notices something new.

May: Joe! He moved in the water! He moved his arms and his legs!

Joe: I didn't see anything.

May: He moved, sure as I'm standing! Let's run back to the house, Joe, and try to stand him up. He'll feel more sure of himself there.

Narrator: They rush home with Leslie, hurriedly adjusting Leslie's hands so that they grip the fence wire. Fearfully, May releases her hold on Leslie. For a moment he seems about to sag as always, his hands slipping and his knees buckling. Then Leslie's hands tighten on the fence and he <u>stands</u>— supporting himself. It lasts only a moment before he collapses as always. But May is overwhelmed by joy.

May: God bless you, love. You did it! Oh, thank you, God—for helping us and especially him.

Continued in the next lesson . . .

2 Understanding the Play. Answer the following questions in good sentence form.

1. Cite evidence that indicates the hospital did not expect Leslie to live very long.

    _____

    _____

2. What connection does May Lemke see between the stunted evergreen tree and Leslie?

    _____

    _____

3. What does Dr. Edwards refer to as "a miracle"?

    _____

    _____

4. Why does Dr. Edwards call May "stubborn"?

    _____

    _____

5. For what reason does May offer a prayer of thanksgiving in the last scene?

    _____

    _____

3 Word Review. Fill in the blanks with the set of words that makes the best sense in each sentence.

1. _____ is the _____ state in the United States.

    a. Missouri—most independent

    b. Rhode Island—smallest

    c. New York—most densely populated

    d. Texas—largest

2. Eddie was pleasantly surprised to find the _____ he had to read for English class

    had been _____ because he couldn't endure reading lengthy accounts of other

    people's lives.

    a. autobiography—published

    b. autobiography—continued

    c. biography—abridged

    d. biography—expanded

3. At the meeting held in the high school auditorium, the guidance counselor was

_____ with angry cries of protest when he announced that scholarship programs

would be _____ cut.

    a. bombarded—drastically

    b. bombed—actively

    c. escorted—severely

    d. hustled—outrageously

4. In order to _____ the false impression given to the jury by the truck driver, the

lawyer decided to use all the _____ to the accident.

    a. analyze—data

    b. appreciate—tests

    c. correct—eyewitnesses

    d. explain—information

5. An example of a beast of _____ is a _____.

    a. burden—burro

    b. mischief—lapdog

    c. South America—camel

    d. the jungle—timber wolf

6. Bill's _____ was so big that he was completely _____

in everything but himself.

    a. salary—absorbed

    b. heart—determined

    c. physique—destructive

    d. ego—disinterested

7. Often, we _____ our way through difficult situations in an effort to hide the fact

that, inwardly, we are _____.

    a. badger—selfish

    b. bluster—cowering

    c. discover—courageous

    d. fidget—restless

8. When the drum majorette _____ under the pressure of drilling constantly for the

state finals, she prayed she would never again have to confront such a(n) _____.

    a. capsized—tragedy

    b. collapsed—ordeal

    c. collided—collision

    d. competed—embarrassment

4 Synonyms and Antonyms. Choose a synonym to fill in the first blank in each sentence. Choose an antonym to fill in the second blank.

Synonyms

awesome

immortal

blossom

meddle

comfortable

noble

confess

random

divine

wretched

fidgety

yield

Antonyms

composed

ignore

deny

joyous

dishonest

purposeful

distressful

resist

fade

temporary

humdrum

worldly

1. Admit and _____ are antonyms for _____.

2. Amazing and _____ are antonyms for _____.

3. Interfere and _____ are antonyms for _____.

4. Bloom and _____ are antonyms for _____.

5. Buckle under and _____ are antonyms for _____.

6. Everlasting and _____ are antonyms for _____.

7. Heavenly and _____ are antonyms for _____.

8. High-minded and _____ are antonyms for _____.

9. Hit-or-miss and _____ are antonyms for _____.

10. Jittery and _____ are antonyms for _____.

11. Pleasant and _____ are antonyms for _____.

12. Sorrowful and _____ are antonyms for _____.

5 Using the Dictionary. Even though many of our words come from Latin, we have borrowed words from other languages as well. Use a dictionary to help you match the words listed below with the languages from which we have borrowed them. Algonquian is a family of North American Indian languages spoken in an area from southern Canada to the Carolinas and from the Atlantic Coast to the Rocky Mountains.

bureau	chipmunk	peso	solitaire
burro	gourmet	possum	strudel
chauffeur	hamburger	raccoon	tomahawk
chili	kindergarten	sauerkraut	tornado

Algonquian

1. _____

2. _____

3. _____

4. _____

French

1. _____

2. _____

3. _____

4. _____

German

1. _____

2. _____

3. _____

4. _____

Spanish

1. _____

2. _____

3. _____

4. _____

6 Word Families. Choose the correct word from each set to complete these sentences correctly.

comfortable
comfortably
uncomfortably

1. Nestled _____ in her mother's arms, the baby slept peacefully, unaware of the commotion going on around her.

appreciated
appreciation
appreciative

2. The sportswriter was _____ of the fact that his editor did not overwhelm him with extra assignments during the World Series.

prudent
prudently
imprudent

3. Even though his boss's invitation to attend the fall harvest festival was hardly Tom's idea of a stimulating afternoon, he thought it would be _____ to refuse the offer.

| mortal |
| immortal |
| immortality |

4. Hoping to make him feel better after he spilled a glass of milk, Molly reminded her young son that he was a mere _____ and that occasional accidents were to be expected.

| moral |
| immoral |
| immorality |

5. Conscious of his responsibilities as a father, Rudolph tried to set a good example of _____ behavior.

| wretch |
| wretched |
| wretchedly |

6. The candidate knew he was a _____ for giving the reporter misleading information about his opponent, but he was desperate in his desire to win the election.

| immense |
| immensely |
| immensity |

7. Unlike May and Joe, many people would have been discouraged by the _____ of the task of raising Leslie Lemke.

| mischief |
| mischievous |
| mischievously |

8. Mrs. Trenton's nine-year-old nephew had acted so _____ in the barbershop that the barber could have sworn he was bewitched.

| develop |
| development |
| undeveloped |

9. Bucky turned crimson upon hearing his sister's announcement that her best friend wanted to _____ a closer relationship with him.

| athletic |
| athletics |
| athlete |

10. As the policewoman snapped the handcuffs on the breathless shoplifter, she remarked cynically, "You're not only a bad crook, but you're a lousy _____ as well. I think a crippled turtle could have given me more of a chase."

Four-Letter Words

alto	helm	liar	dote	dupe
ably	memo	lima	dole	dual
alas	sewn	Lima	gory	lure
arid	rely	Iran	Oslo	burr
lava	defy	Iraq	oboe	null
carp	anew	idol	oral	mull
taco	epic	bias	onyx	suet
Bach	Zeus	tier	Noel	cult

1 Definitions. Match the words listed below with the correct definitions.

arid	dote	gory	idol	ne'er	oral	tier
dole	dupe	helm	lure	null	suet	Zeus

_____ 1. a gift or share of money, food, or clothing given as charity; a handout

_____ 2. a person who is easily deceived or used; to deceive

_____ 3. the main god of the ancient Greeks

_____ 4. anything that tempts or attracts with the promise of gaining pleasure or reward

_____ 5. bloody; characterized by bloodshed or acts of violence

_____ 6. having no legal force; having no value

_____ 7. lacking moisture; parched by heat; dry

_____ 8. one of a series of rows placed one above another

_____ 9. spoken rather than written

_____ 10. a thing that is worshipped as a god; a person or thing that is loved very much

_____ 11. the hard fatty tissues around the kidneys of cattle and sheep, used in cooking and making tallow

_____ 12. the wheel, tiller, or whole steering gear of a ship; a position of leadership

_____ 13. the poetic contraction of never

_____ 14. to express extreme love or fondness, used with on or upon

Words for Study

haltingly	secondhand	insecurely	devotion
Tchaikovsky	musicians	repetition	guttural
concerto	sequence	idiot savant	enthusiastic
attentively	Chopin	serial	solitary

The Woman Who Willed a Miracle: Part II
by Arthur Heinemann

SCENE FOUR

Narrator: Six years later, a 16-year-old Leslie moves with a good deal of effort. Sometimes he shuffles along behind Joe, adjusting his steps to his father's. More often, Leslie walks along the fence, gripping its links for support, placing one foot haltingly in front of the other. One day, Joe and May lead Leslie out to the garden for some fresh air and sunlight. Although the boy's face shows no expression, he tilts his head so that the sun falls fully on his face.

May: That's the sun shining on your face. Doesn't it feel good? Warm and gentle as an angel's kiss.

Narrator: Joe walks slowly with Leslie, holding him from behind. Although Leslie's face shows no sign of understanding, May's talk never stops.

May: Now we're on the grass, passing our favorite tree. Would you like to touch it, Leslie?

Narrator: May takes one of Leslie's hands and holds it out to touch the needles.

May: The needles stick, don't they? (*As they arrive at the fence, May puts Leslie's gloves on.*) Now for your gloves, right hand first, then the left, so you don't tear your hands on the wires. Now both hands on the fence, and off we go!

Narrator: Neighbors often pass Leslie as he beats an unsteady path up and down the grass alongside the fence. Usually they greet Leslie warmly, never expecting an answer. One day, however, a new boy approaches Leslie.

Stranger: Hey, you! What's your name?

Narrator: Leslie stops walking. He still grips the fence, but his body stiffens in reaction to the strange voice.

Stranger: I asked you, what's your name? What's the matter? Are you some kind of retard?

Narrator: Suddenly May becomes aware of the conversation. She looks up just in time to see the boy clumsily mimicking Leslie's walk.

May: Get away from him! Leave him alone! You ought to be ashamed! (*Putting her arms around Leslie, she urges him inside.*) There, Leslie, it's all right. No need to be frightened. He was a stupid stranger who didn't know you. Let's go in and we'll turn on the radio and listen to some pretty music.

Narrator: Then May raises her eyes up to heaven in still another prayer.

May: Dear God, you've got to do something for this lad! It's not fair, letting him be the butt of teasing like that!

Narrator: Inside, May turns on a radio program that features a Tchaikovsky piano concerto. She knits while Leslie and Joe sit nearby listening to the classical music. Suddenly Leslie reaches for a bit of May's knitting wool. Tugging the wool taut, he plucks a sound from it.

May: (*whispering*) What do you make of that, Joe?

Joe: I've seen him do it before.

Narrator: Both May and Joe continue to watch Leslie in silence—as though speaking might break the spell.

May: He likes music, that's for sure. Look how attentively he listens. Do you suppose we could get a piano? I could play for him—and sing.

Joe: He does seem to like music. Maybe a piano would be a good idea.

SCENE FIVE

Narrator: Several days later, a pair of piano movers arrive with a secondhand piano. May ushers them into Leslie's room, where the movers squeeze the piano between the boy's bed and the wall. After the movers leave, May sits at the worn piano bench.

May: Do you know what this is, Leslie? It's a piano—what the musicians on the radio play.

Narrator: Joe helps Leslie up onto the piano bench alongside May. May holds Leslie's hands, striking each note, singing as she does.

May: Come, Leslie, shall we sing?

Narrator: May sings a few folk songs she learned many years earlier in England. As she sings, she guides Leslie's hands over the notes. Then she puts her lips to his cheek to let him know where the singing comes from. In spite of all May's help, Leslie does not respond.

May: (*sadly*) We'll try tomorrow.

Narrator: During the next several days, May and Leslie sit at the piano daily. At each session, May guides Leslie's hands. Though the boy remains expressionless, May never loses hope. Then one night, as moonlight shines through their bedroom windows, Joe and May are awakened by music.

May: Did you leave the TV on, Joe?

Joe: I don't think so.

May: But I hear music. I'll go look.

Narrator: First May checks the television—but it's turned off. Still the music persists. It's the Tchaikovsky concerto, and it's coming from Leslie's room. Not knowing what to think, May hurries to the open doorway of Leslie's room, flicks on the light, and gasps.

May: Joe! Oh, dear God! Come quick!

Narrator: Joe comes sleepily out of the bedroom and stares at Leslie with astonishment. There, sitting in his pajamas, is Leslie—playing a sequence from Tchaikovsky! He sits rather insecurely, and palsy shakes him from time to time—interrupting his playing. But the more he plays, the surer his playing becomes, until he finishes the entire passage.

May: (*weeping*) Oh, dear God. You've shown us a miracle!

Narrator: May and Joe, tears streaming down their cheeks, hug Leslie. In the weeks that follow, Leslie learns song after song, sometimes classical, sometimes popular. Leslie's fame spreads throughout the state. Reporters interview the Lemkes, and scientists also show great interest. One day a brain specialist named Dr. Vince comes. He plays a recording of a Chopin piece on the stereo—a song that Leslie has never played before. After Leslie listens . . .

Dr. Vince: Would you ask Leslie if he would mind trying that?

May: He's heard you, Doctor. Up with you, Leslie. The doctor wants to hear you play.

Narrator: Once Dr. Vince and May have helped Leslie to the piano, the boy begins an almost perfect repetition of the dazzling showpiece played on the record.

Dr. Vince: You're sure he's never played that before?

May: Quite sure.

Dr. Vince: How long has he been doing this?

May: Let's see. It was late in May, I believe.

Dr. Vince: Less than seven months! Amazing! I've read of instances like this. But in all my years as a doctor, this is the first case I've seen. The scientific term for it is *idiot savant*.

May: You mean this has happened to others?

Dr. Vince: Yes. There was one man who would watch a train of freight cars go by. As the last car passed, he could give the total of all the serial numbers on all the cars, instantly.

May: But could any of these people play like Leslie?

Dr. Vince: I don't know of any. May, tell me a bit more about Leslie. He never shows any emotion, does he?

May: Never. Never a smile, or a cry—even when he hurts himself.

Dr. Vince: And he doesn't speak?

May: No, but I'm working on that. Singing to him. Talking to him with my lips up to his cheek. And doctor—he'll speak someday.

Dr. Vince: You're an amazing person, Mrs. Lemke, do you realize that?

May: My Joe is too. I couldn't have done a thing without him.

Dr. Vince: (*overcome by emotion for a moment*) As I was about to say—we really can't explain people like Leslie. It's as if the brain were a bundle of wires—hopelessly jumbled—and somehow two of those wires cross by accident and produce a genius in one specific area. But without doubt, your devotion to Leslie has made this possible.

SCENE SIX

Narrator: Later that week, Gladys and May sit in the kitchen with Leslie, who is finishing a piece of cake.

May: There, Leslie. You've finished the last crumb. Now would you mind playing something for us?

Narrator: Gladys watches as Leslie rises from his chair. Feeling with his hands, he moves along the wall to the door of his room and sits at the piano.

May: (*bursting with pride*) He's been doing that for a week now. And dressing himself as well.

Narrator: From the next room, May hears Leslie play the first English ballad she ever taught him. Suddenly she hears a voice singing as well.

May: Joe, is that you? (*to Gladys*) He was working outside.

Narrator: Then—knocking over a chair, not daring to believe what she's heard—May races to Leslie's room.

Leslie: (*singing in a guttural voice, but on key*) She wheeled her wheelbarrow, Through streets broad and narrow . . .

May: That's just lovely, Leslie. You've got a beautiful voice. Hasn't he, Gladys? And he was hiding it from us all these years!

Narrator: During the weeks to come, Leslie sings and plays constantly. His voice grows stronger, and the neighbors love to sit and listen to him. One night some young neighbors sit on the porch where Joe and May have moved the piano. Joe sits near Leslie while May and Gladys listen from the kitchen. As Leslie finishes a spirited version of Glen Campbell's "Gentle on My Mind," the young people burst into enthusiastic applause. But when the applause dies down, an eerie silence is left. Leslie sits motionless, his hands in his lap, his head bowed.

Joe: (*alarmed*) May, come!

May: (*frightened*) What is it? (*She goes up to Leslie and puts her arms around the boy.*) What is it, Leslie?

Narrator: Leslie turns toward May. He is weeping, his face streaked with tears. In wonder he raises his hands to his cheeks and feels the tears.

Leslie: I'm crying!

May: Yes, you are, love. Let it out. You've held it back for a lifetime.

Gladys: He's never cried before?

May: No.

Gladys: Why now?

May: It was the music—and giving it to the rest of us so we could feel it too. Wasn't that it, Leslie? And your finally being a person like everyone else?

Narrator: Leslie's body language seems to say yes. He reaches up and touches one solitary note. May brushes the tears from the boy's face as Gladys approaches him.

Joe: What does the music mean to you, Leslie?

Leslie: Love.

Gladys: What does love mean?

Narrator: Leslie hesitates—as though he's thinking. Then suddenly his body straightens, his hands shoot forward to the keyboard—and he begins to play, singing out boldly with each note.

Leslie: Amazing Grace,
How sweet the sound
That saved a wretch like me,
I once was lost,
But now I'm found,
Was blind but now can see . . .

Note: This play, adapted from a made-for-TV movie, is based on a real person. Yes, Leslie Lemke does exist.

2 Understanding the Play. Answer the following questions in good sentence form.

1. At the beginning of Scene Four, how many years have passed since Jenny first brought Leslie to May
    and Joe Lemke? _____

2. How do the actions of the stranger prompt May to offer another prayer?

    _____

    _____

    _____

3. Describe how May's prayer is answered.

    _____

    _____

    _____

    _____

4. What is an *idiot savant*?

    _____

    _____

    _____

5. Why does Dr. Vince call May "amazing"?

    _____

    _____

    _____

What do you think? What is the "amazing grace" that Leslie sings of at the end of the play?

_____

_____

_____

3 Which Word Does Not Fit? Choose the word that does not fit with the rest, and write it on the line.

1. oral	spoken	verbal	written	word-of-mouth	_____
2. Erie	Hudson	Huron	Michigan	Superior	_____
3. craving	desire	devotion	passion	urge	_____
4. lasagna	macaroni	pizza	spaghetti	taco	_____
5. Bach	Chopin	Dickens	Mozart	Tchaikovsky	_____
6. foolish	joyous	laughable	moronic	idiotic	_____
7. abridge	analyze	condense	limit	reduce	_____
8. essence	interest	kernel	root	soul	_____
9. Armenia	Brussels	Lima	Oslo	Warsaw	_____
10. awaken	enliven	entertain	kindle	stimulate	_____
11. cautious	prudent	sensible	wise	intellectual	_____
12. curb	decrease	lessen	retard	stop	_____
13. energy	jitters	liveliness	spirit	vitality	_____
14. morbid	unhealthy	poisonous	realistic	unwholesome	_____
15. sole	solitary	unaccompanied	unescorted	unpopular	_____
16. amethyst	bloodstone	onyx	rhinestone	turquoise	_____

4 Problems. Although most people are not disabled in the same way Leslie Lemke is, we all have, or feel we have, our own problems to deal with. Match the words or phrases below with those who most likely think of them as problems. Use each item only once.

ailments	deadlines	dishonesty	inflation	jitters	preservatives	sharks
dandelions	depression	disobedience	injuries	peer pressure	reality	spies

_____ 1. adolescents

_____ 2. athletes

_____ 3. consumers

_____ 4. dreamers

_____ 5. editors

_____ 6. gardeners

_____ 7. IRS

_____ 8. nutritionists

_____ 9. performers

_____ 10. patients

_____ 11. psychiatrists

_____ 12. schoolteachers

_____ 13. sentries

_____ 14. swimmers

5 A Little Latin. Because many of our words come from Latin, by knowing a little Latin, we can increase our understanding of the English language. For example, here are three common Latin prefixes:

uni—which means one

bi—which means two

tri—which means three

Use these prefixes to complete the following exercise. Each prefix is used *four* times. Study the example carefully before you begin.

✓angle	ceps	corn	cycle	focals	form
mester	monthly	ped	pod	sect	verse

_____ **1.** a fabled creature with a single horn

_____ **2.** a vehicle with a single wheel

_____ **3.** all existing things

_____ **4.** always the same

_____ **5.** an animal with two feet

_____ **6.** eyeglasses used for both near and distant vision

_____ **7.** happening every two months

_____ **8.** to cut or divide into two equal parts

_____ **9.** a period of three months

_____ **10.** a three-legged stool, stand, etc.

_____ triangle _____ **11.** a three-sided figure

_____ **12.** a three-headed muscle running along the back of the upper arm

6 On Living and Loving: A Poet's Point of View. Read these two poems by Georgia Douglas Johnson (1886–1966), and then answer the questions that follow.

Your World

Your world is as big as you make it.
    I know, for I used to abide
In the narrowest nest in a corner,
    My wings pressing close to my side.

But I sighted the distant horizon
    Where the sky-line encircled the sea
And I throbbed with a burning desire
    To travel this immensity.

I battered the cordons around me
    And cradled my wings on the breeze
Then soared to the uttermost reaches
    With rapture, with power, with ease!

The Poet Speaks

How much living have you done?
    From it the patterns that you weave
Are imaged:
    Your own life is your totem pole,
Your yard of cloth,
    Your living.

How much loving have you done?
    How full and free your giving?
For living is but loving
    And loving only giving.

1. In "Your World" Johnson compares herself to a(n) _____.
    a. bird   **b.** infant   **c.** pilot   **d.** prisoner

2. *Rapture* in the last line of "Your World" means _____.
    a. detachment   **b.** joy   **c.** security   **d.** speed

3. Which proverb best expresses the theme of "Your World"?
    a. A bird in the hand is worth two in the bush.   **c.** Hitch your wagon to a star.
    b. Haste makes waste.   **d.** Look before you leap.

4. In "The Poet Speaks," Johnson probably asks questions because _____.
    a. she considers this to be the polite way to address her readers
    b. she doesn't have any ready answers
    c. she is curious about our lives
    d. she is challenging us to think about our lives

5. In "The Poet Speaks," the speaker defines *living* as _____.
    a. woven patterns   **b.** a totem pole   **c.** full and free   **d.** loving

6. If the Lemke family read these poems, they would probably _____ Johnson.
    a. agree with   **b.** argue against   **c.** not understand   **d.** question

1 Word Review. Match the words listed below with the correct definitions.

abide	campus	ego	mode
accompany	concerto	elfin	sect
adolescence	devotion	folklore	trestle
ballad	diagonal	guttural	wretch

_____ **1.** a composition for an orchestra and one or more solo instruments, usually in three movements

_____ **2.** an open, braced framework consisting of vertical, slanted supports and horizontal crosspieces used to support a road or railroad tracks

_____ **3.** heartfelt attachment or affection to a person or cause; loyalty

_____ **4.** to wait patiently for; to withstand; to accept the consequences of

_____ **5.** relating to sounds produced in or near the throat

_____ **6.** a poem which tells a story, often of folk origin and intended to be sung, consisting of simple stanzas and usually having a constant refrain

_____ **7.** crossing in a slanting direction from corner to corner or side to side

_____ **8.** a group of people that shares the same beliefs or that follows the same leader or teacher, especially in religious matters

_____ **9.** a miserable, unfortunate, or unhappy person; a mean person

_____ **10.** small and sprightly; mischievous; fairylike

_____ **11.** to go with as a companion

_____ **12.** the grounds of a school, college, or university

_____ **13.** the period of physical, mental, and emotional development from the onset of puberty to maturity

_____ **14.** the self; the part of the personality that is conscious, most immediately controls behavior, and is most in touch with outer reality

_____ **15.** the traditional beliefs, practices, legends, and tales preserved among a people or tribe

_____ **16.** a manner or method of doing or acting; the current fashion or style

2 Who or What Would You Expect to Be . . . ? Match each word below with the person or thing it describes. Use each word only once.

abridged	enthusiastic	mischievous	treacherous
ancient	festive	rhythmical	unwholesome
arid	intellectual	shimmering	verbal
dwindling	invisible	somber	vulnerable

_____ 1. a cheerleader

_____ 2. a desert

_____ 3. a funeral

_____ 4. the Dead Sea scrolls

_____ 5. a philosopher

_____ 6. a pocket dictionary

_____ 7. jazz

_____ 8. a baby bird

_____ 9. a tornado

_____ 10. a wedding

_____ 11. a speech

_____ 12. hydrogen

_____ 13. an endangered species

_____ 14. an imp

_____ 15. junk food

_____ 16. tinsel

3 World Capitals. Refer to the dictionary or other reference book to help you match the world capitals listed below with their countries.

Baghdad	Bern	Damascus	Madrid	Ottawa	Tehran
Beijing	Brussels	Lisbon	Oslo	Stockholm	Tokyo

_____ 1. Belgium

_____ 2. Canada

_____ 3. China

_____ 4. Iran

_____ 5. Iraq

_____ 6. Japan

_____ 7. Norway

_____ 8. Portugal

_____ 9. Spain

_____ 10. Sweden

_____ 11. Switzerland

_____ 12. Syria

4 A Little More Latin. A *root* is a basic word part to which prefixes and suffixes can be added. *Cred* is one of the many roots that come to us from Latin. The root *cred* means *belief* or *trust*. The words below are formed from this root. Use these words to complete the sentences.

credentials	credible	creditor	incredible
credenza	credit	creed	incredibly

1. The little town of Tango was buzzing with excitement as the most _____ murder trial in its history was about to begin.

2. Reporters who had journeyed from far and wide to cover the trial were required to show their _____ in order to be admitted to the section reserved for the press.

3. The defendant was the most unpopular Nick Nichols, who liked to think of himself as a fair-minded _____. But to those who had had dealings with him, he was nothing but a cutthroat loan shark.

4. From the moment of his arrest, Nichols had protested loudly that he was an innocent victim of circumstance—that his fingerprints had gotten on the knife when he had put it on the _____ hours before his right-hand man was stabbed.

5. To their _____ the folks of Tango were not so biased that they automatically assumed Nichols was indeed guilty.

6. Even his worst enemies found his story _____; for it was a well-known fact that Nichols was so squeamish that had he intended to murder anybody, he certainly would have devised a less gory method.

7. If the townspeople could be said to live by any _____, it was this: every person is entitled to a fair chance—even a crook like Nichols.

8. Nevertheless, everyone hoped the trial would be an _____ long one; for nothing this stimulating had ever happened in Tango before and probably never would again.

Note: A *credenza* is a piece of dining room furniture from which food is served. How does this relate to the Latin root *cred*? In the days of old, one or two servants normally tasted the food first in order to detect the presence of poison. If these servants survived the taste test, the family and guests could then trust the food. As you see, life wasn't necessarily safer in "the good old days."

5 More Work with Expressions and Proverbs. Write the letter of the best answer on the line.

1. The proverb "Spare the rod and spoil the child" cautions us to avoid _____ children.
   a. abusing   **b.** disciplining   **c.** nurturing   **d.** pampering

2. "Do a good deed daily" is the Boy Scout _____.
   a. legend   **b.** motto   **c.** proverb   **d.** promise

3. When you read about a "summit" talk in the newspapers, you're reading about a discussion _____.
   a. among people at the peak of their careers
   b. in which world leaders are involved
   d. that is the most important event that has ever happened
   b. that takes place on a mountain

4. When a person "hedges his bets," he _____.
   a. is addicted to gambling   **c.** protects himself against severe losses
   b. tells no one of his schemes   **d.** trims his expenses

5. The proverb "Experience keeps a dear school, but a fool will learn in no other" is addressed to those who are easily _____.
   a. conquered   **b.** educated   **c.** duped   **d.** satisfied

6. "Mum's the word" advises us _____.
   a. to be silent   **c.** to know the password
   b. to honor our mothers   **d.** to plant flowers

7. A person who has a "holier-than-thou" attitude is _____.
   a. humble   **b.** generous   **c.** religious   **d.** judgmental

8. A person might be called a "cold fish" because _____.
   a. he is hard to catch   **c.** he is good at escaping
   b. we don't know anything about him   **d.** he seems unfeeling

9. The proverb "If you would not be forgotten, as soon as you are dead and rotten, either write things worth reading, or do things worth the writing" advises those who crave _____.
   a. immorality   **b.** immortality   **c.** morality   **d.** mortality

6 Find the Quote. Can you decipher this formula for happiness, which May Lemke in *The Woman Who Willed a Miracle* would have probably agreed with? Refer to the directions in Lesson 8 if necessary.

$\overline{}\ \overline{66}\ \overline{15}\ \overline{32}\ \overline{88}\ \overline{24}\ \overline{52}\ \overline{6}$ **1.** the planet closest to the sun

$\overline{11}\ \overline{3}\ \overline{72}\ \overline{67}\ \overline{27}\ \overline{36}\ \overline{47}\ \overline{13}\ \overline{49}\ \overline{78}$ **2.** the flavor of Christmas candy canes

$\overline{18}\ \overline{83}\ \overline{60}\ \overline{75}$ **3.** a garment sometimes worn by men in Scotland

$\overline{40}\ \overline{16}\ \overline{39}\ \ \overline{4}\ \overline{70}\ \overline{50}\ \overline{14}\ \overline{20}\ \overline{64}\ \overline{50}\ \overline{28}\ \overline{69}$ **4.** the first day of Lent (2 words)

$\overline{17}\ \overline{85}\ \overline{46}\ \overline{61}\ \overline{10}\ \overline{76}$ **5.** a homonym for cereal

$\overline{89}\ \overline{45}\ \overline{54}\ \overline{8}\ \overline{57}\ \overline{53}\ \overline{87}\ \overline{17}$ **6.** funny or amusing

$\overline{21}\ \overline{58}\ \overline{44}\ \overline{31}\ \overline{77}\ \overline{68}\ \overline{34}$ **7.** a side view of an object, especially the human head

$\overline{26}\ \overline{43}\ \overline{33}\ \overline{49}\ \overline{5}$ **8.** a mammal of Asia and Africa known for its "laugh"

$\overline{74}\ \overline{23}\ \overline{35}\ \overline{51}\ \overline{42}\ \overline{73}$ **9.** a popular hot beverage

$\overline{12}\ \overline{56}\ \overline{84}\ \overline{63}\ \overline{25}\ \overline{1}\ \overline{59}$ **10.** an antonym for wealth

$\overline{55}\ \overline{13}\ \overline{82}$ **11.** a headpiece of artificial hair

$\overline{80}\ \overline{19}\ \overline{86}\ \overline{37}\ \overline{14}$ **12.** a citrus fruit

$\overline{41}\ \overline{24}\ \overline{71}\ \overline{81}\ \overline{50}\ \overline{8}$ **13.** a formal outfit for men

$\overline{29}\ \overline{9}\ \overline{59}\ \overline{30}\ \overline{2}\ \overline{38}$ **14.** the pattern of sounds in music, dance, poetry, etc.

$\overline{62}\ \overline{48}\ \overline{7}\ \overline{40}\ \overline{68}\ \overline{65}\ \overline{79}\ \overline{22}$ **15.** energy that is characteristic of life; spirit

A formula for happiness:

$\overline{}_{1}\ \overline{}_{2}\ \overline{}_{3}\quad \overline{}_{4}\ \overline{}_{5}\ \overline{}_{6}\quad \overline{}_{7}\ \overline{}_{8}\quad \overline{}_{9}\ \overline{}_{10}\ \overline{}_{11}\ \overline{}_{12}\ \overline{}_{13}\ \overline{}_{14}\ \overline{}_{15}\ \overline{}_{16}\ \overline{}_{17}$:

_____
1   2   3   4   5   6   7   8   9   10 11 12 13 14 15 16 17   :

_____
18 19 20 21   22 23 24 25   26 27 28 29 30   31 32 33 34

_____
35 36 37 38   39 40 41 42 ,   43 44 45 46   47 48 49 50   51 52 53 54

_____
55 56 57 58 59 .   60 61 62 63   64 65 66 67 68 69 .   70 71 72 73 74 75

_____
76 77 78 79 80 81 ,   82 83 84 85   86 87 88 89 .

Answer Key

Lesson 1

1 Definitions

1. hub
2. opt
3. maze
4. yen
5. olive
6. tot
7. imp
8. humdrum
9. impede
10. kindle
11. ebb
12. tote
13. eke
14. rove
15. puny

2 Understanding the Story

1. a
2. b
3. d
4. c
5. b
6. c
7. d

3 What Do You Think?

1. Answers will vary. Possible answer: He is trying to give Kyle some money. He may have stolen it from the ship.

2. Answers will vary. Possible answer: Kyle's decision to accept the envelope will relieve him of worry and keep him from breaking the law to get money. It will help care for Maggie, ensuring she will get good health care. It may get Salama in trouble, perhaps serious trouble, if he has stolen the money and the owners find out.

4 Which Word Does Not Fit?

1. piano
2. romp
3. creative
4. foam
5. fern
6. crawl
7. occurrence
8. thoughtless
9. murmur
10. suddenly

5 More about New York Harbor

busiest, passenger, cargo, serves, manufactured, handle
commercial, recreational, Swimmers
ships, human, common

Lesson 2

1 Definitions

1. nucleus
2. glacier
3. blazer
4. clique
5. blunder
6. Plymouth
7. blemish
8. blunt
9. glee
10. clergy
11. plasma
12. plaster
13. flog

2 Understanding the Story

1. He drove the getaway car for a bank robbery.

2. He says he didn't know the men planned to rob the bank or that they had guns. They paid him to get them out of town and that was all he did.

3. Ernie is a blackmailer.

4. a. Ernie has some letters that George, the vice president of the bank, wrote to Ruthie Watkins. When Judy mentions the letters to George, he arranges an extension on their mortgage payments for them.

   b. Knowing that his mail is read by prison authorities, Walt writes to Judy that something is buried in the south field. The sheriff and his deputies dig up the field looking for what they think will be the money from the bank robbery. Once the field is dug up, Judy can plant a crop.

3 What Do You Think?

1. Walt is not stupid. He figures out ways to get his mortgage extended and to get his field ready for planting while he is in prison.

2. Answers will vary. Accept any reasonable response.

4 Look It Up

1. completely, totally, or any similar word

2. to measure the depth of something; to examine critically; to search

3. Answers will vary. Reasonable responses include: to hang a full-length mirror; to straighten a large picture frame.

5 Standard English

1. a. stupid
   b. dumb
   c. stupid
   d. dumb
   e. stupid

2. a. teaching
   b. teach
   c. learn
   d. teach
   e. learn

3. a. set
   b. sit
   c. sit
   d. set
   e. set

6 Common Expressions

1. goose, chicken
2. fleabag, pig's
3. horse, hog
4. chicken, skunk
5. bug, tigers
6. rat, horse
7. butterflies, bull
8. goat, doghouse

Lesson 3

1 Definitions

1. credentials
2. griddle
3. crocodile
4. prude
5. drama
6. privilege
7. predicament
8. drudgery
9. drowsy
10. brilliant
11. fragrant
12. granola
13. gruff

2 Understanding the Story

1. a
2. d
3. d
4. c
5. a
6. b
7. d
8. a

3 What Do You Think?

Answers will vary. Accept any reasonable response.

4 Synonyms

1. comical
2. attraction
3. inflict
4. mess
5. recently
6. acquire
7. unity
8. possibly
9. effortless
10. reflection
11. generous
12. flimsy

5 Standard English

1. a. may
   b. can
   c. May
   d. may, can

2. a. in
   b. into
   c. into
   d. in, into

3. a. borrow
   b. lending
   c. borrow
   d. borrowing, lending

4. a. about
   b. around
   c. about
   d. about, around

6 Can You Crack the Code?

1. spruce
2. oak
3. maple
4. birch
5. willow
6. pine
7. cinnamon
8. redwood
9. chestnut
10. Judas

Lesson 4

1 Definitions

1. shroud
2. throng
3. strychnine
4. Scrooge
5. sprockets
6. shrapnel
7. shrew
8. sprite
9. strife
10. shrewd
11. scrawny
12. threshold

2 Understanding the Story

1. 5, 4, 2, 6, 7, 9, 10, 1, 3, 8

2. In signing notes to buy the garage and later the auto dealership, Henry gambled that he would be able to pay off the notes without having to use the hidden money.

3. In the second part of the story, Henry's gambling is a legal and ordinary business risk which many people take. His gambling in the first part of the story was done with money that wasn't his, and was therefore illegal.

4. Answers will vary. Reasonable responses include: He was unwilling to destroy the spruce tree in order to get the stolen money. He returned $30,000 plus interest to the bank. His wife and children mattered more to him than the money did.

3 What Do You Think?

Answers will vary. Possible answer: Robert Arthur seems to agree with the saying. When Henry cares more for his wife and children, and for the spruce tree, than he does for the money, he prospers and has a happy life. Jerome Smith, on the other hand, becomes involved in illegal activities in his pursuit of money and ends up in prison, as Henry did earlier.

4 Words That End in -al

1. brutal
2. intentional
3. disposal
4. refusal
5. proposal
6. approval
7. personal
8. regional
9. mechanical
10. behavioral

5 Antonyms

1. impede
2. flustered
3. creditor
4. play up
5. glamorous
6. shrinkage
7. rumor
8. ebb
9. idleness
10. detect
11. approve
12. unity
13. gradually
14. precious

6 Look It Up

1. 75 mph
2. Atlantic
3. a lamp with a glass chimney covering a bulb, wick, or candle

Review: Lessons 1–4

1 Word Review

1. temple
2. suburb
3. Mozart
4. mortgage
5. compost
6. casino
7. plaza
8. burlap
9. gratitude
10. rheumatism
11. reptile
12. rumor
13. Dickens
14. parole
15. credit
16. finance

2 Synonyms and Antonyms

1. wicked, saintly
2. prolong, shorten
3. brilliant, drab
4. nucleus, edge
5. humble, boastful
6. trustworthy, faithless
7. glee, despair
8. frequent, seldom
9. rival, partner
10. humdrum, inspiring
11. puny, strong
12. anxious, calm

3 Word Families

1. finances, financially, financial
2. disunity, unify, unity
3. curiosity, curiously, curious
4. fashionable, fashion, unfashionable
5. graciousness, graciously, gracious
6. shrewd, shrewdly, shrewdness
7. wicked, wickedly, wickedness
8. disagreeable, agreeably, agreeable
9. instance, instantly, instant
10. generous, generously, generosity

4 Which Word Does Not Fit?

1. plod
2. grasp
3. frustration
4. angel
5. disagree
6. amazing
7. silly
8. Illinois
9. spree
10. earthquake
11. option
12. outraged

5 Money

1. inches
2. attempting
3. thankful
4. success
5. budget
6. friend
7. federal
8. government
9. necessary
10. usually
11. don't
12. wealth

6 A Final Note on Love and Money

1. a. He offered her lands, houses, farms, pearls, rubies, laces, dresses, ribbons, and horses, i.e., riches, material things.

   b. He offered her a song, happiness, excitement, strength, gaiety, joy.

2. She chooses the second man.

3. Answers will vary. Reasonable responses include: She was attracted by the excitement, the happiness, the gaiety; she loved him; he made her happy.

4. Answers will vary. Some students may feel that the last line indicates that she regrets her choice. Other students may maintain that the playful tone of the poem indicates that this statement should not be taken seriously.

5. Answers will vary.

Lesson 5

1 Definitions

1. shawl
2. characteristic
3. thoroughfare
4. chauffeur
5. merchant
6. chandelier
7. orchid
8. Chile
9. shanty
10. theory
11. chute
12. shiftless
13. chemistry
14. parched
15. shun

2 Understanding the Story

Answers will vary. Reasonable responses include:

Sam Carr:

puzzled: Mrs. Higgins wasn't reacting the way he expected her to.

softhearted: Mrs. Higgins persuaded him not to call the police.

Alfred Higgins:

blustering: He thought he could bluff his way out of the store.

frightened: Sam Carr caught him with the stolen items in his pocket.

astonished: His mother had been calm and dignified when he had expected her to make a scene.

Mrs. Higgins:

polite: She was quiet and gentle in her manner with Mr. Carr.

angry: Alfred had disgraced her again.

trembling: She had held her distress in check until she was alone.

3 What Do You Think?

1. Answers will vary. Accept any reasonable response.
2. Answers will vary.
3. Answers will vary.

4 Word Relationships

1. cowboy is to herd
2. Egypt is to Africa
3. strategy is to method
4. fixture is to chandelier
5. hymn is to church
6. Memphis is to Tennessee
7. thermometer is to temperature
8. oval is to shape
9. silliness is to gravity
10. bothersome is to convenient

5 Sounds for *ch*

china	chandelier	character
chalk	champagne	ache
chapel	chef	chemical
Cherokee	Chicago	choir
chief	machinery	echo
lynch	Michigan	mechanical
scorch	mustache	strychnine

6 Standard English

1. a. all ready
   b. already
   c. already
   d. all ready
2. a. Besides
   b. beside
   c. Besides
   d. beside
3. a. affect
   b. effect
   c. effect
   d. affect

Lesson 6

1 Definitions

1. skirmish
2. slogan
3. scholarship
4. descendant
5. Scandinavia
6. smithereens
7. microscope
8. telescope
9. slacken
10. snicker
11. scissors
12. descend
13. scurry

2 Understanding the Story

1. b
2. c
3. c
4. d
5. b
6. d
7. d
8. a
9. a
10. d

3 What Do You Think?

1. Answers will vary. Accept any reasonable response.
2. The bullying by the gang and the destruction of the newsstand were events which foretold the great violence against and persecution of Jews which was to come under Hitler's regime. The indifference of the people who witnessed the event and did nothing to stop it was also an indication of the attitudes which made the genocide in Europe possible.
3. Answers will vary. Reasonable responses include: The Silversteins had done nothing wrong, while Alfred Higgins had caused his family's problems. The Silversteins' pressure comes from other people, and it is unfair and unjust, while the pressure on the Higgins family comes from within and is caused by their own actions and reactions.

4 Synonyms and Antonyms

1. antonyms
2. antonyms
3. synonyms
4. synonyms
5. antonyms
6. antonyms
7. synonyms
8. synonyms
9. synonyms
10. antonyms
11. antonyms
12. synonyms
13. antonyms
14. synonyms
15. synonyms
16. synonyms

5 March, 1938

1. schedule
2. plainly
3. than
4. jewelry
5. priest
6. reference
7. beginning
8. helpful
9. Wednesday
10. You'll
11. past
12. committee

In the city, a copy of the daily edition cost 3¢.

6 Who Was General Pershing?

1. John Joseph Pershing
2. September 13, 1860—July 15, 1948
3. the Spanish-American War and World War I (He also fought in several battles against the Indians in the West.)
4. 1914–1918
5. Black Jack

Lesson 7

1 Definitions

1. squadron
2. chromium
3. squabble
4. swab
5. spatula
6. spectacles
7. chronological
8. swine
9. squatter
10. quest
11. whisk
12. tweak

2 Understanding the Story

1. Answers will vary. Alert students may notice the reference to "a white person" in the second paragraph and realize very quickly that prejudice is the theme.
2. Answers will vary. Reasonable responses include: Marian wants to earn her license because she deserves it. Marian knows that offering a bribe would only give the inspector another reason to reject her.
3. Answers will vary. Many students may cite the inspector's referring to Marian as "Mandy" as the first hint.
4. Any three details, including the following: He calls her "Mandy" and "Mandy-Lou." He says she is "old enough to have a flock of pickaninnies." He hints that she wants to sneak out at night to meet "some young blood." He assumes she is from the South. He speaks to her in a phony Southern accent. He makes fun of her for having a college degree.
5. When Marian tells the inspector she got her college degree, her voice was "not quite steady."
6. Marian probably had little chance of passing, since the first inspector had marked mistakes she didn't remember and the second one deliberately goaded her into doing something wrong. He then marked four X's at random. He didn't judge her driving ability at all.
7. Mrs. Ericson doesn't seem to be aware that prejudice is a factor in Marian's inability to get a driver's license.
8. Answers will vary. Students may feel that if Mrs. Ericson had gone with Marian, the inspector wouldn't have goaded Marian into failing.
9. Answers will vary. Reasonable responses include: She fails to keep her self-control. She fails to act inferior, as she is expected to. She fails to hide her emotions. She fails to keep her cool.

3 What Do You Think?

1. Answers will vary. Students may suggest that Mrs. Ericson should stay with her, that they should go to a different town, that she should act the way she is expected to act, etc.
2. Answers will vary.

4 Word Review

1. chandelier	5. ivy	9. sun	13. panther
2. Africa	6. Peru	10. Dickens	14. banana
3. house	7. husk	11. strudel	15. pimple
4. flute	8. machinist	12. spleen	

5 Chronological Order

Presidents	Holidays
Thomas Jefferson	Presidents' Day
Andrew Jackson	Memorial Day
Abraham Lincoln	Fourth of July
James Garfield	Labor Day
Herbert Hoover	Columbus Day
John F. Kennedy	Veterans Day

6 Standard English

1. Change *no* to *any*.
2. Change *than* to *from*.
3. Change *no* to *any*.
4. Change *being that* to *since* or *because*.
5. Delete *here*.
6. Change *off of* to *off*.
7. Change *being that* to *since* or *because*.
8. Change *alright* to *all right*.

Lesson 8

1 Definitions

1. thyroid	6. peeve	10. maim
2. cleaver	7. woe	11. loiter
3. auditorium	8. treacherous	12. heed
4. foe	9. bloat	13. queasy
5. moat		

2 Understanding the Story

1. Any three of the following, or similar details: Laurie was rude to his father and mother. He swaggered and his voice became rough sounding. He used bad language. He spilled his sister's milk. He had to think before he gave Charles's name. He played the "Gee, you're dumb" joke on his father. He filled his wagon full of mud and pulled it through the kitchen.
2. Laurie's mother is curious about Charles's mother. She seems to pity her and wonders how Charles's mother could cope with such a child.
3. Answers will vary. Possible answer: She doesn't like Laurie's swaggering toughness and corrects his bad grammar. But she doesn't scold or punish him for his rudeness, and she believes his bad behavior is a result of Charles's influence.
4. Laurie created Charles to be able to tell his parents about the things he did in school without having them punish or scold him for being so naughty. He could witness his parents' reactions to his behavior without being held accountable for his actions.

3 What Might You Use if You Wanted to . . .

1. explosives	6. compost	11. scraper
2. scissors	7. grid	12. spectacles
3. cleaver	8. burlap	13. slogan
4. stereo	9. telescope	14. sauna
5. microscope	10. plasma	15. griddle

4 Spelling

1. shakily	5. thriftily	9. nastily
2. hungrily	6. sturdily	10. hastily
3. bossily	7. stockily	11. ordinarily
4. fancily	8. naughtily	12. extraordinarily

5 The Suffix -*ly*

1. evident, evidently	6. indignant, indignantly
2. responsibly, responsible	7. earnest, earnestly
3. probable, probably	8. physically, physical
4. furiously, furious	9. casual, casually
5. spiritual, spiritually	10. smug, smugly

6 Find the Quote

1. footnote
2. shoe
3. dynamite
4. telephone
5. bottle
6. itchy
7. one-third
8. scooter
9. litterbug
10. dud
11. New England
12. deflate
13. timetable
14. boulevard

Quote: I do not intend the children to be schooled, but to be allowed under the gentlest treatment to develop freely.

Review: Lessons 1–8

1 Word Review

1. lapse
2. prejudice
3. fragment
4. nursery
5. schedule
6. stampede
7. New Zealand
8. Iceland
9. decree
10. republic
11. mull
12. memorial
13. scope
14. dignity
15. charity

2 Word Review

1. a
2. c
3. d
4. b
5. d
6. b
7. a
8. c
9. c
10. a
11. c
12. b
13. d
14. a

3 Sound Review

1. senator
2. plaid
3. discharge
4. thyself
5. science
6. chapter
7. broadcast
8. laughter

4 Word Families

1. apology, apologetic, apologize
2. disloyally, disloyalty, disloyal
3. incompetent, competent, competence
4. official, unofficial, officially
5. Unacquainted, acquaint, acquaintance
6. observer, observations, observed
7. residence, residential, resident
8. familiar, Familiarity, unfamiliar
9. respectful, respect, disrespect, respectable
10. determined, determine, determination, undetermined

5 Standard English: A Review

1. 2
2. 3
3. 1
4. 4
5. 5
6. 1

6 A Poet's Thoughts

1. Rossetti seems to consider pressures and problems common, as she speaks of the road winding uphill "all the way," the journey taking "the whole long day," and coming to the end "travel-sore and weak," seeking a resting-place.
2. Night represents the end of life.
3. The inn and the beds represent the shelter, comfort and rest of the afterlife in which Rossetti believed.
4. a. Answers will vary. Reasonable responses include: a young person looking for assurances; a disappointed, dejected or bereaved person.

b. An older, wiser person who believes in the continuation of life after death.

Lesson 9

1 Definitions

1. grievance
2. typhoon
3. virtue
4. spouse
5. reign
6. revenue
7. residue
8. hygiene
9. siege
10. oust
11. vouch

2 Understanding the Story

1. a
2. b
3. d
4. c
5. a
6. c
7. b
8. b

3 What Do You Think?

1. She asks Framton questions when he first arrives. She learns that his sister was in the neighborhood four years before, so she wouldn't know about any events that did or did not happen three years ago.
2. No, they are living people. We know because the men enter the room and talk to those present, including the niece. We also know that the niece likes to tell stories, like the one she tells about Framton's fear of dogs.
3. Answers will vary. Many students will say that the niece was very clever and would have fooled most people.
4. She means that the niece likes to make up stories very quickly.

4 Word Relationships

1. b
2. c
3. a
4. a
5. d
6. b
7. c
8. a
9. c
10. d

5 More about Standard Usage

1. a. altogether
   b. altogether
   c. all together
   d. all together, altogether
2. a. latest
   b. latest
   c. last
   d. latest, last
3. a. between
   b. among
   c. among
   d. between, among
4. a. preceded
   b. proceeded
   c. precedes
   d. preceded, proceeded

Lesson 10

1 Definitions

1. purgatory
2. proverb
3. narcotic
4. irksome
5. urban
6. rural
7. wary
8. threadbare
9. convert
10. inert
11. lurk
12. garment

2 Understanding the Story

1. c
2. a
3. a
4. c
5. d
6. b
7. c
8. b
9. b
10. d

3 What Do You Think?

1. She doesn't realize that people always stand with their feet down toward the center of the earth. She thinks people on the other side of the earth will be upside-down.

2. Answers will vary. Students might say she will figure out how to make herself shut up like a telescope so she is small enough to fit through the door.

4 Alice in Wonderland

1. casually, outing, including, daughters, rowed, occupied

2. basis, originally, pestered, Eventually, expanded, version

3. author, actual, assumed, profession, mathematics, instructor

4. edition, handwritten, illustrated, popular, encouraged, publish

5. expense, immediate, success, famous, novel, continuous

5 Spelling Check

1. laundromat	5. neighbor	9. innocent
2. October	6. allowance	10. tulip
3. respectable	7. endurance	11. hospital
4. identify	8. delightful	

First daughter's name: Lorina

Second daughter's name: Edith

Lesson 11

1 Definitions

1. boar	5. bleary	8. lair	11. impair
2. endearment	6. eerie	9. weary	12. veer
3. tourniquet	7. gourmet	10. yearn	13. coarse
4. gourd			

2 Understanding the Story

1. a	3. d	5. c	7. c
2. d	4. b	6. b	

3 What Do You Think?

1. Many students will say it is a dream because the story seems to describe a reality in which Anika goes to the lab as a test patient, works at the insurance agency, and steals the blue capsules. Other students may say the antelope chase is a reality that exists in another dimension. According to Dr. Webster, "dreams are as real as the lives we live every day; they're simply lived in another dimension, or plane of existence."

2. Answers will vary. Possible answer: Anika and Dr. Anika Webster are the same person. Anika is the woman who is a patient in the sleep study; Dr. Anika Webster is the woman who lives in Anika's dreams and is a doctor working in the sleep lab.

4 Word Review

1. eerie — omen	7. Pilgrims — dull
2. wavering — resources	8. courteously — bluntness
3. lion's — lair	9. completed — betrayed
4. irksome — courtship	10. agreeable — frustrated
5. Pearl Harbor — Hawaii	11. prude — displeased
6. New York City — New York	12. instill — boldly

5 Words That Describe

1. severe	5. scarlet	9. eerie
2. classified	6. romantic	10. beige
3. treacherous	7. feeble	11. hoarse
4. dismal	8. steadfast	12. sincere

6 Words That *Don't* Describe

1. frizzy	5. heartfelt	9. relaxed
2. unintentional	6. persistent	10. nourishing
3. savage	7. hasty	11. distinct
4. apparent	8. generous	12. deafening

Lesson 12

1 Definitions

1. kilt	6. culprit	10. fowl
2. almanac	7. stowaway	11. hew
3. bolster	8. pulpit	12. jolt
4. widower	9. cultivate	13. jilt
5. brawl		

2 Understanding the Story

1. The narrator is someone who has lived in the area since he was a child. He learned the secret of the boarded window from his grandfather, who lived nearby and knew Murlock.

2. As a young man, he was eager to build a home in the wilderness. He built a cabin and cleared land for farming. Due to events surrounding his wife's death, he withdrew, lost enthusiasm for farming, let the cleared land grow up, and took on the appearance of someone much older than he was.

3. He fires his gun, and in the flash of the discharge sees a panther dragging his wife's body toward the window.

4. He passes out, probably from shock at what he has seen combined with exhaustion at his long day and sorrow over the death of his wife.

5. a. There was a pool of blood from his wife's throat. She wouldn't have bled if she were already dead.

   b. The ribbon that he had used to tie her hands together was broken and the hands were tightly clenched.

   c. Between his wife's teeth was a piece of the panther's ear. She must have bitten it off while fighting for her life.

3 What Do You Think?

1. Answers will vary. Possible response: He thinks the ghost of his wife is in the room. He feels the table shake and hears what he thinks are bare feet on the floor. He tries to speak the woman's name, but can't. A heavy body seems to be hurled against the table. He hears something on the floor. He loses control of his faculties and is in terror.

2. Answers will vary. Possible response: The panther killed her. Apparently, she is not dead when Murlock prepares her for burial. In the morning, he finds evidence that she fought against the panther.

3. Answers will vary. Possible response: Murlock may have been so terrorized by events of that night that he irrationally boards it up in order to protect himself from the horror that happened because of the open window.

4. Answers will vary. Possible response: Yes, because if he had not fallen asleep and later passed out, perhaps he could have saved his wife from the panther.

4 Proverbs

1. d	4. c	7. b	9. d
2. a	5. a	8. d	10. c
3. b	6. c		

5 The Suffix -ness

1. suddenness, bluntness
2. drowsiness, feebleness
3. skimpiness, thriftiness
4. graciousness, queasiness
5. idleness, scornfulness
6. earnestness, casualness
7. scrawniness, sturdiness
8. cleanliness, godliness

6 More about Standard English

1. Change *could of* to *could have.*
2. Change *had ought* to *ought.*
3. Change *might of* to *might have.*
4. Change *The reason . . . is because* to *The reason . . . is that.*
5. Change *kind of a* to *kind of.*
6. Change *the reason is . . . because* to *the reason is . . . that.*
7. Change *It don't* to *It doesn't.*
8. Change *could of* to *could have.*

7 Word Families

1. unrehearsed, rehearsed, rehearsal
2. achieved, unachieved, achievements
3. unnourishing, nourishing, nourishment
4. mournful, mournfully, mourning
5. unapparent, apparent, apparently
6. courteous, courteously, courtesy
7. sincerity, sincerely, sincere
8. suitably, unsuitable, suitable
9. persuasive, persuasion, persuade
10. misfortune, unfortunate, fortune, unfortunately

Review: Lessons 1–12

1 Word Review

1. volume	7. awkward	12. zeal
2. circuit	8. motive	13. verdict
3. vice versa	9. erratic	14. solitaire
4. delicatessen	10. receptionist	15. kayak
5. bristle	11. tragedy	16. marmalade
6. prairie		

2 Which Word Does Not Fit?

1. solitaire	5. marrying	9. grieve	12. report
2. jilt	6. qualified	10. riddle	13. wield
3. withdrawn	7. unsafe	11. scissors	14. advertise
4. Australia	8. antelope		

3 A Review of Sounds

1. chemistry	4. gourd	7. weary	9. thorough
2. tow	5. bout	8. bargain	10. issue
3. profile	6. sleigh		

4 Speaking in Idioms

1. die laughing
2. kick the bucket
3. not on your life
4. scared to death
5. the life of the party
6. I didn't sleep a wink, I slept like a baby
7. let sleeping dogs lie
8. takes your breath away
9. a dream come true

5 A Review of Standard Usage

1. 2	3. 1	5. 3
2. 2	4. 4	6. 5

6 "Life is real."

1. Answers will vary. Accept reasonable responses.
2. Answers will vary. Reasonable responses include: Framton in "The Open Window" believes that after people die they can return as ghosts because he is terrified that the returning hunters are ghosts. Mrs. Sappleton's niece tells Framton that her aunt believes her dead husband is returning, so she is claiming that Mrs. Sappleton believes the dead can come back to life.
3. Answers will vary. Reasonable responses include: Alice lives life to the fullest because she seems to have no fear. She is curious and adventurous, and she takes each moment as it comes.
4. Answers will vary. Accept reasonable responses.

Lesson 13

1 Definitions

1. gelatin	7. spigot	12. genuine
2. agenda	8. tragedy	13. bigot
3. generator	9. fungus	14. vogue
4. hostage	10. outrageous	15. gangrene
5. legend	11. fatigue	16. haggle
6. logic		

2 Understanding the Play

1. He lifted and carried the heavy box full of china.
2. Most of their relatives and dearest friends have died.
3. They put Norman's book back on the shelf to be read next summer.
4. Answers will vary.

3 What Do You Think?

Answers will vary.

4 Tone of Voice

1. innocently	6. persistently
2. mysteriously	7. formally
3. coaxingly	8. grudgingly
4. encouragingly	9. wisely
5. grimly	10. absent-mindedly

5 Vacations around the World

1. Boston
2. Las Vegas
3. Philadelphia
4. Atlantic City
5. Amsterdam
6. Washington, D.C.
7. Jamestown
8. Black Sea
9. Ireland
10. Utah
11. Austria
12. Greece
13. Dead Sea
14. Hawaii
15. New York City

6 Synonyms and Antonyms

1. swarthy, fair
2. eternal, temporary
3. carefree, worried
4. descendant, ancestor
5. counterfeit, genuine
6. zesty, tasteless
7. aimless, deliberate
8. outrageous, sensible
9. withdrawn, outgoing
10. courteous, crude
11. callous, warmhearted
12. fatigued, energetic

Lesson 14

1 Definitions

1. zinc
2. jaundice
3. cavity
4. fabric
5. tonic
6. vacuum
7. disciple
8. columnist
9. Sicily
10. civilian
11. citrus
12. menace
13. majestic
14. mimic
15. larceny
16. malice

2 Understanding the Reading

1. c
2. b
3. c
4. d
5. a
6. c
7. d
8. a
9. c
10. b

3 Which Word Does Not Fit?

1. knowledge
2. whimper
3. certain
4. courteously
5. sphere
6. propose
7. enfold
8. coconut
9. folly
10. erratic
11. cultivate
12. reality
13. mourn
14. plague
15. distinct
16. vast

4 Look It Up

1. tsar, czar
2. An emperor or king, particularly one of the former rulers of Russia
3. 1868–1918
4. 1894
5. 1894–1917
6. He abdicated the throne in 1917 and was executed by revolutionary forces in 1918.

5 Who Might Know Most about…?

1. receptionist
2. pianist
3. columnist
4. artist
5. colonist
6. humorist
7. tourist
8. violinist
9. motorist
10. florist
11. psychiatrist
12. naturalist
13. pharmacist
14. chemist
15. nutritionist

Question: -*ist* means a person who does something.

6 The Mystery Tzar

CRATE	ASIDE	THERE	CANOE
16	2	11	5
TRACE	IDEAS	ETHER	OCEAN
BLEAT	ANGLE	STALE	LEAFS
9	7	6	12
TABLE	ANGEL	LEAST	FLEAS
WEEPS	SHORE	CAROB	SLIDE
8	10	3	13
SWEEP	HORSE	COBRA	IDLES
TONES	CAUSE	FLIER	SHORN
1	15	14	4
NOTES	SAUCE	RIFLE	HORNS

The Mystery Tzar: Nicholas the First

Lesson 15

1 Definitions

1. synagogue
2. hydrogen
3. Syria
4. sentry
5. syringe
6. hypocrite
7. cypress
8. ebony
9. cynical
10. Sydney
11. foyer
12. analyze
13. waylay

2 Understanding the Story

1. 212° F
2. the doctor and the father
3. 100° C
4. Schatz
5. Schatz is waiting to die.
6. Schatz knows his temperature is 102°, and he believes that people can't live with a temperature above 44°.
7. Answers will vary. Reasonable responses include: Schatz wasn't responding to his company. He thought Schatz might relax and sleep if he were left alone. The father may have wanted some fresh air and exercise. He knew Schatz wasn't seriously ill.
8. He tells his father that he believes he is going to die because his temperature is 102°. His father explains the difference between the Fahrenheit and centigrade thermometers and convinces him that he isn't going to die.
9. Answers will vary. Accept any of the following or similar details: He didn't sleep or move. He stared at the foot of the bed. He wasn't interested in the story his father read to him. He wouldn't let any others come into his room.

3 Working with Measurements

1. 80.45
2. 1,000
3. 39.37 inches
4. 0
5. 32
6. Gabriel Daniel Fahrenheit
7. Germany
8. 1686–1736

4 Word Relationships

1. cider is to pudding
2. nightstick is to patrolman
3. prowler is to lurk
4. fragment is to piece
5. advise is to listen
6. clove is to garlic
7. Denver is to Colorado
8. ordinary is to everyday
9. ivory is to white
10. nutty is to cuckoo

5 Multiple Meanings

1. b
2. d
3. a
4. c
5. a
6. c

6 Homonyms

1. add, ad
2. lessen, lesson
3. Shoot, chute
4. aid, aide
5. horse, hoarse
6. fowl, foul
7. butt, but
8. vary, very
9. bawl, ball
10. weekly, weakly
11. fir, fur
12. sheer, shear
13. plum, plumb
14. sense, cents, scents
15. cite, sight, site

Lesson 16

1 Definitions

1. lymph
2. phosphorus
3. asphalt
4. phobia
5. prophecy
6. saxophone
7. pamphlet
8. amphibian
9. pheasant
10. dolphin
11. graphic
12. philosophy
13. autobiography
14. decipher
15. triumph

2 Understanding the Story

1. c
2. d
3. b
4. a
5. c
6. b
7. b
8. a
9. b

3 What Do You Think?

1. Answers will vary. Johnsy probably would have expressed remorse and guilt.
2. Schatz was very tense and probably afraid of dying. He really didn't want to die. Johnsy was tired of trying to stay alive and was willing to let death take her. She didn't appear to fear death.
3. Schatz was filled with disbelief at first (as was Fyodor in "The Execution"). As he realized he wasn't going to die, he began to relax. Johnsy realized that giving up was wrong, and she began to eat and try to get better. She regained hope and started to make plans for the future.

4 Hyphenated Words

1. all-round
2. down-to-earth
3. well-built
4. thick-skinned
5. bird's-eye
6. absent-minded
7. self-conscious
8. full-fledged
9. tongue-in-cheek
10. self-critical
11. high-strung
12. red-handed
13. two-faced
14. hunky-dory
15. far-reaching

5 The $24 Swindle

unsettling
official, colonies, particularly, colony
purchase, claim
intelligent, outright
rival, quibble, chuckling
settled, absolutely, betrayed, situation

Review: Lessons 1–16

1 Word Review

1. a
2. c
3. d
4. b
5. b
6. c
7. b
8. d
9. b
10. c
11. a
12. a
13. d
14. a
15. a
16. c

2 Find the Homonym

isle
beet
Cokes
chord
doe
jeans
scene
soar
tents
vein
we'd
yolk

1. chord
2. we'd
3. doe
4. scene
5. beet
6. isle
7. vein
8. jeans
9. Cokes
10. tents
11. yolk
12. soar

3 Word Review

1. penguin — bird
2. bigot — enraged
3. mechanical — electrical
4. beagle — hound
5. coarseness — embarrassed
6. jaundiced — brilliance
7. narcotics — menace
8. conceive — unpleasant
9. protective — tragedies
10. parade — majestic
11. hardheaded — cement
12. analysis — cynical

4 Word Sound Review

1. gospel
2. halter
3. Polish
4. powder
5. thaw
6. hyena
7. vocal
8. jaguar
9. reception
10. residue
11. heyday
12. symbol

5 A Poet's View of Dying

1. Death is something to be fought and resisted. The speaker doesn't want to die; she will cling vehemently to life. Accept any of the various phrases as evidence.
2. Answers will vary. Accept any reasonable responses.

Lesson 17

1 Definitions

1. khaki
2. rhinestone
3. wreath
4. gherkin
5. knoll
6. ghoul
7. salve
8. porridge
9. wretched
10. ghastly
11. Wright
12. bustle
13. jostle
14. wrangle
15. abridge
16. widget

2 Understanding the Story

1. They don't want the uncle to see them because, if he does, he will make them go in.
2. They know that she has orders to bring them in and isn't going to leave until they come.

3. He lies on the floor in the parlor and watches for Mangan's sister to leave for school because he has a crush on her.

4. He likes being around her and he wants her to be aware of him, even though he is afraid to talk to her.

5. He is in love with her and wants to give her something that will make her happy and cause her to think of him.

6. His uncle is very late coming home from work. The narrator cannot go until his uncle gets home and gives him some money.

7. She is wrapped up in conversation with two men and would rather spend her time with them than in helping some boy.

8. No, the narrator doesn't give Mangan's sister a gift from Araby. The stalls are closing and he doesn't know what to get her. He is as shy and indecisive in dealing with the stall clerks as he is in talking to Mangan's sister.

3 Character Descriptions

1. wrangling
2. aimless
3. courageous
4. solemn
5. ghastly
6. weary
7. heartbroken
8. humble
9. bustling
10. indifferent
11. innocent
12. God-fearing
13. sly
14. boastful
15. bewitched

4 What Do You Think?

1. Answers will vary, but students should give reasons for their answers based on what they know about the main character.

2. Answers will vary. Many students may say the narrator may be too shy and embarrassed to talk to Mangan's sister, preferring to withdraw and suffer.

3. Answers will vary. Many students may say they doubt Mangan's sister even remembers the conversation. She is probably unaware of the narrator's infatuation with her and doesn't give him much thought.

5 Occupations

Playwrights
acts
casts
dialogue
scenery

Biographers
chapters
dates
diaries
personal letters

Poets
rhyme
rhythm
stanzas
verse

Sportswriters
headlines
play-offs
scores
trades

6 More about Ireland

prehistoric, conquered, culture, civilization, flourished, scholars, missionaries

warfare, vulnerable, invaders, attacked, established

numerous, loyal, conflict

compromise

Lesson 18

1 Definitions

1. motto
2. eddy
3. burrow
4. essay
5. jimmy
6. nugget
7. asset
8. giddy
9. fodder
10. rubbish
11. commerce
12. summit
13. essence
14. Sabbath
15. pollute
16. shimmer

2 Understanding the Reading

1. c
2. a
3. c
4. b
5. c
6. d
7. b
8. a
9. d

3 What Do You Think?

1. The narrator in Lesson 17 is in the *being* mode because he is so focused on Mangan's sister instead of himself. He goes out of his way to see her, to be near her, and to try to give her a gift. Even though he doesn't succeed, all his activity is focused on the girl.

2. Answers will vary. Accept any reasonable response.

3. Answers will vary. Accept any reasonable response.

4 Word Relationships

1. d
2. a
3. b
4. d
5. a
6. c
7. d
8. c
9. d
10. a

5 On Latin and Language

1. influence, persists, calculated, roots
2. Romance, derived, tongue, ancient
3. Hemisphere, independent, political, three
4. inscription, buckle, century, BC
5. scholars, established, grammar, pore
6. peak, language, throughout, large
7. conquered, unconquered, conquerors, conquer
8. traditional, despite, testify, presence
9. however, exceedingly, translate, translation
10. importance, circumstances, phrases, objects

6 State Search

Lesson 19

1 Definitions

1. crimson	6. textile	11. surpass
2. kernel	7. drastic	12. flounder
3. goblin	8. verbal	13. nurture
4. mascot	9. festive	14. plunder
5. ordeal	10. bombard	

2 Understanding the Play

1. They sent very few supplies along with Leslie when he was brought to the Lemkes' from the hospital.
2. Both had been expected to die within a short time. Both needed care that May was willing to give.
3. Dr. Edwards says it is a miracle that the Lemkes have kept Leslie alive for 10 years.
4. May has never given up hope for Leslie even though there has been little progress or improvement in his condition.
5. Leslie has briefly stood alone for the first time.

3 Word Review

1. Rhode Island — smallest	5. burden — burro
2. biography — abridged	6. ego — disinterested
3. bombarded — drastically	7. bluster — cowering
4. correct — eyewitnesses	8. collapsed — ordeal

4 Synonyms and Antonyms

1. confess, deny	7. divine, worldly
2. awesome, humdrum	8. noble, dishonest
3. meddle, ignore	9. random, purposeful
4. blossom, fade	10. fidgety, composed
5. yield, resist	11. comfortable, distressful
6. immortal, temporary	12. wretched, joyous

5 Using the Dictionary

Algonquian	French
chipmunk	bureau
possum	chauffeur
raccoon	gourmet
tomahawk	solitaire

German	Spanish
hamburger	burro
kindergarten	chili
sauerkraut	peso
strudel	tornado

6 Word Families

1. comfortably	5. moral	8. mischievously
2. appreciative	6. wretch	9. develop
3. imprudent	7. immensity	10. athlete
4. mortal		

Lesson 20

1 Definitions

1. dole	6. null	11. suet
2. dupe	7. arid	12. helm
3. Zeus	8. tier	13. ne'er
4. lure	9. oral	14. dote
5. gory	10. idol	

2 Understanding the Play

1. Sixteen years have passed.
2. The stranger was making fun of Leslie, and May doesn't want Leslie to be the butt of teasing by thoughtless people.
3. When they get a piano for Leslie they discover that he can play any piece of music he hears. Later, he begins to sing the words to songs, and he eventually starts to talk, as well. His musical talent makes him someone to be admired, not teased.
4. It is a person who is generally mentally deficient but who has an exceptional talent or skill in some special area or field.
5. Dr. Vince calls May "amazing" because she has ceaselessly worked to help Leslie and has faith that he will continue to grow and to learn. She believes he will learn to speak someday.

What do you think? Answers will vary. Accept any reasonable response.

3 Which Word Does Not Fit?

1. written	7. analyze	12. stop
2. Hudson	8. interest	13. jitters
3. devotion	9. Armenia	14. realistic
4. taco	10. entertain	15. unpopular
5. Dickens	11. intellectual	16. rhinestone
6. joyous		

4 Problems

1. peer pressure	6. dandelions	11. depression
2. injuries	7. dishonesty	12. disobedience
3. inflation	8. preservatives	13. spies
4. reality	9. jitters	14. sharks
5. deadlines	10. ailments	

5 A Little Latin

1. unicorn	5. biped	9. trimester
2. unicycle	6. bifocals	10. tripod
3. universe	7. bimonthly	11. triangle
4. uniform	8. bisect	12. triceps

6 On Living and Loving: A Poet's Point of View

1. a	3. c	5. d
2. b	4. d	6. a

Review: Lessons 1–20

1 Word Review

1. concerto
2. trestle
3. devotion
4. abide
5. guttural
6. ballad
7. diagonal
8. sect
9. wretch
10. elfin
11. accompany
12. campus
13. adolescence
14. ego
15. folklore
16. mode

2 Who or What Would You Expect to Be . . . ?

1. enthusiastic
2. arid
3. somber
4. ancient
5. intellectual
6. abridged
7. rhythmical
8. vulnerable
9. treacherous
10. festive
11. verbal
12. invisible
13. dwindling
14. mischievous
15. unwholesome
16. shimmering

3 World Capitals

1. Brussels
2. Ottawa
3. Beijing
4. Tehran
5. Baghdad
6. Tokyo
7. Oslo
8. Lisbon
9. Madrid
10. Stockholm
11. Bern
12. Damascus

4 A Little More Latin

1. incredible
2. credentials
3. creditor
4. credenza
5. credit
6. credible
7. creed
8. incredibly

5 More Work with Expressions and Proverbs

1. d
2. b
3. b
4. c
5. c
6. a
7. d
8. d
9. b

6 Find the Quote

1. Mercury
2. peppermint
3. kilt
4. Ash Wednesday
5. serial
6. humorous
7. profile
8. hyena
9. coffee
10. poverty
11. wig
12. lemon
13. tuxedo
14. rhythm
15. vitality

A formula for happiness: The way to happiness: keep your heart free from hate, your mind from worry. Live simply. Expect little, give much.